MAN-MADE MINDS

MINDS

The Promise of Artificial Intelligence

M. Mitchell Waldrop

Walker and Company

The following publishers have generously given permission to use extended quotations from copyrighted works: From *Science* magazine, copyright 1983 by the American Association for the Advancement of Science. Reprinted by permission of Richard O. Duda and the publisher. From *The Handbook of Artificial Intelligence, Vol. 1*, edited by Edward Feigenbaum and Avron Barr, copyright 1981 by Addison Wesley Publishing Company. Reprinted by permission of the publisher. From *Computer Power and Human Reason* by Joseph Weizenbaum, copyright 1976 by W. H. Freeman and Company. Reprinted by permission of the publisher. From *The Second Self*, by Sherry Turkle, copyright 1984 by Sherry Turkle. Reprinted by permission of the publisher, Simon and Schuster. From *Newsweek* magazine, copyright 1985 by Newsweek, Inc. Reprinted by permission of the publisher. From *Next-Generation Computers*, ed. Edward A. Torrero, copyright 1985 by The Institute for Electrical and Electronics Engineers. Reprinted by permission of the publisher. From *The Best of Jack Williamson*, copyright 1978 by Jack Williamson. Reprinted by permission of the publisher, Ballantine Books, Inc., a division of Random House.

Figure credits: Figure 2–4 adapted from John R. Anderson, *Cognitive Psychology, 2d. Ed.*, copyright 1984 by W. H. Freeman and Company. Reprinted by permission of the publisher. Figure 4–1 adapted from *Artificial Intelligence: an MIT Perspective, Vol. 2.*, ed. Patrick H. Winston and Richard H. Brown, copyright 1979 by the Massachusetts Institute of Technology. Reprinted by permission of the publisher. Figures 4–2 and 4–3 from *Proceedings of the Royal Society of London*, copyright 1980 by the Royal Society of London. Reprinted courtesy of Ellen Hildreth and the Royal Society of London. Figures 4–6 and 4–7 from David Marr, *Vision*, copyright 1980 by W. H. Freeman and Company. Reprinted by permission of the publisher. Figure 4–8 from *Proceedings of the Royal Society of London*, copyright 1978 by the Royal Society of London. Reprinted courtesy of Keith Nishihara and the Royal Society of London.

Parts of chapters, 2, 3, 4, 5, and 8 appeared in slightly different versions in *Science* magazine, copyright 1984 by the American Association for the Advancement of Science.

First published in the United States of America in 1987 by the Walker Publishing Company, Inc.

Published simultaneously in Canada by John Wiley & Sons
Canada, Limited, Rexdale, Ontario.

Library of Congress Cataloging-in-Publication Data

Waldrop, M. Mitchell.
  Man–made minds.

  Bibliography: p.
  Includes index.
  1. Artificial intelligence. I. Title
Q335.W35 1987   006.3   86-22370
ISBN 0-8027-0899-4
ISBN 0-8027-7297-8 (paper)

Printed in the United States of America

10 9 8 7 6 5 4 3 2 1

Text design by Lorraine Mullaney

Acknowledgements

To Robert Abelson, Hayward Alker, Saul Amarel, John Anderson, Isaac Asimov, Jon Barwise, Daniel Bobrow, David Brandin, Rodney Brooks, John Seely Brown, Bruce Buchanan, Charles Buffalano, Jaime Carbonell, Lynn Conway, Robert Cooper, Randall Davis, Ned Dearborn, David Dickson, Scott Fahlman, Edward Feigenbaum, Rollie Frye, Michael Genesereth, Eric Grimson, Barbara Grosz, Peter Hart, Barbara Hayes-Roth, Frederick Hayes-Roth, Carl Hewitt, Ellen Hildreth, Daniel Hillis, Geoffrey Hinton, Dennis Jennings, Robert Kahn, Ronald Kaplan, Clint Kelly, Rob Kling, Thomas Knight, Jill Larkin, Douglas Lenat, Victor Lesser, Thomas Malone, Claudia Mazzetti, John McCarthy, Pamela McCorduck, Marvin Minsky, Allen Newell, Keith Nishihara, Ray Perrault, John Pinkston, Raj Reddy, Louis Robinson, Stanley Rosenschein, Roger Schank, Charles Seitz, Terry Sejnowski, Herbert Simon, Brian Smith, Paul Smolensky, Mark Stefik, Gerald Sussman, David Sylvan, John Walsh, David Waltz, Joseph Weizenbaum, Langdon Winner, Terry Winograd, Patrick Winston, Steven Wolfram, and Lofti Zadeh: Thank you. You freely gave of your time and patience to help me understand what artificial intelligence is all about. I hope you will like what I have written here.

To Beth Adelson, Robert Kahn, and Rick Weingarten: Thank you for reading portions of the manuscript. You made this a better book than it otherwise would have been.

To Tomaso Poggio: Thank you for reading portions of the manuscript— and for hospitality and friendship beyond the call of duty.

To Barbara Culliton: Thank you for suggesting, long ago now, that I do a series on computers for *Science* magazine; that suggestion was the real origin of this book.

To Richard Winslow: Thank you for your patience and for your insistence that this book deserved the best I could give it.

And to Amy: Thank you. For everything.

TO A. E. F.
Who went through it all

and

TO P. R. W.
Who wasn't here to see it,
but who would have been proud

CONTENTS

CONTENTS

CONTENTS

INTRODUCTION
The New Land of Fairie

For we are, all of us, children with respect to the future
—ALLEN NEWELL

According to one popular definition, artificial intelligence—or AI, as it's generally known—is the art of making computers do smart things. And that definition does seem to capture the spirit of AI. On the other hand, it's not very informative. So let's try some others:

- As a branch of software engineering, AI is simply a collection of programming techniques that make a computer do certain tricks: communicate with its operator in natural-sounding English, for example, or diagnose diseases as if the computer were an expert physician. Of course, people are beginning to make lots of money using these tricks.
- As a theory of computer science, however, AI is a unique conception of what programming is all about. Instead of telling the computer precisely what to do in every conceivable situation, as conventional programmers do, an AI programmer will tell it what to *know*—facts, skills, and rules of thumb that the machine can apply to changing situations as it goes along. Thus, the machine can perform flexibly and sensibly instead of rigidly and mechanically.
- As a branch of philosophy, AI is a kind of experimental epistemology: What is knowledge? How can knowledge be represented in a computer—or in the mind? What does it mean to know? What does it mean to understand? What does it mean to *mean*?
- As a science of the mind, AI embodies a controversial and compelling idea: that the mind—the part of us that reasons, perceives, and thinks—is basically a mechanism for processing information. In effect, it is a kind of program running on a flesh-and-blood computer called the brain. In-

deed, at the deepest level AI comes to grips with one of the great unsolved mysteries of science: How can mind arise from nonmind? How can the brain, an object made of ordinary matter subject to ordinary physical laws, give rise to feeling, purpose, thought, and awareness?
- And finally, on a practical, everyday level, AI is the technology of enchantment.

COMPUTERS AND ENCHANTMENT

Admittedly, that last definition demands some explanation. It has the sound of overwrought ad copy. And it is certainly not how AI researchers themselves would describe what they do (most of them, anyway). On the other hand, as the science-fiction writer Arthur C. Clarke is fond of pointing out, any sufficiently advanced technology is indistinguishable from magic. And in that sense, the phrase *technology of enchantment* does seem to express something essential about AI.

Consider that computers are a potent form of Clarkean magic all by themselves. The revolution in information technology has been underway for more than forty years now, ever since computers were developed during World War II. Lately, in fact, that revolution has come to seem more like an explosion, encompassing not just computers, but telecommunications networks, fiber optics, optical discs, satellite communications, programmed robots, automated factories, and more. Information technology has become a multibillion-dollar industry. And yet, unlike many other industrial products, computers don't pollute the environment. They require very little in the way of natural resources to build. They take up minimal space and use a negligible amount of electricity. And they continue to defy all common sense by getting smaller, cheaper, and more capable every year—with every indication that the process will continue until every office, every government agency, every factory, every restaurant, and indeed every home can afford to have a computer thousands of times more powerful than anything that exists today.

That's magic.

AI, of course, is only one part of this information-processing revolution. However, it is fast emerging as the most interesting and important part, precisely because AI is the software that promises to endow all that hardware with *sense*. So instead of having to put up with the kind of computers we have now—machines that are perfectly capable of dunning a business's clients with bill after bill for $0.00—we could have computers that use knowledge and judgment, that understand human affairs, and that can see why a bill for $0.00 is ludicrous.

The first wave of such software is already on the market, with emphasis on the so-called expert systems that give advice like a human specialist in such areas as medicine, law, and accounting. Before too much longer, given the pace of hardware and software development, we should be seeing machines that can, for instance, talk to us in English or Japanese, rather than in rigid programming codes written in FORTRAN or BASIC. We can expect to have machines that give us instant advice about our income taxes or tell us what to do when the baby has a fever. We can expect to see silicon tutors that will help a child understand the enthralling possibilities of geometry and numbers. Ultimately we can even expect trucks that drive themselves through the night and unload themselves at their destinations. Indeed, we can one day expect to have machines that do almost anything that now requires human intelligence.

Moreover, unlike conventional computers, these artificially intelligent machines will no longer be like imbecilic slaves who sit passively until ordered to do something—and then do precisely that and nothing more. They will be like trusted assistants. They will understand what it is they have been asked to do. They will even help us decide, through questions and suggestions, what it is that we *want* them to do.

And perhaps most important of all, they will no longer be an implacable, alien presence in our lives. These machines will be our servants, our tutors, our advisers, perhaps even our friends.

Thus, AI promises to bring enchantment into the world in much the same sense that the Brothers Grimm meant enchantment: The ordinary objects that surround us will be given animation and the power of speech. Indeed, AI pioneer Allen Newell, who was the first to use this enchantment metaphor, describes a future that has an eerie resemblance to a pagan, animistic world, in which every rock and tree is inhabited by its own spirit. AI provides the capability, he says,

> For little boxes that make out your income taxes for you.
> For brakes that know how to stop on wet pavement.
> For instruments that can converse with their users.
> For bridges that watch out for the safety of those who cross them.
> For streetlights that care about those who stand under them—who know the way, so no one need get lost.

In short, he says, "the aim of technology, properly applied, is to build a Land of Fairie."[1]

Fairy Tales and the Future

In a sense, fairy tales are always about the future—because they are always, the experts tell us, about growing up. Adulthood is a fascinating place in a child's eyes. But it is also strange, new, and frightening. Fairy tales are compelling precisely because they speak to those feelings, because they provide both lessons and reassurance. Thus, Little Red Riding Hood learned a painful lesson about temptation, devotion to duty, and the perils of trusting in

3

strangers. Hansel and Gretel had to leave home and find their own way. And Jack, who climbed the beanstalk, had to prove that he could succeed when everyone thought he would fail.

Perhaps we adults find fairy tales compelling for the same reason: because we are both fascinated and anxious about what tomorrow will bring—because, as Newell points out, we are all children with respect to the future. So perhaps we, too, can find some important lessons in the Land of Fairie.

Certainly the most important thing to remember is that the Land of Fairie is not all happiness and buttercups. Think of J.R.R. Tolkien's Middle Earth: one finds beauty and joy there, but also confusion, strife, evil, and heartbreak. And so it is with our modern fairy tale. Japan, Europe, and the United States, for example, have all launched billion-dollar research projects to create a new generation of artificially intelligent computers: the so-called Fifth Generation machines. Yet these projects are motivated not just by the vision of a glorious future but also by a grim kind of international rivalry. Japan is determined to win respect in the world, while Europe and the United States are gnawed by anxiety about their own political power, their high-tech prowess, and the prospect of once again losing out in the economic competition.

Meanwhile, just as enchantment can be used as a weapon of war in the Land of Fairie, so can AI. In the United States, at least, its funding has always been dominated by Pentagon's Defense Advanced Research Projects Agency (DARPA), although historically the agency has stressed open, unclassified basic research. Since 1983 and the beginning of the agency's Strategic Computing Initiative, however, DARPA's goals have turned more explicitly toward the arts of war. The project's ten-year goals include an autonomous land vehicle capable of roving over rough terrain at high speed, an R2D2-like pilot's assistant, and a naval battle-management system. To many people in the AI community, the implications of this shift are troubling.

At the same time, the Pentagon's very different Strategic *Defense* Initiative—"Star Wars"—has the potential for becoming the biggest supporter of AI research and ultimately the biggest consumer of AI and information technology. After all, assuming that a space-based missile defense system can be made to work at all—a big assumption—then in a crisis that system will have to respond to a missile attack within minutes, far too fast for human intervention, which means that it will have to be guided by a system of artificially intelligent computers. As we shall see, this leads to some serious questions about the nature of responsibility. For instance: Do we have the right to sign over the fate of civilization to machines?

Finally, it's important to remember that the power of enchantment is not necessarily the same thing as wisdom. Consider the Sorcerer's Apprentice, who learned enough magic to put his broom to work hauling water from the river to his master's cistern—but not enough to stop it. Or consider the jinn who was released from his bottle in *A Thousand and One Nights:* He proved to be not a magical servant but a demonic and wrathful spirit who refused to go back in again.

Thus, many people are deeply concerned about what kind of world this new Land of Fairie will be. Quite aside from any concerns about nuclear Armageddon, there is the sense that a world given over to computers and other machines will inevitably become *like* a machine: cold, dark, rigid, and unfeeling; a gray kind of place, devoid of freedom, individuality, or humanity—not unlike Tolkien's Middle Earth if the Dark Lord of Mordor had won the War of the Rings.

That fear is very apparent in the Orwellian vision of computer scientist Joseph Weizenbaum of the Massachusetts Institute of Technology:

> I see an increasingly homogeneous and therefore very dull world, and a further stratification of society, most particularly of Western society. We will have an information society populated by those whose lives are characterized by their plastic machine-readable cards. As time goes by, people's poverty of inner resources will be rendered invisible by the humanly irrelevant power of their plastic cards. Great masses of people will live out their lives alternating between obeying the imperatives of machines at work and in their free time suckling at the breast of the great bitch entertainment.[2]

In short, there is nothing in the rules that says high technology has to be benign. And in the real world, unfortunately, there is no guarantee of a happy ending.

The Uses of Enchantment

Fairy tales, of course, usually *do* give us a happy ending—otherwise many of them would be horror stories. (Imagine *Little Red Riding Hood* if the story ended before the hunter came to cut her out of the belly of the wolf.) They reassure us, without lying to us about how easy the path will be.

"In fairy stories there are great trials to be performed before the happy ending," Newell points out. "Great dangers must be encountered and overcome. . . . In fairy stories, the hero (or the heroine)—the one who achieves finally the happy ending—must grow in virtue and in mature understanding. No villains need apply for the central role. The fairy story [of technology] will not come true automatically. We must earn it."[3]

This book is written in much that same spirit—not because it is a fairy tale, but because I side with the optimists. Whatever concerns people may have—and those concerns are real—AI, along with information technology in general, strikes me as being ultimately a source of hope, not of despair. The child psychologist Bruno Bettelheim might have been writing about AI in *The Uses of Enchantment,* his book about fairy tales:

Each fairy tale is a magic mirror that reflects some aspects of our inner world, and of the steps required by our evolution from immaturity to maturity. For those who immerse themselves in what the fairy tale has to communicate, it becomes a deep, quiet pool which at first seems to reflect only our own image; but behind it we soon discover the inner turmoils of our soul—its depth, and ways to gain peace within ourselves and with the world, which is the reward of our struggles.[4]

Artificial intelligence is just such a mirror. Because it asks how computers can be made intelligent, it leads us to look inward at ourselves and ask how it is that *we* are intelligent. And because it promises us an enchanted world, it challenges us to take responsibility for the kind of world we want to live in.

A Word About Organization and Chronology.

Man-Made Minds is a book about the meaning and promise of AI, and as such it is not intended primarily as a history of the field. In general, however, the chapters do follow in chronological order, so it seems useful to give a summary of AI's history here:[12]

- *Prehistory:* the 1930s and 1940s. The electronic computer was born in World War II, almost concurrent with the developments in formal logic, information theory, and cybernetics that would lay the foundations for AI. A fundamentally new concept of *mechanism* was emerging, one based not on gears, grease, and engines, but on communication, control, and the flow of information. Speculations sprang up immediately about the computer's ability to mimic the mind.
- *Dawn:* early 1950s to mid-1960s. AI began to emerge as an identifiable discipline. In 1956, Allen Newell and Herbert Simon of the Carnegie Institute of Technology (now Carnegie-Mellon University) created the first true AI program, Logic Theorist, and thereby demonstrated that a computer could perform a genuine intellectual task: It could prove theorems in symbolic logic. In effect, Newell and Simon were saying that the mind is best understood as a mechanism for processing information; independently and almost simultaneously, that same idea made itself felt in philosophy, psychology, linguistics, anthropology, neuroscience, and sociology. Thus, the foundations were laid for what people are now calling *cognitive science*. Meanwhile, Stanford University's John McCarthy coined the name *artificial intelligence* and began the theoretical work that led to LISP, still the most widely used computer language for AI. Within a few years, major AI research groups had been founded at such institutions as Carnegie-Mellon, MIT, and Stanford University.
- *Dark Ages:* the late 1960s. After a period of early euphoria, a certain disillusionment and stagnation set in as AI researchers began to realize that creating intelligence was a much bigger challenge than they had thought. Such everyday tasks as recognizing a face or walking across the

room turned out to be far tougher to program than such "hard" intellectual tasks as mathematical theorem-proving and chess playing. Indeed, the kind of mental information processing involved in everyday common sense turns out to be nothing short of awesome. It requires a vast and complex body of knowledge about the world, far exceeding the capacity of any existing computer.

- *Renaissance:* the 1970s. The dark ages of AI gradually gave way to a rebirth based on a new insight: that a fundamental ingredient of intelligence—perhaps *the* fundamental ingredient—is knowledge. Much of the research in AI since that time has therefore focused on finding practical answers to questions such as: What is knowledge? How do you represent knowledge in a machine so that you can get at it and use it? And how do you get a computer to learn? The most obvious expression of AI's preoccupation with knowledge has been the invention of expert systems, programs that attempt to capture the knowledge of human specialists and then give expertlike advice in response to specific questions. But this preoccupation has also provided the foundation for more-sophisticated natural language systems, computer-image understanding, and even robotics. Now, more than a decade later, the approaches pioneered in the 1970s renaissance are just beginning to enter the marketplace.

The chapters in Part I, *Thinking About Thinking,* follow this sequence fairly closely, with special emphasis on the developments just mentioned in expert systems, natural language, and vision. Before continuing, however, I pause for some reflection on the inevitable question: "Can a machine think?" *Really* think? In the end, of course, I return to the inevitable answer: "Nobody knows." But there are some marvelously entertaining arguments along the way—and some serious reflection about what it means to be human.

In Part II, *Visions of a New Generation,* I turn to the upheavals that have taken place in AI since about 1980. This is an era that might be called "The Age of the Entrepreneur" or perhaps "The Age of the Fifth Generation." AI had the good fortune—or in some people's opinion, the bad luck—to reach a certain level of technical maturity just in time to get caught up in the larger information-processing revolution. At this time, AI was discovered by technocrats and venture capitalists in much the same way that an out-of-the-way restaurant is sometimes discovered by trendy gourmets. The result has been a boom in commercial AI applications—particularly expert systems—and an upheaval in the AI research community. Given the fabulous success of Apple Computer Company, and other such high-tech start-up firms, there are obviously fortunes to be made. But just as important, given the remarkable strides being made in the power and affordability of computer hardware, the community has been fired by the vision of a new kind of computing that can change the world in much the same way that Edison and Ford changed theirs.

At the same time, as I pointed out earlier, Japan, Europe, and the United States have mounted ten-year, billion-dollar projects to turn that vision into a reality. Indeed, out of a complex amalgam of anxiety and global ambition, these projects have created something unique in the history of computing: For the first time, researchers have begun to think on a ten-year time scale. For the first time, they've begun to look beyond the next piece of hardware or software and instead ask what it's all *for*.

And thus we return to the New Land of Fairie. Part III of this book, *The Shape of the Future,* is a personal meditation on just what this world of the future may be like. In broad terms, intelligent machines do seem to have the potential for taking on two kinds of roles. As *facilitators,* they can help people cope with complexity, explore new ideas, heighten creativity, and organize work in new and more fulfilling ways. As *robots,* or *agents*—machines that can take action on their own, without direct supervision—they can relieve human beings from drudgery, danger, and mind-numbing routine. In either role, intelligent machines have the potential to affect human society in ways we can only dimly foresee—which leads us to perhaps the most important question about the uses of AI: How much responsibility should intelligent machines actually be given? It may be that in answering that question we will have to endow these machines with an electronic code of ethics. It may be that in trying to define such a code we will learn a great deal about our own sense of right and wrong, just as the pursuit of artificial intelligence in general has taught us a great deal about intelligence itself.

Indeed, as we work out how intelligent machines are supposed to fit into society, we may very well gain new insight into what society—and human beings—are all about.

P A R T   I
THINKING ABOUT THINKING

1

The Birth of a New Idea

It's been said that AI has a short history but a long past. And fair enough: Its direct ancestry can be traced well back into the nineteenth century, to the efforts of philosophers and mathematicians to forge the ancient rules of logic into rigorous "laws of thought." Its spiritual ancestry goes back even farther, beyond Aristotle, Plato, and Socrates to the first human beings who wondered about the nature of knowledge and the nature of mind. But its own life as a separate discipline began just over three decades ago, on the campus of Dartmouth College in Hanover, New Hampshire, in the summer of 1956.

Taken by itself, the Dartmouth Summer Research Project on Artificial Intelligence was actually a rather inconclusive event. John McCarthy, then a young assistant professor of mathematics at Dartmouth and a prime mover in organizing the two-month workshop, recalls being disappointed. People had begun writing AI-like programs almost as soon as they'd had computers to run them on, of course. But with the Dartmouth conference, McCarthy hoped to bring together virtually all the researchers then active in the field—all ten of them—and forge some kind of new consensus on what the field was and where it was going. Unfortunately, he says, things didn't quite work out that way. Not everyone came for the full time. People stubbornly persisted in their own approaches. And no one really changed their research interest as a direct result of the conference.[1]

Nonetheless, taken in context, the Dartmouth conference's reputation as the birthplace of AI is accurate. Its symbolic importance far outweighs anything that did or did not happen there. Simply by bringing people together, the conference underscored the conviction that their hitherto vague and philosophical musings were beginning to coalesce into something real. Not incidentally, the conference also gave the emerging field a name. Until then it had been known as "complex information processing," "automata studies," and various other names. McCarthy had concocted the term *artificial intelligence* when he was writing the proposal for the workshop, and somehow it seemed to fit.★

The Dartmouth gathering also provided a debut of sorts for four young men who were to play a critical role in shaping the field:

John McCarthy, the principal organizer of the conference, left Dartmouth within a year for MIT, where he became the cofounder of a new AI research laboratory. A few years later, in 1962, McCarthy moved to Stanford University, where he organized yet another AI laboratory. Along with Carnegie-Mellon University in Pittsburgh, these two laboratories are still the leading AI research centers in the United States. Meanwhile, in 1958, McCarthy devised a programming language known as List Processor, or LISP, which is still the most widely used language for AI research.

Marvin Minsky, then a Harvard junior fellow in mathematics and neurology, was McCarthy's cofounder at the MIT center; he was for many years the laboratory's leader. Less a programmer than a brilliant and provocative thinker, Minsky has made his influence felt in every subfield of AI—in part because he has served as mentor to a cadre of talented students, many of whom have gone on to become important AI researchers in their own right.

Allen Newell and *Herbert Simon,* both from the Carnegie Institute of Technology (now Carnegie-Mellon University) in Pittsburgh, were virtual unknowns to the others at the Dartmouth conference. But, working independently, they had devised a program known as Logic Theorist, which could prove theorems in mathematical logic. The first true AI program, Logic Theorist established many of the themes that have dominated AI ever since. Newell and Simon, together with their students at Carnegie Tech, formed the nucleus of the third of the three major AI laboratories.

Beyond symbolism and introductions, however, the Dartmouth conference was important mainly because it happened at the right time. The conference was not an isolated event, nor was the emergence of AI in the midfifties just a matter of happenstance. Those same years saw intellectual upheavals taking place along a much broader front. In virtually all the sciences of mind—in psychology, linguistics, neuroscience, anthropology, and even philosophy—old assumptions were being shaken by a new concept of what the mind was all about.

THE BEGINNINGS OF A COGNITIVE SCIENCE

In that same year, for example, the Harvard psychologist George Miller published an essay entitled "The Magical Number Seven, Plus or Minus Two: Some Limits on Our Capacity for Processing Information." In it, he asserted

---

★It was not to everyone's taste. The word *artificial* was thought to carry connotations of *ersatz,* of being not as good as the natural kind, while the term *artificial intelligence* sounded like science fiction rather than serious research. But for better or worse, artificial intelligence was the name that stuck.

---

on the basis of considerable empirical evidence that human beings can deal consciously with only about seven items of information at a time. Thus, a seven-digit telephone number or a five-digit zip code is easy enough to remember, but longer sequences are much harder. A sentence shorter than about seven words is easy to repeat verbatim, but longer sentences tend to get scrambled.

It is true, asserts Miller, that people often group things together into "chunks," so that they can deal with them as units. Sentences, for example, tend to be remembered as phrases or units of meaning, rather than as abstract strings of words. Indeed, according to Miller, "This kind of linguistic recoding that people do seems to me to be the lifeblood of the thought process." Nonetheless, he says, no matter how big the chunks, the conscious mind can deal with only seven at a time.[2]

Thirty years later this idea seems interesting, but innocuous. In 1956, however, Miller's paper was downright subversive. In those years American psychologists were only just beginning to break loose from the doctrine of behaviorism, which had dominated their science since the early part of the twentieth century. The behaviorist argument was that no one, not even a psychologist, could observe what was really going on in someone else's head, which was effectively a black box. All we could know was input and output, stimulus and response. So those were the only things a scientist should study; the "mind" was unscientific and off limits. Indeed, in psychology journals it was considered bad form even to use the word *mind*. (The truly radical behaviorists, such as Harvard's B. F. Skinner, have been known to assert that the mind doesn't even exist.)

As a standard of rigor and precision, behaviorism once served as a healthy antidote to the vague technique of "introspection" that characterized psychology at the turn of the century. As a rigid orthodoxy, however, it prevented two generations of psychologists from learning anything interesting about the black box—such as what goes on inside. All it allowed was a list of empty correlations between such-and-such a stimulus and response. So naturally, in the post–World War II years, more and more psychologists began to rebel. And thus, in 1956, the widespread excitement over Miller's magical number seven. It was apparent to everyone in the field that Miller was coming to grips with the human mind, and not just as a bundle of responses to external stimuli. Simply by trying to find the limits of what the conscious mind could handle, Miller was implicitly talking about an entity that was active, an entity that could take information and *do* something with it—an entity that, in short, could think.

Meanwhile, the staid discipline of linguistics was undergoing its own upheaval, thanks to a brash and argumentative young man from MIT named Noam Chomsky. Chomsky's theory of "formal" grammar, also developed in those eventful midfifties, provided linguists with the first rigorous mathematical framework for analyzing the structure of language. And his theory of "transformational" grammar provided a new system of thinking about the way language is actually used. As we'll see more fully in Chapter 4, Chomsky argued that at the heart of each sentence lies a deep structure, a concept such as *John kissed Mary*. To reach the sentence that is actually spoken or written, claims Chomsky, certain transformation rules are applied to the deep structure to produce what he called a surface structure—derived sentences such as *Mary was kissed by John* or *Whom did John kiss?*

Once again, these seem like utterly reasonable things to be thinking about—in retrospect. But at that time Chomsky's ideas were even more revolutionary than Miller's. Suddenly, linguistics was no longer just a collection of interesting, but isolated facts. Because of Chomsky, the discipline was on its way to becoming a theoretical science with an empirical basis approaching that of physics. Indeed, with so much emphasis being placed on the relationships, transformations, and grammatical manipulations underlying language, Chomsky's theoretical linguistics took on an eerie resemblance to the theory of data processing in a computer.

Anthropologists, meanwhile, were beginning to find deep underlying similarities in the way people from widely different cultures classify colors and objects, and in the way they form concepts. And neuroscientists were beginning to realize that the nerve cells of the brain are not simply woven together in a single homogeneous mass but that several different types of cells each respond to extremely specific, different pieces of information. Indeed, a given neuron in the visual cortex might respond to visual input if and only if the input consists of a line falling in a specific orientation at a specific position on the retina.

Thirty years later, as these ideas have continued to mature, people have come to think of all these scattered activities as integral parts of a single new discipline, known as cognitive science.[3] Today there are journals of cognitive science, and a cognitive science society. Currently, the National Science Foundation has begun to develop a special new program to fund research in cognitive science. But even in the midfifties, it was clear to all concerned that these various developments were related to each other and to the fledgling discipline of AI by a single common concept: information processing. Furthermore, that concept implied the possibility of a whole new way to think about thinking. Somehow, whether the human mind was busy proving theorems in mathematical logic, or producing grammatical sentences, or paying attention to chunks of data, it seemed to be manipulating symbolic information in much the same way that computers do.

THE ROOTS OF AI

It's obviously no coincidence that AI and its fellow cognitive sciences began to emerge less than a decade after the invention of the computer in

World War II. But then, computers hardly sprang out of a vacuum, either. In their 1972 book, *Human Problem Solving,* Newell and Simon look back on those years and pay homage to a "powerful, growing Zeitgeist" in the decades just preceding and just following the war, a dawning awareness that ideas, in the form of symbols, could be manipulated "quite as readily as pine boards in a carpenter shop."[4]

Logic and Computers

Newell and Simon particularly stress the importance of the prewar developments in symbolic logic, which had been a preoccupation of mathematicians and philosophers since 1854, when the English mathematician George Boole introduced the basic concepts in his book *The Laws of Thought.*

In flavor and style, symbolic logic bears a strong resemblance to ordinary high-school algebra. But instead of dealing with mathematical equations such as $5x^2 + 2x - 3 = 0$, and operations like addition and subtraction, logic deals with the process of deduction.

As a simple example, the statement *The dog is ready for dinner, or else the dog wants a walk* can be written in symbolic notation this way: Let the symbol *P* stand for the phrase *The dog is ready for dinner;* let the symbol *Q* stand for the phrase *The dog wants a walk;* and let the symbol *v* stand for *or.* The statement then becomes:

$$P \text{ v } Q$$

As another example, suppose we are given these two facts: (1) *Socrates is a man* and (2) *If Socrates is a man, then Socrates is mortal.* Most of us are able to draw the obvious conclusion: *Socrates is mortal.* This elementary bit of reasoning can be written in symbolic form by letting the symbol *R* stand for the assertion *Socrates is a man,* while letting the symbol *S* stand for *Socrates is Mortal.* In addition, the logical relationship of *IF-THEN* can be represented symbolically as an arrow: $\rightarrow$. We can then represent the deduction about Socrates this way:

$$R \text{ is true}$$
$$R \rightarrow S \text{ is true}$$
$$\text{Therefore, } S \text{ is also true}$$

Once a statement is in symbolic form, it can be manipulated by the rules of inference in much the same way that an algebraic equation can be manipulated by adding or subtracting terms from each side. And just as algebra is a tool for solving complex mathematical equations, symbolic logic is an essential tool for exploring the realm of pure reason. Though that parallel may now seem obvious to many of us, it was only at the beginning of this century, over the years 1910–1913, that Alfred North Whitehead and Bertrand Russell published (in parts) their *Principia Mathematica,* demonstrating that all of mathematics is founded on logic—that mathematics is in fact just another form of logic.

In the years prior to World War II, the development of logic entered a new phase. As logicians strove for ever increasing exactitude in their work, they found themselves asking how their symbols were supposed to be manipulated. What steps would be required? What rules would you use? This inquiry culminated in 1936 through the work of the English logician Alan Turing, who described a hypothetical logic machine of deceptive simplicity: Imagine an infinitely long tape divided into squares, as if it were a roll of postage stamps. Each square is either blank or has a symbol on it. It doesn't matter what the symbols are. They could be numbers, letters, colors, coins, or anything else. All that matters, said Turing, is that each square contains at most one symbol, and that the symbols themselves come only in a finite variety. In addition to the tape, said Turing, imagine a scanning device that can move forward and backward along the tape. (To use a modern analogy, it would function very much like the record/play head in a magnetic tape recorder.) When the machine is in operation, this scanning device looks at the tape and scans one square at a time. Depending on what it finds there, it can do one of four things: write a symbol, erase a symbol, move one square forward, or move one square back. And that is all.

On the face of it, this machine seems simple-minded indeed. However, Turing was able to show that in principle his imaginary machine was capable of computing anything that *can* be computed—which meant that any logical reasoning process, no matter how complicated, could be done automatically on a real, physical device. In fact, certain kinds of thinking could be done without the use of a human brain.[5]

A year later, in 1937, a young engineering student at MIT named Claude Shannon wrote a master's thesis in which he applied the notions of formal reasoning to quite a different domain: He showed that the operation of electrical relays and switching circuits could be analyzed to yield such logical elements as *True, False, Not, And,* and *Or.*[6]

And then, in 1943, the neurophysiologist Warren McCulloch and a young mathematician from the University of Illinois, Walter Pitts, showed how hypothetical networks of nerve cells could perform all the operations of formal logic.[7] It later turned out that their mathematical neurons were too idealized to duplicate the action of real neurons in the human brain. But their work was nonetheless a provocative demonstration of how a mechanistic brain might be able to reason automatically.

Of course, it soon became apparent that all these ideas were not unrelated at all. In effect, Turing, Shannon, McCulloch, and Pitts had been laying down a fundamental theory of computing machines.

The Cybernetics Revolution

With the rise of the cybernetics movement in the 1940s, the nebulous Zeitgeist referred to by Newell and Simon began to crystallize into a single set of ideas.[8] Its underlying themes were *communication* and *control* (the word *cybernetics* itself comes from the Greek word *kybernetes,* meaning "steersman"), and its most visible champion was the flamboyant mathematician Norbert Weiner of MIT. In his book *Cybernetics,*[9] published in 1948, Weiner stressed three major elements in defining this new field.

The first was the theory of feedback systems, which Weiner himself had introduced in 1943, in collaboration with Arturo Rosenblueth and Julian Bigelow.[10] The concept of feedback is one of those brilliantly simple ideas that seems utterly obvious once someone has pointed it out. Consider a thermostat, for example: Whenever the room gets too cold, a strip of metal bends, closes a contact, and turns the furnace on; when the room warms up again, the strip straightens out, releases the contact, and cuts the furnace off. Or consider the process of picking up a pencil with your eyes closed: You reach for it and almost certainly miss by a fraction. Open your eyes, however, and your brain can continuously make corrections by using information from your eyes and fingertips. Picking up the pencil becomes much easier. Stated a bit more abstractly, the system has a goal: pick up the pencil. If any deviations arise, they are "fed back" into the system so as to move it back toward the goal.

In a world where nothing is ever perfectly accurate or reliable, some such self-correcting mechanism seems essential for doing anything. Indeed, Weiner and his colleagues pointed out that the feedback mechanism is found everywhere, both in man-made systems and in biology.

But their theory went even further. Imagine an anti-aircraft gun that tracks a target, correcting its aim after every shot with feedback from radar. (Weiner and Bigelow originally conceived of feedback when they were working on artillery during the war.) No matter how the plane twists and evades, the gun tracks and fires, tracks and fires. It's completely automatic, and yet the gun seems guided by a grimly determined intelligence.

Through feedback, said Weiner, Bigelow, and Rosenblueth, a mechanism could embody *purpose*.

As Newell said recently, "The instant rise to prominence of cybernetics occurred because of the universal perception of the importance of this thesis. AI has added the weight of numbers and variety to the evidence, but has not produced any qualitatively different argument."[11]

The second element in Weiner's concept of cybernetics was information theory, which was first set down in its modern form by Claude Shannon in 1948.[12] Shannon's work attracted widespread interest because he had finally managed to devise a precise mathematical definition for *information,* which had previously been a very elusive concept. To do so, unfortunately, he had to give up any reference to *meaning*; in his theory the information content of a message was defined by the number of symbols required to encode it, and not by what the message actually said. The payoff, however, was a deeper understanding of what it takes to communicate. Shannon's concept of information provided a rigorous mathematical underpinning for modern communications systems, and found applications in fields ranging from computer science to thermodynamics.[13] But perhaps just as importantly, Shannon's information theory inspired certain young psychologists, such as George Miller, to begin asking heretical questions—such as, How much information gets processed in the human mind?

The third element in Weiner's cybernetics was, of course, the electronic computer.

A New Kind of Machine

The computer itself was invented during World War II, not once but three times: once for calculating artillery tables (the United States), once for breaking German military codes (Great Britain), and once for calculating airplane wing flutter (Germany).[14] It was cast in its modern form immediately after the war by the brilliant Hungarian mathematician John von Neumann, one of the many European scientists who had fled to the United States in the dark days of the 1930s.

In von Neumann's conception, a computer fundamentally consists of three parts: a memory unit, a central processing unit, and a data channel connecting them (Figure 1-1).

The memory unit, which corresponds roughly to the tape of Turing's machine, stores data and instructions using a simple code. The code consists of two symbols, which can be thought of as *1* and *0*, *yes* and *no*, *up* and *down*, *red* and *green*, or whatever. These symbols, which are known as *bits*, are grouped together in strings to form code words. (Often the words consist of eight, sixteen, or thirty-two bits, but there are many variations.) Depending on context, these words may denote numbers, symbols, or commands. Thus, the

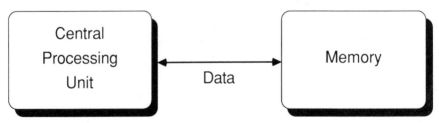

Fig. 1–1
The logical structure of a computer

sequence 01000001 might denote the number *65*, the capital letter *A*, or an instruction to tell the central processing unit what to do next.

The central processing unit, which corresponds roughly to the read/write head on Turing's machine, is the heart of the computer. And, like Turing's machine, it is fundamentally simple-minded. In operation it goes through an endless cycle: fetch the next chunk of instructions or data from memory, execute the appropriate operation, then send the results back. Fetch, execute, return. Fetch, execute, return.

At one level, this is clearly absurd. It's a bit like trying to make a dinner salad the hard way: go out to buy the lettuce, bring it home, and chop it up. Go out to buy the carrots, bring them home, and chop them up. Go out to buy the celery. . . . Of course, the inefficiency of the process doesn't matter if the computers are fast enough. Even the vacuum-tube computers of the 1940s, which were lumbering dinosaurs by modern standards, could crunch numbers a lot faster than humans can.*

But the speed of the computers, or their lack of it, was beside the point. The brilliant stroke in von Neumann's design was that the machine could treat data and program instructions in precisely the same way. They both used the same codes. They were both stored in the same memory unit. They both traveled back and forth over the same data channel. In fact, they were both simply two aspects of the same thing: The program in a von Neumann-style computer is basically just another kind of data.

Thus, for the first time, it became possible to imagine programs that could treat *themselves* as data, that could rewrite themselves on the fly.** In principle such programs could evolve and grow, becoming richer with time and experience—rather like a mind.

After the war, as computers became more widely known, the machines were dubbed "electronic brains" or "giant brains." And along with all the other technological marvels that came out of the war—the atomic bomb, radar, rockets, the jet airplane—they became the subject of sensationalized magazine and newspaper articles, lurid Sunday supplements, and gloomy science fiction. People were both fascinated and horrified. For the first time in history, here was a machine that could do arithmetic, break codes, and solve all sorts of other problems that humans found very hard and intellectually demanding. Had scientists uncovered the secrets of the mind at last? Could it be long before robots ran the world? Were humans already obsolete?

Weiner and von Neumann themselves both felt compelled to give public warnings against making too much of computers. Despite the use of provoca-

*As we'll see in later chapters, however, this serial, one-step-at-a-time operation—the "von Neumann bottleneck"—has now become a severe constraint on advanced AI applications. For that matter, it has become a severe constraint on high-speed computations of all kinds. Thus, a great deal of effort is currently going into devising new kinds of computer architectures that will circumvent the bottleneck.

**LISP and other modern languages used in AI are designed to do exactly that.

tive words like *memory,* they pointed out, the resemblance between brains and computers is really quite superficial. The brain has no "central processing unit," so far as anyone can tell, nor does it store discrete bits of information in individual memory cells the way a computer does. And it certainly doesn't use a binary code for storing information.

Nonetheless, as Weiner, von Neumann, and their contemporaries were also well aware, the computer and the brain *were* analogous in a deeper and more important sense. Obvious physical differences to the contrary, they both seemed to be able to do the same kinds of mental tasks, in much the same way that a sparrow and a B29 both performed the same task of flying. Indeed, to those who contemplated its nature in those early days, the computer seemed to be saying something very important about the mind, although it was not entirely clear what. Moreover, the computer provided a rich source of new metaphors for thinking about the mind, and for framing new kinds of questions about the mind. Instead of trying to think about the mind as a black box with inputs and outputs, or as a chemical reactor, or as plumbing (Freud's theories of pent-up drives, repressions, and outlets had a distinctly hydraulic tone), scientists could begin to ask much more specific questions about communication, control, and the flow of information. As Weiner writes in *Cybernetics,* "The mechanical brain does not secrete thought 'as the liver does bile,' as the earlier materialists claimed, nor does it put it out in the form of energy, as the muscle puts out its activity. Information is information, not matter or energy. No materialism which does not admit this can survive at the present day."[15]

THE DAWN OF AI

Attempts to create "intelligent" programs began almost immediately after the invention of the computer. Arthur Samuel, now professor emeritus at Stanford, began writing a checkers-playing program as early as 1948. Shannon was already sketching some ideas for a chess-playing program in 1950.[16] Yet progress was slow, partly because in those days computers were still sluggish, limited, difficult to program; and rare. Moreover, the ones that did exist were mostly dedicated to defense work.

But just as important, progress was slow because people were still groping. They had no clear idea of how to proceed. It was not until the midfifties and the work of Newell and Simon that the inchoate ideas began to crystallize.

The Computer as a Processor of Symbols

Herbert Simon can still remember the moment of insight. It was in 1952, just after he had arrived at the Rand Corporation in Santa Monica, California, to spend the summer as a consultant on a study of man–machine interactions that the company was doing for the Air Force. The machines in this case were the radar sets and fighter planes under the control of a regional air defense center, and the men were the plotters who traced the location and direction of each aircraft on a large Lucite screen. The problem was what to do about unidentified aircraft. Should a fighter be scrambled to go out and look at every one? That would be expensive. On the other hand, letting an enemy plane through could be even more expensive. It was a tense and hectic job that no one was performing very well.[17]

For Simon, however, the problem itself wasn't nearly as fascinating as the way the Rand people were studying it. Taking what was then a strikingly original approach, they had modeled the entire air defense center with a computer simulation.

Simon was particularly intrigued by an old card-programmed calculator being used to produce the simulated radar maps: "What was remarkable about this application," he recalls, "was that the computer was being used not to generate numbers, but locations—points—on a two-dimensional map. Computers, then, were not merely number-crunchers; they were general symbol manipulators, capable of processing symbols of any kind—numerical or not!"[18]

This insight may seem obvious now, when computers are routinely being used for word processing and data manipulations of all kinds. But at a time when computers were almost universally viewed as superfast arithmetic machines, it was startling. And to Simon, especially, it had far-reaching implications. At the age of thirty-six, Simon had already established a formidable reputation for his work in the theory of management and organizational decision-making. A few years earlier, in fact, he had helped found Carnegie Tech's new Graduate School of Industrial Administration, which was well on its way toward a national reputation for science-based professionalism in business education. His book *Administrative Behavior,* first published in 1947, had immediately been hailed as a classic—and would be among the works cited by the Swedish Academy of Sciences in 1978 when Simon was awarded the Nobel prize in economics.

Administrative Behavior was based on two interrelated ideas that have formed the core of Simon's whole intellectual career. The first is his concept of bounded rationality. Human beings are nothing at all like the omniscient, godlike, utterly rational beings imagined by economists, Simon points out. For instance, real people can rarely afford the time and effort it takes to make the "best" decisions. Instead, they settle for satisfactory decisions. When shopping for a new pair of shoes, for example, very few people will systematically visit every shoe store in town to find the lowest possible price. The savings just aren't worth it. Most of us simply visit two or three of the most convenient stores and settle for the best buy we can find. Simon coined a new word for this kind of behavior—*satisficing*—and pointed out that it is ubiquitous in human decision-making. Life is too short, and the human mind too limited, to insist on perfection.

Simon's second fundamental idea was that human beings, because of their cognitive limitations, tend to identify with subgoals rather than ultimate goals. In a human organization such as a corporation or a government agency, for example, different individuals in the organization work from different premises. A salesman will tend to see every problem in terms of maximizing sales. But a production engineer will see the same problem in terms of optimizing production—and may reach a very different conclusion. As a result, says Simon, one can predict the kind of decisions people in an organization will make by looking at their positions in the organization. In short, "Where you stand depends on where you sit."

By the time he arrived at Rand in that summer of 1952, Simon had already begun to think about organizational decision-making in terms of the way individual humans solve problems; it was clear to him that the two processes were inseparable. "My original quest was for a language in which to systematically express these social science concepts," he says. "The question was, What language? Classical math was not the right language. So I took my lantern around, and looked in all sorts of nooks and crannies."[19] It was at Rand that he found the answer in the symbol-processing capabilities of computers.

Simon was greatly helped toward this realization by another discovery he made at Rand: a young man of boundless energy and enthusiasm named Allen Newell. Newell had come to Rand two years before, in 1950, after a year of graduate work in mathematics at Princeton had convinced him that he didn't have the temperament for that kind of arcane research. "I was a problem solver," he recalls, "and I wanted problems that I could go out and solve."

Newell had already been struck by the way that a change in the organization of Rand's air control center could drastically change how well the people there performed. Furthermore, he had begun to notice strong similarities between the way humans communicated and made decisions in the center and the way information was processed in his computers. Thus, within five minutes of his meeting Simon, the two men discovered their ideological affinity. "We launched at once into an animated discussion," says Simon, "recognizing that, though our vocabularies were different, we both viewed man's mind as a symbol-manipulating, or information-processing system. I think the phrase 'symbol-manipulating' was mine, and 'information-processing' was Al's."[20]

But it took a long time for their ideas to fully gel. Not until 1954, during one of Simon's subsequent summers at Rand, did he and Newell first say it out loud: "Well, if you're really going to have a good theory of what goes on in human problem-solving, why not simulate it on the computer?"[21] And even then, they made no specific plans. It was only much later in the year, on a November afternoon after Simon had returned to Carnegie Tech, that Newell experienced his own moment of epiphany.

Oliver Selfridge of MIT had come to Rand that day to give a talk about a pattern-recognition program he was developing. As it happens, this program itself was to be a dead end in terms of AI. But it worked: Not only could it recognize patterns such as the letter *A*; it could modify itself and learn to recognize the patterns better than it had before.

And for Newell, Selfridge's talk was a revelation. He couldn't get over the way in which a set of simple, easy-to-understand subprocesses, once they were organized and interacted the right way, could produce highly complex behavior. Suddenly, he recalls, building a system that exhibited intelligence not only seemed possible but had become an appropriate scientific task. "Those guys [Selfridge and his coworkers] had developed a mechanism that was so much richer than any other mechanism that I'd been exposed to that we'd entered another world as far as our ability to conceptualize went," says Newell. "And that turned my life around. I mean that was the point at which I started working on artificial intelligence. Very clear—I mean it all happened one afternoon."[22]

So in 1955 Newell left Rand for Carnegie Tech, officially to complete his Ph.D. as Simon's student (which he did) but in fact to work as Simon's colleague in the design of a program that could exhibit intelligence.

The Importance of Heuristic Reasoning

Ultimately, their project became Logic Theorist, the first true AI program. As the name indicates, the program proves theorems in symbolic logic—a task chosen in part because it seemed simpler than Newell's first topic, chess, and in part because the material was ready at hand: Simon happened to have a copy of Whitehead and Russell's *Principia Mathematica* in his home library.

A proof in logic proceeds just like a high-school geometry proof. The starting point is a set of statements known as the *premises,* and the goal is another statement known as the *theorem.* To get from one to the other, you simply combine and modify the premises by using the rules of inference. (There are about half a dozen of them.) Eventually, if the rules are applied in the right order, the manipulations will produce the theorem.★

The trick is to figure out the right order. A proof in its final form is obviously "logical." But the process of *discovering* that proof is not at all logical. Ask a mathematician how he does it, and you're likely to hear words such as *intuition* and *hunch,* as if the proofs were brewed in his subconscious by some kind of magic. Newell and Simon's challenge was to reduce that magic to a system that could be programmed into a computer.

★Anyone who has ever tried to solve a Rubik's cube has a good idea of what the process is like: Take a mixed-up Rubik's cube (the axioms), twist the faces this way and that (apply the rules of inference) until all the faces have their proper colors (the theorem is proved).

Of course, they could have proceeded by brute force. All they had to do was to program the computer to start from the given premises, then doggedly apply every rule in sight. That approach is guaranteed to produce the theorem eventually. The problem is that "eventually" might not come for a very, very long time.

Newell and Simon dubbed this brute-force method "the British Museum Algorithm," in honor of the legendary monkeys who work at the typewriters of the British Museum. (The monkeys type, and type, and type; one day, completely at random, they will type out the complete works of Shakespeare.) Newell and Simon then estimated how many proofs the algorithm would have to generate before it found all the sixty-odd theorems in Chapter 2 of the *Principia*. Their answer—"Almost certainly greater than 10^{1000}"—is a number so vast as to defy all metaphor. There is no computer that could generate so many proofs. There is no way even to conceive of a computer that could do it. There haven't been that many microseconds since the Big Bang. There aren't that many atoms in the observable universe.

As Newell and Simon noted with admirable understatement, "something more effective than the British Museum Algorithm is needed." Whatever it is that mathematicians (and high-school students) are doing when they prove theorems, it obviously isn't that.[23]

In fact, this problem of insanely multiplying possibilities turns out to be *the* critical issue in understanding how computers (or people) can adapt to changing circumstances. Known as the "combinatoric explosion," it crops up everywhere, not just in logic but in games. Claude Shannon once calculated, for instance, that there are some 10^{120} possible moves in a game of chess. It even occurs in everyday life. As an illustration, try calculating how many conceivable outfits you could put on tomorrow morning, counting every combination of shirts, slacks, underwear, socks, and so forth, that you own. For my own closet I estimate about a billion, and it's not a big closet. So here is the problem in a nutshell: How do you even manage to get dressed in the morning?

The answer, obviously, is that you *don't* stand there and try to debate all of your one billion–odd options systematically. (At least, I hope you don't.) Instead, most of us half-consciously apply Simon's satisficing strategy: We think things like *Those two look good together* and *Do these shoes match?* and *I can't wear that to work!* And very quickly, using a few rules of thumb, we've whittled down the choices to something manageable.

Such rules of thumb are known as *heuristics*, from the Greek word *heuriskein*, meaning "to invent" or "to discover."* Newell and Simon accordingly made heuristic reasoning the central strategy of Logic Theorist: At each decision point, instead of blindly and systematically trying to follow all the

---

*This word was first popularized in the 1940s by the mathematician George Polya, who had been one of the few people to study human problem-solving before Newell and Simon;[24] he had also been one of Newell's teachers at Stanford.

paths, the program would apply what were, in effect, rules of thumb. Its reasoning process could be paraphrased, "First try approach A; if that doesn't work, try approach B; and so on." For example, Logic Theorist might start with *substitution*, simply replacing one symbol with another symbol, or perhaps another whole expression. If that did not produce the desired theorem right away, the program might then try such things as working backward from the theorem to find intermediate expressions that might be easier to prove.

As straightforward as it seems, Newell and Simon's use of heuristic reasoning was in fact a profound step. In mainstream computer science, the emphasis was (and is) on algorithms, which are precisely defined, step-by-step procedures that are guaranteed to give you an answer. A good example is the algorithm for subtraction taught in elementary school: Start in the right-hand column, borrow from the top number in the next column if necessary, and so on. Algorithms are ideally suited to numerical calculations. And of course, most people in the 1950s still thought of computers as numerical machines.

But heuristic procedures are very different. They are *not* guaranteed to work. They are only guaranteed to be worth trying. Their outcome is *not* predictable, because there is no way to know in advance what kinds of situations they will encounter. And they are *not* precise and tidy. In fact, there is something fundamentally messy and ad hoc about heuristics.

But then, the world is a messy, ad-hoc place. The unique power of heuristic reasoning lies in its ability to cope with the complex and the unexpected, to make choices when there is no time to make a choice, to hunker down and keep on going when a precisely defined algorithm would be overwhelmed by the combinatoric explosion. In effect, Newell and Simon were programming a computer to cope with its world through satisficing. In effect, they were asserting that even computers are subject to bounded rationality.

"It Works!"

By October 1955, Newell and Simon had begun to get a feel for how problem-solving heuristics would work in theorem-proving, and were moving on to rough out the design of Logic Theorist. "My method of working," says Simon, "was to take theorems in the *Principia* and work out proofs while trying to dissect as minutely as possible, not only the proof steps, but the cues that led me to each one. Then we tried to incorporate what I had learned into a flow diagram. We repeated this day after day, with the flow diagram steadily approaching a description that could be programmed on the machine. On December 15, 1955, I simulated by hand a proof of Theorem 2.15 of *Principia* in such detail that we agreed the scheme was programmable. I have always celebrated that date as the birthday of heuristic problem-solving by computer."[25]

Newell recalls their elation: "Kind of crude, but it works, boy, does it work."[26] A few weeks later, when classes had resumed after Christmas break, Simon walked into his course on Mathematical Models for the Social Sciences and announced, "Over Christmas Allen Newell and I invented a thinking machine."★

However, there remained the problem of actually programming Logic Theorist into a machine. Newell was running up a horrendous telephone bill ($200 per month) with incessant calls to J. Clifford Shaw, who was doing most of the actual programming on the JOHNNIAC computer back at Rand. Shaw had been working with Newell and Simon on the programming part of the problem since 1954, when they were still thinking in terms of a chess-playing machine. It wasn't easy. As Shaw later explained, programming in those days was still pretty much a matter of writing out numerical codes: "It was very painful to try to program anything, to make progress towards a chess-learning machine, because we didn't have an adequate language for communicating. . . . As programmers, we had a creative task each time with trying to invent a representation in the machine corresponding to what we were communicating fairly loosely in English. The natural direction then was to suggest interpretive languages, higher-level languages, trying to approach something where Al and Herb could specify more completely the complex concepts of chess."[28]

The idea of a programming language seems obvious now, at a time when BASIC and PASCAL are being taught in our high schools. But in the mid-1950s it was a major challenge. Everything had to be done from scratch. The systems designed by Newell and Shaw—a series of Information Processing Languages, as they called them—were not only the first programming languages designed specifically for AI applications; they were very nearly the first high-level languages of any kind. (FORTRAN, still widely used in scientific programming, was being developed at almost exactly the same time.)

The programming and refinement of Logic Theorist thus consumed most of the spring. By June 1956, however, it was working well enough that Newell and Simon could exhibit preliminary runs at the Dartmouth Conference. On August 9, 1956, it produced its first complete proof of a theorem: *Principia*'s Theorem 2.01. And a month later, on September 11, 1956, Newell and Simon presented the first formal report on Logic Theorist to an audience of leading computer and social scientists gathered at MIT for the Symposium on Information Theory. Here, beyond any argument, they said, was proof that certain kinds of intelligent behavior—theorem-proving—could arise from simple, comprehensible mechanisms.

Logic Theorist caused a sensation. But then, the day itself was something

---

★One of the students in that class was an undergraduate named Edward Feigenbaum, now a senior AI researcher at Stanford. No one in the room could figure out exactly what Simon meant by a "thinking machine," Feigenbaum recalls. But it sounded intriguing; Simon gave him some manuals, and that night Feigenbaum began to learn about computers.[27]

of a sensation. Newell and Simon led off the proceedings. They were followed by linguist Noam Chomsky, who exhibited his own new approach to grammar based on linguistic transformations. And not long afterward came psychologist George Miller, who outlined his claim that the capacity of human short-term memory is limited to approximately seven items.

Indeed, if the Dartmouth conference can accurately be called the birthplace of AI, then the first formal report on Logic Theorist fell on a day that can fairly be called the birthdate of cognitive science. As Miller later recounted, "I went away from the Symposium with a strong conviction, more intuitive than rational, that human experimental psychology, theoretical linguistics, and computer simulation of cognitive processes were all pieces of a larger whole, and that the future would see progressive elaboration and coordination of their shared concerns."[29]

Human Problem Solving

Logic Theorist continued its runs throughout the autumn of 1956 and went through several major revisions. But simultaneously, Newell, Simon, and Shaw were already designing its successor: GPS, the General Problem Solver.

By that point Newell and Simon had learned of the research done at the Naval Research Laboratory by psychologists O. K. Moore and Scarvia B. Anderson, who had begun using logic theorem-proving several years earlier in their own research on human problem-solving. Moore and Anderson's innovation was to have the subject think aloud as they worked through each test problem; these "protocols," as they were called, provided a trace of the reasoning process. (Example: "Well, my first feeling is that we want to get R on the left and somehow invert P and Q, so. . . .")

"As soon as we got the protocols they were fabulously interesting," recalls Newell. "They caught and just laid out a whole bunch of the processes that were going on."[30]

However, what quickly became clear was that Logic Theorist, while obviously capable of doing "intelligent" things, did not fit the details of human problem-solving very well. In the transcripts, the subjects were using problem-solving techniques that Newell and Simon had never thought of—to which no one had even given a name. Chief among them was what Newell and Simon dubbed "means-end analysis": In essence, "If you're over *here* and your goal is over *there*, take steps to reduce the difference." In their book *Human Problem Solving*, Newell and Simon give a common-sense example:

I want to take my son to nursery school. What's the difference between what I have and what I want? One of distance. What changes distance? My automobile. My automobile won't work. What is needed to make it work? A new battery. What has new batteries? An auto repair shop. I want the repair shop to put in a new battery; but the shop doesn't know I need one. What is the difficulty? One of communication. What allows communication? A telephone . . . and so on.[31]

By 1957, they had distilled their work with protocol analysis into the first version of GPS, also programmed by Shaw. In all its various incarnations, GPS was to dominate their research for the next ten years. *Human Problem Solving*, published in 1972, is a massive, 920-page retrospective of that work.

GPS was explicitly intended as a model of human thought processes, as revealed in the protocols. In fact, Newell and Simon saw their work as being psychology as much as anything else; it was no accident that their book was called *Human Problem Solving*. Nonetheless, GPS was also a major advance in AI, and it bequeathed a great deal. Not only did it introduce means-end analysis, which is now a standard reasoning technique in AI programs, but it was able to make plans—it could rough out its problem-solving strategy in broad outline before filling in details.

Finally, as the name implies, GPS was *general*; Newell and Simon eventually applied it not just to logic but to various kinds of games and puzzles as well. "We learned more than most people want to know about Missionaries and Cannibals, cryptarithmetic problems, chess, and the Tower of Hanoi," says Simon.[32] GPS was thus the first program to attempt a clean separation between the general problem-solving heuristics that were supposed to apply across the board, and specific rules of thumb that applied only to the task at hand—the so-called domain-specific knowledge.

As we will see in the next chapter, this division is a common feature in modern AI programs. In effect, it represents a fundamentally new concept of what programming is: Instead of writing an algorithm that tells the computer in excruciating detail what to *do*, step by step by step, tell the computer what to *know*. Give it a body of knowledge about the world so that it can use general reasoning heuristics to solve the problem at hand—without knowing in advance what the problem will be.

SYMBOLS AND THE COMPUTATIONAL PARADOX

Newell and Simon were hardly the only pioneers in AI. Indeed, the late 1950s and early 1960s were something of a golden age, vibrant with enthusiasm and a sense of the possible. People were writing programs for playing chess, for playing checkers, for recognizing patterns, even for doing the psychologists' nonsense syllable tests. John McCarthy devised LISP, still the most popular programming language for AI. Major AI research groups began to form at Carnegie Tech, MIT, and Stanford, as well as at consulting firms such as SRI International. Even the Defense Advanced Research Projects Agency (DARPA) became interested in the possibilities of AI; starting in 1962, in fact, DARPA began to express that interest with money, thus inaugurating its long and ongoing relationship as the primary funding agency for the field.

But for all that, it was Newell and Simon more than anyone else who gave shape and direction to the field. The themes they laid out with Logic Theorist and General Problem Solver have dominated AI ever since. As Simon's student Edward A. Feigenbaum says, "We're still waiting for our Newtons and Einsteins in AI. But we've had our Galileo, and he was Newell and Simon."

With the perspective of thirty years, we can point to two key legacies of their work, one of which has to do with method, the other with content.

Laboratories of the Mind

As Newell and Simon are quick to point out, the resemblance between brains and computers is superficial at best. Neurons, after all, are living cells, each one as unique as a snowflake; at any one instant there are billions of them working independently. Computers (at least in their modern form), are geometric arrays of integrated circuits etched on silicon, all marching in lockstep.

However, the analogy is more subtle than it seems. The presumption in AI is that the obvious physical differences between computers and brains are irrelevant; at some level computers can still perform the same information processing *tasks* as the brain, much as a B29 and a sparrow can both fly.

As Newell and Simon demonstrated with Logic Theorist and General Problem Solver, the computer can serve as a kind of laboratory. To continue with the flight metaphor, doing AI research is a bit like doing aeronautical engineering at a wind tunnel: First turn a set of abstract speculations about the mind into a computer program (build a model airplane for the wind tunnel); then make the program perform (turn on the wind). If it works, then maybe your speculations had something to do with reality. If not, then try again.

If nothing else, this approach does weed out fuzzy ideas and unspoken assumptions. The computer's reputation for literal-mindedness is well deserved; the programmer has to explain *everything*, step by step by step. "Computers keep you honest," says Simon. "When human beings reason verbally they can convince themselves of a lot of fallacious things because it's really hard to be aware of all the premises they're sticking in. So thinking is very loose. [But with a computer,] if you say that such and such processes will produce such and such a phenomenon, and you write the program, and they don't—well, bad luck. You'd better find out what to do about it. You have no way of fooling yourself."[33]

However, even as the computer-as-laboratory approach enforces scientific integrity, it also changes the whole way AI researchers think about the human mind. We'll see this again and again in the chapter to come: Instead of talking about an abstract, disembodied mentality, as philosophers have for three thousand years, AI researchers talk about a mind that is mechanistic, finite, operating in real time. "It can be summed up in one word," says Yale University's Roger Schank, a pioneer in natural language understanding. "Process: Seeing what the steps are, seeing what the inputs are, and providing algorithms to get from place A to place B."

Finally, and perhaps most importantly, a computer isn't human (obviously), which means that it isn't limited to doing things the human way. So an AI researcher can in principle explore other mechanisms of thinking, and thus put human intelligence in a wider context in much the same way that the Wright brothers put sparrows and eagles into a wider context. In fact, AI offers the vision of someday constructing a general theory of intelligence, whether human, silicon, or anything else.

What Is a Symbol?

Newell and Simon's second legacy, of course, was a clear articulation of the symbol-processing paradigm, which has served as the basic conceptual framework for AI ever since—and for that matter, as the framework for cognitive science as a whole.

While it's common to hear people talk about AI as "symbol processing," however, it's much less common to hear an explanation of exactly what that means. The phrase itself has an odd sound, as if the computer were pasting electronic labels on electronic file cards, and then shuffling the cards around. It's hard to see how that kind of "symbol processing" could ever express the meaning of a Mozart symphony or the full implications of a concept such as *family*.

However, while the file-card image is true in a sense, it misses the point. As philosophers have pointed out for centuries, we ourselves have no access to the world, only to our minds and to the information that our sense organs bring into our minds. We can't even think about the world until we make a symbolic model of the world in our head. Moreover, we obviously do use symbols as a powerful way of organizing our world-model, as a way of packaging and unpackaging ideas so that we can focus our attention at the appropriate level. A set of concepts such as *furniture, plumbing,* and *groceries* can be subsumed into a single concept—*home,* for example. Or a concept like *furniture* can be expanded into *dining-room table, bedroom dresser, living-room couch,* and so on.

And so it is with the symbols in an AI program. As we'll see more fully in the next chapter, they aren't just electronic file cards but the components of an electronic model of the world. They have structure and associations. Moreover, they are active: As the program runs, the symbols have the power to interact with each other, to make and break connections with each other, and thus to capture some of the flexibility and expressive power of human symbol-making. General Problem Solver, for example, had a symbol for *goal,* which was a complex data structure. It contained information about methods the program might use to attain that goal, as well as a history of the program's previous attempts to reach it. So the symbol was an active object. It had associations and meaning. It grew and changed with time.

The Computational Paradox

No one denies that in comparison to the brain, current-generation computers are very simple machines. Cast in such a light, they are almost trivial; despite their speed, they are essentially plodding, step-by-step devices governed by a rigidly precise logic. And yet that very fact underscores what Harvard psychologist Howard Gardner has called the computational paradox: By trying to model the mind on linear, logical computers, scientists have had to face just how vast, complex, and *non*linear the mind really is.[34]

Consider, for example, that life is largely a matter of making choices— which is just another way of saying that almost every cognitive act is a form of problem-solving. We've already seen what that takes. Even in a domain as straightforward and as well-defined as symbolic logic, the array of choices that Logic Theorist faced was vast beyond imagining; it had to use heuristics, uncertain rules of thumb, to find its way. And the uncertainties only get worse out in the real world, where things are *never* straightforward and well defined.

For many people, the idea that a computer can prove theorems and do other "hard" intellectual tasks is terrifying. Somehow it conjures up an image of omniscient and malevolent mentalities that will somehow take over the world and run it "logically"—and in the process stamp out all the messy, illogical, human things such as "feelings."

But the message of Logic Theorist, General Problem Solver, and their descendants isn't that at all. In fact, it's just the opposite. An intelligent machine operating in the real world *can't* be omniscient and logical; the world is simply too complex. There is too much data pouring in, too many choices to be made, too many gaps to be filled, too much that is unexpected, ambiguous, and unknowable. It may very well be that as computers become more intelligent, more flexible, and more sensitive to their surroundings, they will necessarily come to share many of the same confusions and uncertainties that we humans have.

In the same vein, consider the oft-heard statement that "a computer only does what you tell it to do." On a superficial level, this is undeniably true: A computer has to follow whatever rules the programmer writes down. But in a deeper sense, it is not true. The actual behavior of an AI program can be incredibly complex, especially when there are heuristic rules involved. After a certain point, the only way to find out exactly what the computer will do is to run the program.

Logic Theorist, for example, was a very simple AI program by today's standards. And yet it managed to discover a proof for one theorem, *Principia*'s theorem 2.85, that was shorter and more elegant than the proof given by Whitehead and Russell.★ Nobody had ever programmed Logic Theorist to do that; as primitive as it was, it already had a glimmer of something that might be called spontaneity.

Simon takes this idea even further. At some fundamental level, he maintains, even the human mind is quite simple, in the sense that there are only a few basic processes at work. What gives the human experience its infinite variety, he says, is design—the vast number of ways in which these processes can interact with each other, and in which the organism can interact with its environment.[35]

"To take my favorite analogy," says Simon, "are proteins simple, or are they complex? They are made up of very simple components, the amino acids. But you can get all sorts of wonderful behavior out of those simple components, just as you can get Shakespeare's works out of the twenty-six letters of the English alphabet. All you have to do is combine them right. *Design is all!*

"So if you want to understand human behavior, what you should try to do is look beneath the complexity. Our problem is not in simulating a human being but in finding out what it is we ought to be simulating."[36]

Of course, one could be forgiven a certain skepticism about all this. As Newell and Simon themselves freely admitted, Logic Theorist, General Problem Solver, and their brethren operated only in the very narrow domain of puzzles and games. And even then these programs were concerned only with problem-solving behavior. The programs said very little about learning, and nothing at all about perception or motor skills. Nor did they address verbal skills, intellectual development with age, or that complex of factors known as personality.

On the other hand, as Simon suggests, no one in AI was (or is) trying to create an artificial human being in full intellectual glory. The available computers were (and are) far too primitive for that, to say nothing of the researchers' level of understanding. What Logic Theorist and its successors *have* provided is a provocative hypothesis about the nature of mind: the symbol-processing hypothesis. And while this idea is far from being universally accepted (we will see in later chapters just how vociferously some people object to it), it has undeniably moved the debate about the nature of mind into a whole new realm.

As Newell says, "There is an underlying concern about the aspects of mentality that can be exhibited by machines. This shows itself at each historical moment by denying to machines those mental abilities that seem problematical at the time." Thus, he points out, the great rationalist philosopher René Descartes asserted in the 1640s that *mind* was something fundamentally different from the base matter of the body, largely out of a belief that

---

★The editors of *The Journal of Symbolic Logic* refused to publish the proof, on the grounds that if a machine did it, it couldn't possibly be real mathematics!

material objects could not have purpose. So after the cybernetics movement in the 1940s showed that machines *could* have purpose through the mechanisms of feedback, the debate shifted. In the 1950s it was said that machines could never be intelligent. Then, in the 1960s, after AI's early progress in problem solving, one heard that machines might mimic some kinds of "intelligence," but that they could never really learn.

"Thus, the basic issue simply continues," says Newell, "undergoing continuous transformation."[37]

2

The Necessity of Knowledge

It is not my aim to surprise or shock you. . . . But the simplest way I can summarize is to say that there are now in the world machines that think, that learn, and that create. Moreover, the ability to do these things is going to increase rapidly until—in a visible future—the range of problems they can handle will be coextensive with the range to which the human mind has been applied. . . .

[I predict]

1. That within ten years a digital computer will be the world's chess champion, unless the rules bar it from competition.

2. That within ten years a digital computer will discover and prove an important new mathematical theorem.

3. That within ten years most theories in psychology will take the form of computer programs, or of qualitative statements about computer programs.

—Herbert Simon[1]

Simon's words, delivered in a 1957 speech to the Operations Research Society of America, bear witness to the sense of optimism that pervaded those early years of AI. Logic Theorist had proved that machines really could reason and do intellectual tasks. General Problem Solver and its brethren were well underway. The nascent AI community was vibrant with enthusiasm and a sense of the possible.

And yet in 1967 the tenth anniversary of Simon's speech went by unnoticed, his prophecies unfulfilled. Indeed, they seemed to be more unlikely than ever. The brutal fact was that by the mid-1960s AI had sunk into a kind of dark ages, dogged by a sense of frustration and stagnation. Creating intelligence was turning out to be far more difficult than anyone had ever imagined.

AWE IN THE FACE OF THE ORDINARY

A big part of the problem was that no one, not even Simon, had fully appreciated the magnitude of the task. It's one thing to teach a computer how to prove theorems, or to play games and solve puzzles. The computer's "world" is sharply limited in such problems, and the rules are well defined. But in the midsixties people began trying to work in more realistic domains, and they began to realize that "easy," everyday tasks actually require an appalling amount of computation.

As an illustration, try writing down everything a child has to do to stack up three blocks in a little tower—*everything,* including how she finds the next block, how she moves her hand toward it, how she positions her hand to pick it up, how hard she grasps the block, which direction she moves it, ad infinitum. And then try to figure out how *she* figures out what to do next.

This sort of thing still leads to all kinds of incomprehension about AI, simply because to most of us, theorem-proving programs look impressive and block-stackers don't. When an AI researcher shows a layman his proudest accomplishment, a program he has slaved over for years, the reaction is often "So what?" In the late sixties and early seventies, for example, the AI group at MIT really did tackle the block problem: On command, a simulated robot arm would manipulate simulated blocks on a simulated tabletop. Blocks World, it was called, and at various times dozens of people worked with it. Graduate students wrote theses about it, some of them major milestones in natural-language understanding, planning, and computer vision. And yet after years of programming effort, the system could stack and unstack the blocks about as well as a human three-year-old. (Among other things, the computer had to be told that when building a tower, you don't try to pick up the block on the bottom of the tower and put it on top. . . .)

One admittedly crude way of measuring how much knowledge it takes to do something is to count how many rules of thumb are required. This inspiration came again from Newell and Simon. In the late 1960s they pointed out that much of human reasoning ability can be represented rather simply by IF-THEN rules: for example, "IF it's a tiger, and it looks hungry, and it's headed your way, THEN run," or "IF it looks like a duck, and walks like a duck, and quacks like a duck, THEN it probably is a duck."

As we'll see later on, such IF-THEN rules turn out to be ideal for capturing the kind of specialized expertise used by a doctor, say, in diagnosing a disease. However, while the computers in general use for AI in the mid-1980s are hard put to handle more than a few thousand rules at a time, Simon has estimated that a human expert—say, a chess master—uses the equivalent of about fifty thousand rules in his or her domain of expertise. And everyday common sense, which is a kind of diffuse expertise about the world in general, probably involves millions or even billions of rules.

The upshot is that AI researchers have come to regard common sense and everyday human abilities with some of the same awe that astronomers reserve for contemplating the enormity of the universe. "We shouldn't be intimidated by our Beethovens and Einsteins," writes MIT's Marvin Minsky in his essay "Why People Think Computers Can't." "We're simply so accustomed to the marvels of everyday thought that we never wonder about it."[2]

KNOWLEDGE AS A KEY TO INTELLIGENCE

But it wasn't just the enormity of common sense that was causing the problem. In retrospect, Newell, Simon, and their colleagues in the early years of AI had actually been making problem-solving harder for machines than it was for people. Their assumption was that an intelligent program ought to be general—notice the name General Problem Solver—and that it ought to be able to reason its way through problems by using a few very powerful heuristic principles, such as means-end analysis, or by working backward from goals to subgoals. It shouldn't be necessary to give the program a great deal of specific knowledge about the problem at hand. In fact, it was somehow cheating if you did. After all, how intelligent is a student who just regurgitates a set of canned answers on a test?[3]

In all fairness, general-purpose reasoning *is* very important. How else can we reason our way through unfamiliar problems when we don't have any rules of thumb or prior experience to guide us? Nonetheless, by the latter half of the sixties the limitations of general-purpose reasoning were becoming increasingly clear. An AI program that relied on general methods and nothing else was intellectually crippled, condemned to being an eternal beginner at everything. There was no way for the machine to "learn the ropes" of a job, so to speak, no way for it to employ specialized shortcuts or tricks of the trade.

As an illustration, consider the recent studies by Simon and his colleagues at Carnegie-Mellon University on the different ways that experts and novices solve physics problems. Novices do reason—frantically. They work out elaborate strategies, complete with goals and subgoals, and solve every equation in sight. At each step they ask, "What do I do next?" And yet for all the energy they expend, they are not very efficient at solving the problems. The more experienced physics students, by contrast, seem to have built up a store of special-purpose tricks and skills. They can usually just look at a problem and see right through to the solution: "Aha! That's a conservation of energy problem," or "Aha! That's an ideal gas law problem."[4]

Or consider that classic testbed of AI, chess. Simon and his coworkers have shown in a number of experiments that chess masters don't reason any better or any faster than anybody else; their mastery comes from having learned thousands of board positions and strategies, and from having learned how to put that knowledge to use when needed.[5]

"General problem-solvers are too weak to be used as the basis for building high-performance systems," write Stanford University AI researchers Edward Feigenbaum and Bruce Buchanan, along with Nobel laureate geneticist Joshua Lederberg, reflecting on their experience in the development of an early expert system known as Dendral. "The behavior of the best problem-solvers we know, the human problem-solvers, is observed to be weak and shallow, except in the areas in which the human problem-solver is a specialist. And it is observed that the transfer of expertise between specialty areas is slight. A chess-master is unlikely to be an expert algebraist or an expert mass-spectrum analyzer."[6]

In a 1977 article, AI researchers Ira Goldstein and Seymour Papert of MIT echo that point: "Today," they write, "the fundamental problem of understanding intelligence is not the identification of a few powerful techniques, but how to represent large amounts of knowledge in a fashion that permits their effective use and interaction."[7]

In short, it isn't enough just to reason. To be intelligent, you also have to *know*.

This insight, which came to dominate the field in the early 1970s, was arguably the major conceptual shift in the short history of AI. And by no coincidence, it came at a time when the dark ages of the 1960s were giving way to a renaissance—a new wave of advances in natural-language understanding, in computer vision, and in the ability of machines to learn, make plans, reason, and draw conclusions. In one way or another, all such advances were the product of this new appreciation of the importance of knowledge, and of the development of new techniques for representing knowledge in the computer and for reasoning with it.

THE RISE OF EXPERT SYSTEMS

The most dramatic success story of the AI renaissance was undoubtedly the development of expert systems, which are programs designed to give advice and make informed judgments much as a human expert would. Expert systems have hardly solved all the problems of AI; as we'll see a bit further on in this chapter, their limitations are often as interesting and illuminating as their capabilities. Nonetheless, they have played a seminal role in the development of AI, for two reasons.

First, when expert systems were first developed, in the late sixties, they epitomized the very philosophy of this new, knowledge-rich programming: Their "expertise" consisted of hundreds of rules of thumb that had been laboriously distilled by consultation with human experts. Indeed, the news that such systems could perform as well as or better than the human experts themselves was crucial to establishing the knowledge-programming philosophy as conventional wisdom in AI.

Second, the rise of expert systems reinforced a marked change that was already taking place in the tone, style, and direction of AI. During the first decade or so after the Dartmouth conference, AI researchers had focused most of their energies on trying to model human cognition; this is sometimes known as the "scientific" approach to AI. By the late 1960s, however, the field had developed a strong cadre of programmers who were less interested in cognition than in writing AI programs that worked and worked well, by whatever means necessary. In other words, they were thinking less like scientists than like engineers. The programmers who wrote the first expert systems were squarely in that camp.* Stanford's Feigenbaum, who was one of the pioneers, cheerfully acknowledged this attitude when he coined the term *knowledge engineering* to describe what he and his colleagues were up to. At the same time, the programmers on the engineering side of AI were much less interested in games and puzzles than in the practical problems of such fields as medicine and oil prospecting. This focus was popular partly because the field's major funding agency, DARPA, put increasing emphasis on real-world pay-offs. And it had partly to do with personal taste and style: "My methodology has been to work on difficult real-world problems, not toy problems," says Feigenbaum, "because your system is inevitably going to break down, and you need to know where it breaks so you can fix it. That way you learn something."[8]

The scientific component of AI hardly died out in the late sixties; understanding human thought processes continued to be an important item on the AI research agenda. Nonetheless, the emphasis on real-world applications increasingly came to dominate AI during the seventies, not least because of the success of expert systems. Indeed, it was this very shift in emphasis that ultimately gave rise to the commercial AI boom of the eighties, a topic I'll return to in Chapter 7.

MYCIN: Doctor's Consultant

It's hard to point to the first expert system, simply because so many AI researchers were working on the same ideas at the same time. But certainly the most energetic center of expert-system development has been Stanford's Heuristic Programming Project, founded by Feigenbaum and Buchanan in 1965. Their first effort was Dendral, which was designed to do chemical

---

*This difference of approach between AI scientists and AI engineers actually dates back to the beginning: As soon as Newell and Simon finished Logic Theorist in 1956, having explicitly written it as a model of human problem-solving, the program was criticized as being inefficient, and people went out to write theorem-proving programs that could do better.

analyses by interpreting the output of a mass spectrometer.* Developed in collaboration with Nobel laureate geneticist Joshua Lederberg and completed in the late 1960s, Dendral was ultimately able to analyze certain families of compounds even better than human specialists could. A variant, Genoa, is still widely used in chemical laboratories.[9]

However, while Dendral was impressive, the real landmark program was Mycin, which was developed by the Stanford team in the midseventies in collaboration with the Infectious Diseases Group at Stanford Medical School.[10] First implemented as the Ph.D. project of Edward H. Shortliffe (now an M.D. as well), Mycin's task was to advise physicians on the diagnosis of blood and meningitis infections, and on the selection of drugs for treatment. Like Dendral, it proved highly effective; indeed, it was the first program to have its expertise acknowledged by the experts themselves. In one formal test, a team of evaluators rated Mycin's prescriptions correct in 65 percent of its cases, whereas the accuracy of human specialists given the same cases ranged from 42.5 to 62.5 percent.[11]

Although Mycin was developed as an experimental system and was never intended as a commercial product, it is still in use at Stanford Medical Center; moreover, its structure and design philosophy have been followed in virtually every expert system built since then. An excerpt from one Mycin run is shown below. The patient under discussion is denoted Pt219; he or she has meningitis, which is an inflammation of the membranes surrounding the brain and spinal cord. Such inflammations are often caused by bacteria, but in Pt219's case the specific bacteria is as yet unknown. The numbered entries are Mycin's requests for more information on the case. The doctor's replies are shown in capitals.[12]

34) Is the meningitis a hospital-acquired infection?
** NO
35) Is Pt219's clinical history consistent with EPIGLOTTITIS?
** NO
36) Is Pt219's clinical history consistent with OTITIS MEDIA?
** NO
37) Has the patient ever been to an area that is endemic for coccidiomy-
    coses?
** UNKNOWN
38) Is Pt219 a burn patient?
** WHY

---

*Mass spectrographs are widely used in chemical laboratories to identify complex molecules and to determine their structure. The way they do these tasks sounds counterproductive at first: Essentially, they will take a sample of pure material, smash its molecules, and sort the pieces by weight. However, since molecules tend to break where they are weakest, like anything else, and since each kind of molecule has its own unique pattern of weak links, the array of fragments is as individual as a fingerprint.

[i.e., WHY is it important to determine whether PATIENT-219 has been seriously burned?]

[4.0] This will aid in determining the organisms (other than those seen on the cultures or smears) which might be causing the infection.

It has already been established that

[4.1] the infection which requires therapy is meningitis, and

[4.2] organisms were not seen on the stain of the pending csf culture, and

[4.3] the type of infection may be bacterial

Therefore, if

[4.4] Pt219 has been seriously burned

then

there is suggestive evidence that *Pseudomonas aeruginosa* might be one of the organisms (other than those seen on cultures or smears) causing the infection

Author: Yu [Rule 578]

[Back to question 38 ..]
** HOW 4.3

[i.e., HOW was it established that the type of infection may be bacterial?]

The following rules concluded about: the likelihood that the type of infection may be bacterial

	Rule	Yes	No
[4.5]	Rule500	(.4)	
[4.6]	Rule501		(.17)
[4.7]	Rule502	(.1)	
[4.8]	Rule524	(.42)	
[4.9]	Rule504	(.28)	

Thus, it has been established that the type of infection may be bacterial.

To understand better what is going on here, it helps to look at how Mycin is organized. In simplest terms, shown in Figure 2-1, the program can be thought of as having a four-component structure.

- The *working memory* is a data base roughly equivalent to the current patient's medical history, which doctors ordinarily carry around on paper forms affixed to clipboards. Included in the working memory are the patient's age, sex, test results, and clinical history. In questions 35 through 38 in the example, Mycin is gathering still more information to put in its working memory.
- The *knowledge base* is the heart of Mycin, the place where it keeps the knowledge about infectious diseases that a doctor ordinarily carries

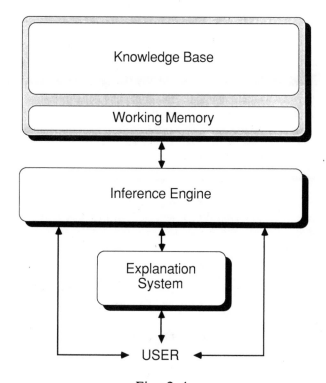

Fig. 2–1
The basic structure of an expert system

around in his head. Working with his consultants at Stanford Medical School, Shortliffe developed about five hundred short rules, each one roughly corresponding to what the physicians thought of as a single piece of knowledge. The one quoted in the example as Rule 578 is typical:

IF   (i)   the infection is meningitis, and
     (ii) organisms were not seen in the stain of the culture, and
     (iii) the type of infection may be bacterial, and
     (iv) the patient has been seriously burned,

THEN   there is suggestive evidence that *Pseudonomas aeruginosa* might be one of the organisms causing the infection.

In AI such rules are often called *productions*, while rule-based programs such as Mycin are known as *production systems*. Whatever the terminology, however, Mycin's rules have the twin advantage of being intuitive and easy to understand (at least to physicians) and of working independently. Thus they are modular: A programmer can change or delete old rules from the knowledge base, and can add new ones, without having to pull the whole program apart. In this way, the system can be developed in an incremental, step-by-step fashion.

- The *inference engine* is the part of the program that takes specific facts from the working memory, puts them together with rules from the knowledge base, and tries to reason its way to a diagnosis. If more data are needed, as is often the case, Mycin will ask the user questions—for example, questions 34 through 38 in Figure 2-1. On the other hand, if the user doesn't know some of the answers (notice that the reply to question 37 is *Unknown*), Mycin can still carry on. The ultimate diagnosis may be less certain, but it will still be made.

  Mycin's inference engine is analogous to the broad reasoning principles used in General Problem Solver, in the sense that it contains no information at all about diseases or treatments. The major difference between the two programs is one of emphasis: In General Problem Solver the stress was on the reasoning principles themselves; the special-purpose knowledge about the domain was assumed to be secondary. In Mycin, as in other expert systems, the emphasis is just reversed. It is the inference engine that is secondary. The power lies in the knowledge base; the bigger, the better.

  Mycin's clean separation between inference engine and knowledge base is also a matter of practicality. As Feigenbaum and Buchanan had learned the hard way in developing Dendral, a knowledge base that mixes general-reasoning heuristics with domain knowledge has a way of turning to concrete. After a while it becomes next to impossible to add or modify rules without drastically—and unpredictably—changing the behavior of the whole system. Thus, in Mycin they made sure that the two were kept separate.[13]

  An added virtue to this approach is that Mycin's inference engine can be reused for other expert systems. Shortly after Mycin was completed, in fact, the Stanford group developed Emycin, which stands for Empty or Essential Mycin. Emycin was the hollow shell of an expert system in that it contained only the inference engine and explanation system of Mycin; the knowledge base itself was left empty, so that it could be filled in with rules from a new domain.[14] The Stanford group subsequently used Emycin to develop new expert systems in areas such as structural analysis (Sacon), pulmonary dysfunction (Puff), and psychiatric disorders (Headmed).[15] More recently, as we'll see in Chapter 7, Emycin has become the basis of a number of commercial products for expert-systems development.

- Finally, the *explanation system*, while not essential to Mycin's operation, is crucial to its credibility. Unlike Dendral, which provided merely a result, Mycin is supposed to provide its users with a *consultation*, which means that they need a way to evaluate its advice. In the sample dialogue, the physician at the keyboard is curious as to why Mycin wants to know if patient Pt219 is a burn patient (question 38). So instead of simply answering the question, he types WHY. Mycin's explanation system then responds by quoting rule 578, which is the rule it had been trying to apply at that moment. However, the physician is still curious: In line 4.3, how does Mycin know that the infection was likely to be bacterial? So he interrupts Mycin's attempt to return to question 38 by typing *HOW 4.3?* The explanation system thus responds with a list of the five rules Mycin has applied, four of which support the conclusion that the infection was bacterial and one of which does not. (The numbers in the table, known as *certainty values*, refer to how strongly each rule does or does not support the conclusion.) So, the user has a firmer basis for understanding what Mycin is up to, and why it reaches the conclusions it does.

The Siblings and Descendants of Mycin

The development of Mycin was something of a watershed in the history of AI. Before Mycin, the vast majority of AI programs had stayed within the benign environment of the laboratory. After Mycin, it was clear that AI could survive and prosper on the outside as well, in the real world where knowledge is incomplete, time is short, and users are skeptical. Corporate executives and venture capitalists began to pay closer attention. By 1980, money was pouring in at a startling rate, and as we'll see in more detail in Chapter 7, AI began to go commercial.

The optimistic mood of the late 1970s was reinforced by the success of a number of other expert systems, which had either descended from Mycin or been developed almost simultaneously. Some notable examples:

- *Prospector.* Developed as an experimental system in the late 1970s by SRI International, which is located in Menlo Park, California (only a few miles from Stanford), Prospector is designed to advise geologists on whether or not a given site might have ore-grade deposits. The process is quite similar to that of diagnosing a disease, except that in this case the "symptoms" are the geological characteristics of the site.★ In 1980, Prospector identified an ore-grade molybdenum deposit at Mount Tolman, in Washington State, which makes it the first knowledge-based system to have a major commercial success.
- *Caduceus.* This is the collective name of a series of expert systems under development at the University of Pittsburgh by Harry E. Pople and Jack D. Myers, M.D. Begun in the early 1970s as Internist, it is generally regarded as the most comprehensive and successful decision-support system in medicine. And because Pople and Myers are attempting to cover *all* of internal medicine—including the possible interactions of different diseases in the same patient—Caduceus is undoubtedly the most complex knowledge-based system ever conceived.[16] With some five

---

★A sample: "There is pervasively biotized hornblende"; "There is an alternation favorable for the potassic zone of a porphyry copper deposit."

hundred diseases in its data base so far, it covers approximately 25 percent of internal medicine as a whole.

- *Xcon*, originally known as *R1*. This was probably the first commercial expert system, developed in the late seventies and early eighties by John McDermott and his colleagues from Carnegie-Mellon University for the Digital Equipment Corporation in Maynard, Massachusetts. Xcon routinely devises configurations for the company's VAX series of mini-computers, in much the same way that a new car salesman might write up a list of options for a new car. The reason DEC needs a computer to do this, however, is that the VAX line has hundreds of components available; it had previously been an exceedingly time-consuming business for humans to get everything straight. Xcon's input is a customer's order, and its output is a diagram showing what components go where. The technicians then use that diagram to physically assemble the system.

THE QUEST FOR COMMON SENSE

From the foregoing list, it's clear that expert systems have power and value in a surprisingly wide range of applications. And, as the last few years have shown, they have considerable commercial appeal. But the one thing expert systems do *not* have is any semblance of common sense. Indeed, their very popularity has only served to focus attention on their limitations, and on the more fundamental issues involved in getting machines to work with knowledge. In this section we'll look at some of the most prominent of these issues.

Knowing How to Break the Rules

Mycin knew a lot about diagnosing diseases. But it understood nothing whatsoever about anatomy or physiology and could not conceive that its patient was a human being. One of its rules told it to avoid giving tetracycline to patients under eight years of age. So it never did. But Mycin had no way of knowing *why* the rule was valid. (Tetracycline can produce dental staining during tooth development and may depress bone growth.) So Mycin couldn't explain the rule to the user or know when to break the rule (when, for instance, the child's life was so threatened that the cosmetic side effects were negligible).[17]

In a word, Mycin was shallow. So are all its successors. Expert systems are the very models of a modern AI program: rich with knowledge, practical, and oriented to real-world problems. But, paradoxically, they also represent a culmination of the earlier games-and-puzzles approach to AI. They work by carving out a piece of the real world and treating it as a self-contained game— subtle and complex perhaps, but nonetheless a game with its own set of rules. Mycin was therefore able to be a good diagnostician because it didn't have to know anything about the patient as a human being. All it had to do was play with the symptoms, the patient's history, and the test results.* As Buchanan says, "We operate, reluctantly, with a 'closed world' assumption—that nothing outside the program is relevant."

At MIT's AI laboratory, Randall Davis likes to explain the shallowness problem by comparing today's expert systems to an old-time TV repairman: You bring your set into the shop. It doesn't work. The repairman looks it over for a while. Then he backs off and carefully bangs it in a certain spot. Suddenly the TV starts playing again. "How did you know to do that?" you ask. "Always worked before," says the repairman with a shrug.

Now, that approach works fine, says Davis, but only when you have a problem that can be fixed by banging. But what happens when your TV set has a problem that this repairman has never seen before? What you need then is a factory-trained technician who knows when to leave off banging the set and go in with some serious diagnostic equipment.

In much the same way, he says, a genuinely *expert* system ought to be able to shift gears and reason from first principles. A medical expert system, for example, ought to know as much about physiology, anatomy, and biochemistry as it knows about symptoms. But therein lies the basic dilemma: How can the computer represent such knowledge? How can it relate one kind of knowledge to another—and to the observed symptoms? And just how does it know when to leave off reasoning at one level and go to a more fundamental level?[18]

Learning How to Learn

One of the basic conceptual problems a programmer faces in building an expert system is the nature of human expertise. As Feigenbaum writes, "Experience has shown us that [expert] knowledge is largely heuristic knowledge, experiential, uncertain—mostly 'good guesses' and 'good practice' in lieu of facts and rigor. Experience has also taught us that much of this knowledge is private to the expert, not because he is unwilling to share publicly how he performs, but because he is unable. He knows more than he is aware of knowing. . . . Why else is the Ph.D. or the Internship a guild-like apprenticeship to a presumed 'master of the craft'? What the masters really know is not written in the textbooks of the masters."[19]

Thus the process of building an expert system is a painful experience for all concerned. In fact, as Jon Doyle of Carnegie-Mellon University points out, it is very similar to putting the computer through a medieval apprenticeship: "The master cobbler [the expert] would take an ignorant apprentice [the

---

*Expert systems may not be so different from human experts in that respect. After all, patients often complain that human doctors treat them like bundles of symptoms. Perhaps it's also significant that people so often refer to their profession as "the game I'm in."

computer] and demonstrate the construction of a shoe, perhaps with a few comments about his actions. The apprentice then attempted to duplicate the feat. But being an ignoramus, and having been fascinated by the master's gold ring instead of by his awl, the apprentice completely botches the intended shoe. The master beats and curses the lout and demonstrates the other shoe, perhaps making special note of the places where the apprentice made errors. After enough repetitions of these steps, the apprentice becomes a journeyman. At this point he is moderately competent."[20]

In modern terms, this means that the expert sits down with the programmer—the *knowledge engineer* in Feigenbaum's terminology—and goes through a painstaking back-and-forth process: Put some rules into the program. Try the program out on some test cases. See how it goes wrong. Fix the rules. And try again.★

Needless to say, this procedure is slow. Mycin had some five hundred rules, and it took roughly twenty man-years to build. Of course, the process has sped up considerably with the accumulation of experience and the development of programming tools designed to help things along. Teiresias, for example, developed by Randall Davis as his 1976 doctoral project at Stanford, was an effort to automate as much of the knowledge-engineering process as possible. Thus, if the expert found the system making a diagnosis he did not agree with, Teiresias would help him back up through the reasoning chain until he reached the spot where things had gone awry; it would then help him modify the rules until the diagnosis came out right.[21]

Nonetheless, this is still a far cry from the machine's being able to learn things on its own. So far, the practical problems of building expert systems have only served to reemphasize the fundamental theoretical problems: What is learning? How can a machine modify its knowledge according to experience? How can it be taught to learn from its mistakes? And what can machine learning tell us about the learning process in humans?[22]

Reasoning by Analogy

When knowledge engineers and experts sit down to write a new expert system, the experts very often find themselves expressing what they know in terms of examples ("You know, I remember this one client who. . . ."). This is especially prevalent in fields, such as law, that rely heavily on cases. The knowledge engineers then go crazy trying to recast these examples as

---

★As painful as this experience is, the experts themselves generally find it worthwhile. Indeed, they often confess at the end that they've learned a great deal, simply because the knowledge-engineering process has forced them to make their intuitive knowledge explicit. It seems likely that this kind of codified intuition will eventually find its way back into textbooks and classroom lectures. In other words, expert systems will not only be the receptacles of human expertise but may well serve as catalysts for improving it.

IF-THEN rules. It would help a great deal if a program could just accept the cases as is, and then use analogical reasoning to apply them in similar situations. By the same token, a system that can reason by analogy from cases should also be able to learn from its own mistakes—because a mistake is simply another kind of case.

More generally, this ability to reason by analogy—to recognize that one thing is like another and to draw conclusions from that fact—seems to be one of the most important components of common sense. Not only do people reason by analogy, but they learn by analogy (imagine a children's book explaining that "a motorcycle looks like a bicycle"). They even come up with creative new ideas by analogy. Furthermore, verbal analogies—metaphors—are ubiquitous in human language: "The SS-20 missile *tips the balance* in favor of the Soviets"; "The Zenith Data Systems Corporation last week *walked away* with a $27 million award to supply portable microcomputers to the IRS"; "The announcement is expected to *spur* sales to corporations"; "Unemployed farmers must *find their way back* into the labor force." A statement such as "John is a *hog*," for example, can tell us some very pertinent things about a man we may never have met. A statement such as "The new evidence *weighed heavily* in the defendant's favor" tells us a lot about how the trial is going without requiring us to know any of the details.

One mark of intelligence in humans is the ability to get the point of an example, to catch on to things quickly without a lot of coaching. The trick is to get a computer to exhibit such intelligence. "Since computer programs perform much better in simple, elegant, abstract domains than in 'scruffy' experience-rich human domains," write Jaime Carbonell and Steven Minton of Carnegie-Mellon University, "it is evident that a fundamental reasoning mechanism is lacking from the AI repertoire."[23] And that mechanism, they maintain, is the ability to make analogies.

So what, exactly, *is* an analogy? How is a computer supposed to recognize a metaphor or an analogy when it sees one? And how is a computer supposed to *understand* that analogy? If we say, "Sam is a bear of a man," is the computer supposed to conclude that Sam is covered with fur?

Coping With Uncertainty

At first glance the process of diagnosis and treatment seems simple enough—rather like theorem-proving or chess, in fact. One has an initial state: the patient with such-and-such a disease. One has a goal: the healthy patient. And one has various "operators" that can be applied to change the state of the patient step by step: various drugs, physical therapies, surgical procedures, and so forth. So why not just use some of the standard AI problem-solving procedures to search through all the options and find the right cure?

Unfortunately, it doesn't work like that. Not only is it hard to be absolutely sure what disease a patient has, but the treatments aren't guaranteed to work even when the disease *is* known. A fact or a definition is absolute, but a rule of thumb is only plausible. So how much reliance can a heuristic program place in its own conclusions?

In Mycin the rules were given numerical certainty values, which were then combined to produce an estimate of the reliability of the final diagnosis. This worked tolerably well. But unfortunately, it wasn't always clear what the numbers meant.

Other researchers have tried to apply classical probability theory by using statements such as "Rule 212 has a 58 percent probability of being true." They have had little success. The laws of probability apply when things happen essentially at random, as in the throw of dice. But most of the time the uncertainty in our knowledge is less a question of randomness than of vagueness. Consider a rule of thumb such as *Be pleasant to your waiter and he'll give you better service:* How do you assign a probability to such a rule?

One approach to reasoning with uncertainty and vagueness is a system called *fuzzy logic*, first developed by Lofti A. Zadeh of the University of California, Berkeley, in the 1960s. Fuzzy logic deals with such relative concepts as "old" and "big" by abandoning sharp yes-no categories in favor of "fuzzy," context-sensitive definitions. For example, instead of saying that someone is either *young* or *old*, you would assign each age-group a mathematical ranking. Thus, a nine-month-old baby might have a ranking of 0.99 on the *young* scale, which means that it is almost certainly young; likewise, its great-grandparents, both in their nineties, might have rankings around 0.01, which makes them almost certainly *not-young* (that is, old). But the baby's parents, both of whom are in their midthirties, might have an intermediate ranking of, say, 0.45, which makes them old relative to a teenager, and young relative to most residents of a retirement home.[24]

Still, this is clearly not the whole answer, and many open questions remain. How is a program supposed to proceed in the face of ignorance, for example? Or how can it even learn to recognize the limits of its knowledge?[25]

Reasoning by Default

Consider a bit of common-sense reasoning, otherwise known as Marvin Minsky's Dead-Duck Challenge:[26]

"If Charlie is a duck, then Charlie can fly."

"But Charlie is dead!"

"Oh, then Charlie can't fly."

Minsky's point is that humans have the common-sense ability to change their conclusions if new information requires it. But computers can't, at least not if their reasoning is confined to standard forms of logic; once they reach the conclusion that Charlie can fly, the standard rules of inference offer them no way to back up and reach the opposite conclusion. Of course, you could always put a rule in the knowledge base that said, "Ducks can fly unless they are dead." But then, what if Charlie has a broken wing? What if he's in a cage? What if he's sick with the duck flu? What if. . . .

Clearly, this way lies insanity, not to mention that trying to list every conceivable exception to every rule would rupture your computer's memory capacity. What's needed is a way of reasoning by default, of supplementing the standard rules of inference with rules that allow you to say, "Ducks can fly unless there's some reason they can't."

This turns out to be a surprisingly delicate thing to do. Meddle with the rules of logic, and it's all too easy to end up proving that Charlie is simultaneously a duck and a frog. So how, exactly, is a computer supposed to reason by default?

AI researchers have by no means answered all these questions. On the other hand, they have made a great deal of progress, most notably by pursuing a deeper understanding of knowledge itself, and by studying how it can be represented in the computer. So that is what we turn to next.

A FRAMEWORK FOR REPRESENTING KNOWLEDGE

Whatever else knowledge may be, it is not simply a mass of data. Consider a telephone book or an encyclopedia or, for that matter, the entire Library of Congress. Without a reader, none of them is anything more than ink marks on paper. In the same sense, the electronic data stored in a computer's memory cells represent knowledge only if a program can use them to behave in a knowledgeable way.

Thus the importance of representation: Imagine a library where all the books were just dumped on the shelf at random, without any attempt to catalog or cross-reference them. A scholar would have a devil of a time trying to get any work done in such a library. He would spend all his time trying to find the next book and very little time thinking about what the book actually says. For much the same reason, a computer can easily get bogged down in a large knowledge base unless the knowledge has some kind of indexing system to guide it.

In 1974, in his seminal paper "A Framework for Representing Knowledge," Marvin Minsky proposed that precisely this sort of indexing system could be provided by a new kind of data structure he called a *frame*:

> It seems to me that the ingredients of most theories both in artificial intelligence and in psychology have been on the whole too minute, local, and unstructured to account . . . for the effectiveness of common sense thought. The "chunks" of reasoning, language, memory, and perception ought to be larger and more structured; their factual and procedural

contents must be more intimately connected in order to explain the apparent power and speed of mental activities.[27]

As an example, he says, consider a children's birthday party. A dictionary might define this event as "a party of children assembled to celebrate another child's birthday." It might define the word *party*, in turn, as "people assembled for a celebration." But any child knows that there's more to a party than that, says Minsky. No sooner does the invitation arrive than she's bursting with questions: "What do I wear?"; "What kind of present should I buy?"; "What will they give us to eat?"—and so on.

Now, some of these questions are straightforward and have standard answers, he says. Unless there is some reason to think otherwise, the answer to "What do I wear?" is "Sunday best." And likewise, the answer to "What will they give us to eat?" almost certainly includes "cake and ice cream." Other questions, however, require quite a bit more thought. "What kind of present should I buy?" involves considerations such as "Would he [the birthday boy] like a kite?" and "Where will I get the money?"

In any case, says Minsky, the *frame* that describes such a situation would be a kind of electronic file folder that summarizes all the standard questions and all the standard answers. Or, to put it another way, the frame would simply codify one's expectations about that situation. So the frame for a typical children's birthday party might look something like this:

CHILDREN'S-BIRTHDAY-PARTY Frame:
DRESS:	Sunday best
PRESENT:	Must please host
	Must be bought and gift-wrapped
GAMES:	Hide-and-seek
	Pin-the-tail-on-the-donkey
DECOR:	Balloons; Favors; Crepe Paper
PARTY-MEAL:	Cake; Ice cream; Soda; Hot dogs
CAKE:	Candles; Blow-out; Wish; Sing Happy Birthday
ICE-CREAM:	Standard Three-Flavor

Minsky wasn't the first to talk about organizing knowledge in this way, as he himself freely acknowledges. In fact, most of the ideas in his paper were already part of the Zeitgeist of the AI community. They were in the air. But Minsky's work was widely influential nonetheless; not only did he give the concept a name—frames—but he also articulated it more clearly and completely than anyone had before. Moreover, he showed that the frame idea, despite its apparent simplicity, is a rich source of new insights about learning, language, language understanding, vision, reasoning, and the workings of memory. Indeed, in the years since Minsky first circulated his paper, frames have proved to be one of the most fruitful methods of overcoming the problems and limitations alluded to earlier.

Frames and Scripts

At the most basic level, frames codify stereotypes, our expectations about familiar events. *Stereotype* is admittedly a loaded word, with ugly connotations of racism, sexism, and other forms of repression. And yet the more benign forms of stereotyping are absolutely essential if we're going to function in the world. Consider the smooth, efficient competence that most of us display at a gas station or a restaurant: That competence is possible only because we do have certain stereotyped ideas about what to expect and what to do. Or, as Minsky would put it, we know what questions to ask and what many of the answers will be. Now compare that with the uncertainty, panic, and downright silliness that people often exhibit at the scene of an automobile accident, where they have no idea what to expect or what to do.

To see how a computer might represent stereotyped expectations, here is a sample frame describing a restaurant, taken from Edward Feigenbaum and Avron Barr's *The Handbook of Artificial Intelligence*:[28]

Generic RESTAURANT Frame
    Specialization-of: Business-Establishment
             Types:
               range: (Cafeteria, Seat-yourself, Wait-to-be-seated)
           default: Wait-to-be-seated
        if-needed: IF plastic-orange-counter THEN Fast-food,
                    IF stack-of-trays THEN Cafeteria,
                    IF wait-for-waitress-sign or reservations-made
                        THEN Wait-to-be-seated,
                    OTHERWISE Seat-yourself
           Location:
               range: an ADDRESS
        if-needed: (Look at the MENU)
             Name:
        if-needed: (Look at the MENU)
        Food-Style:
               range: (Burgers, Chinese, American, Seafood, French)
           default: American
         if-needed: (Update alternatives of Restaurant)
    Times-of-operation:
               range: a Time-of-Day
           default: open evenings except Mondays
      Payment-Form:
               range: (Cash, Credit Card, Check, Washing-Dishes
                    Script)

Event-Sequence:
        default: Eat-At-Restaurant Script
    Alternatives:
        range: all restaurants with same Food-Style
    if-needed: (Find all Restaurants with the same Food-Style)

In practice, of course, this would all be written in computer code. But the logical structure would be as we see it here. Each subheading of the frame—usually referred to by AI researchers as a *slot* or *terminal*—is a signal to the computer that a certain kind of information can be expected. In fact, the slots are a bit like the spaces in an application form for bank credit or for a driver's license. Each one is like a little question that requires a certain type of answer.

In this case, of course, the form is already partially filled in. Or, more precisely, many of the slots list a DEFAULT value, which tells the machine what to assume if no other information is available. Thus, after consulting the Times-of-Operation slot, the machine would assume that unless it was specifically told otherwise, a restaurant is open in the evenings except on Mondays. Furthermore, in almost all slots the frame lets the machine know the range of possibilities; thus, the options for Food-Style include Burgers, Chinese, American, and so forth. But dog food isn't on the list, so the machine knows that that choice is absurd.

Some of the slots in this frame also refer to *scripts,* a concept developed in the early 1970s by Yale University's Roger Schank and Robert Abelson in the course of their work on natural-language understanding.[29] A script is like a frame in that it codifies a certain set of expectations. However, it is different from a frame in that doesn't describe a static set of facts; as the name suggests, it describes what to expect in a stereotypical sequence of events. (In the next chapter, where I discuss scripts in more detail, I'll show an Eat-At-Restaurant script to go with this *Restaurant* frame. See page 00.)

Two other features of the *Restaurant* frame are worth noting. The first is the presence of several if-needed slots. Unlike the other spaces in the frame, which simply contain information, these slots contain little programs that tell the computer what to do when a slot needs filling and none of the available options seems to fit. Under Types, for example, the frame provides the computer with a kind of thumbnail guide for how to identify a restaurant. This technique of attaching procedures to frames turns out to be quite important in practical programs. With procedures, a frame (or a script) can be more than just a static list of facts. It can make decisions for itself. It can take action and interact with other frames. As the program runs, the embedded procedures allow the frame to monitor the changing situation and decide for itself when it is relevant—or else decide what to do when it ceases to be relevant. In short, procedures allow frames and scripts to become dynamic, active objects.★

The other notable feature of the *Restaurant* frame is the specialization-of-slot. As the name suggests, this slot states that restaurants are members of an even larger class of entities called *Business-Establishments*, which have a frame of their own. In much the same way, if we had frames for *Grocery-Store, Hardware-Store,* and so on, they, too, would be specializations of the frame *Business-Establishments.* Furthermore, because of that specialization relationship, the computer knows that each of these entities automatically shares all the properties of *Business-Establishments,* such as that businesses exist to make money. This turns out to be a very efficient way to store knowledge in the computer, because the most basic and general facts have to be stored only once instead of many times.

The relationships between frames are sometimes clearer when they are shown diagrammatically. To take a different example, consider a frame for *Fred-the-Elephant.* Obviously, this frame would include the fact that *Fred* is a member of the class *Elephant* (see Figure 2-2).

The *Elephant* frame, in turn, would include the fact that elephants have a part known as a *trunk,* that elephants are members of the class *mammal,* and that elephants live (among other places) in *Kenya.* Mammals in turn have *hair,* and so on. These relationships can be diagrammed as in Figure 2-3.

In this diagrammatic form, the idea of structured knowledge actually predates Minsky's description of frames by nearly a decade. Under the rubric of semantic networks, the concept was pioneered in the midsixties by Ross Quillian of the consulting firm Bolt Beranek and Newman as a way of modeling one of the most striking things about human memory: the way one idea reminds us of another.[30] When we think about Fred the elephant, for example, the chain of associations might go something like this: "*Fred* is an

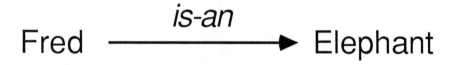

Fig. 2–2
A very simple semantic network

---

*According to some researchers—Minsky, for example—human memory is less like a quiet, orderly library than like the floor of the New York Stock Exchange: The unfilled slots in our mental frames are always frantically calling out for information, while our sense organs and conscious minds are constantly offering up new information to whomever needs it. Embedded procedures allow frames represented in a computer to behave in much the same way.

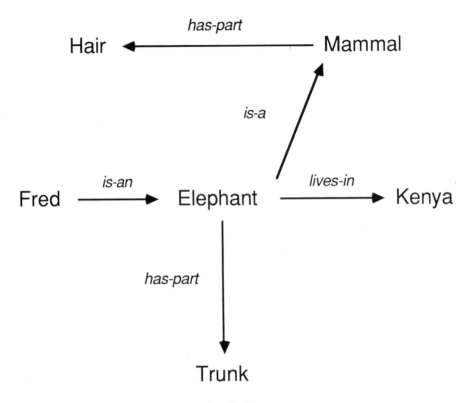

Fig. 2–3
A slightly more complex semantic network

elephant, and *elephants* live in *Kenya,* and *Kenya* is a good place to take a *vacation,* and boy, I sure need a *vacation.* . . ." But from looking at the semantic network in Figure 2-3, it's easy to see how these associations come about: The process of reminding is simply a matter of following the links. Indeed, a number of researchers, starting with Quillian in the late 1960s, have experimentally measured the time it takes for one concept to remind you of another concept; such an interval is measured in seconds and fractions of a second, but it turns out to be roughly proportional to the number of links you have to follow to get there.[31-32]

Quillian's insight has inspired a number of cognitive psychologists to attempt more detailed models of human memory. One of the most ambitious such projects was begun in the early 1970s by Carnegie-Mellon University cognitive psychologist John R. Anderson and his colleague Gordon H. Bower, who elaborated the semantic network idea into a computer program they called HAM, which stands for Human Associative Memory.[33] A few years later, Anderson extended HAM into a more comprehensive program, which he called ACT.

Whereas HAM was essentially a model of human long-term memory—the things that we can remember for years at a time—Act also encompassed short-term memory, that handful of things that we can remember and pay attention to in any given moment. By activating certain nodes (thus the name of the program) and by allowing the activation to spread from node to node through the links of the network, Act was able to shift its focus of attention from subject to subject, just as humans do.[34] Anderson has since programmed Act to perform a wide variety of cognitive tasks; most recently, he has been applying the theories resulting from his work on Act to understanding the human learning process, with particular emphasis on computer-aided education.[35]

Semantic network and frame ideas have also been used to great effect in natural-language research. Consider this sentence: *Nixon gave a beautiful Cadillac to Brezhnev, the leader of the U.S.S.R.*[36] Grammatically, of course, it is one sentence. Psychologically, however, it can be broken down into three independent concepts:

1. Nixon gave a Cadillac to Brezhnev.
2. The Cadillac was beautiful. . . .
3. Brezhnev was leader of the U.S.S.R.

We'll see in the next chapter how each of these concepts can be represented as a certain kind of frame, known as a *case frame*. But they can just as well be diagrammed as in Figure 2-4, with each numbered oval representing a concept.

Looking at this diagram, we can immediately see one reason why natural-language understanding is so complex: The same words can play several different grammatical roles simultaneously, even in a straightforward sentence. Furthermore, the roles may have very little to do with the kind of grammar we learned in high school. "Brezhnev," for example, takes the role of *recipient* in the first concept and *agent* in the third. "Cadillac" is the *object* in the first concept and the *subject* in the second. Indeed, as we'll see later on, it's only when AI researchers started paying very careful attention to such nuances that their programs began to show impressive performance in language understanding.

Another intriguing point about Figure 2-4 concerns the words themselves: *Nixon, Brezhnev, USSR, Cadillac, give,* and so forth. On the diagram, each one is shown simply as a word, a label. Yet when we read them, they aren't just words. We know that the act of giving implies a special set of relationships between two people. We know that the implications of *give* are particularly striking when one of those people is the president of the United States and the other is the premier of the Soviet Union. We know that a Cadillac has a significance of its own as an emblem of opulence and luxury. In short, every word in the diagram is redolent with meaning and associations—

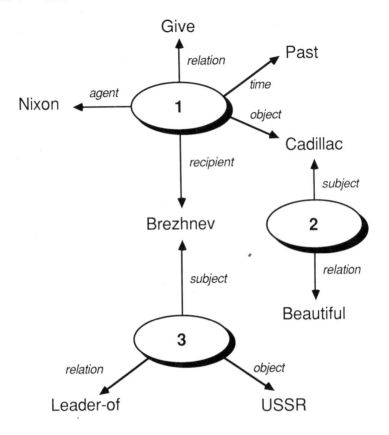

Fig. 2–4
A sentence in semantic network form

none of which appear in the diagram. So something crucial seems to be missing.

On the other hand, that rich set of associations could easily be incorporated, at least in principle, if each word were not really a word but a frame. *Nixon, Brezhnev, Cadillac,* and the others would accordingly be made into structures something like the *Restaurant* frame we saw previously, each listing the same kind of information and associations the words generally convey to us. Furthermore, each of these frames would in turn be linked to still other frames: *Nixon-Watergate-Vietnam-Kissinger-China,* and so on, in a complex network of relationships.

Thus we have the challenge of natural-language understanding in AI: For a computer to understand a sentence or a story, it not only must analyze the grammatical relationships of the words, as we did in the Nixon-Brezhnev-

Cadillac example, but must also match the words to the appropriate frames.* In short, it has to take the incoming stream of language and fit the concepts into a large, preexisting framework of knowledge. Needless to say, this is hard. But as I'll demonstrate in the next chapter, remarkable progress is being made.

From the process of understanding a story, it's only one small step to the process of learning. Indeed, it's hardly a step at all. Merely by comprehending a sentence such as *Nixon gave a Cadillac to Brezhnev*, we've probably learned something we didn't know before. In fact, learning does seem to proceed by exactly the same mechanism as language understanding. We learn new facts and skills by linking them to associations with things we already know. This is why we spend most of our childhood learning common sense; before we can learn how to tie our shoes, for example, we must first know what shoes are and what it means to have them tied or not tied. This is also why people have to study for years to master a subject such as law or quantum-field theory. Memorizing the jargon is easy, but it takes a great deal of time and effort to build the network of mental relationships that allows a physics student to understand not only what a concept such as *antimatter* means but also how it relates to such other concepts as *Dirac equation* and *Lorentz group*.

By thinking of memory as a kind of mental network, we can also understand why analogies and metaphors are so useful in describing new ideas: They provide guidance for how the ideas ought to be fitted into the network. In general, it seems that our cognitive processors would prefer not to work out a whole new pattern of linkages from scratch if they can help it. They would rather adapt an existing pattern, in much the same way that an architect might design a new building by adapting the blueprints from an old one. Analogies and metaphors simply point the way to where useful blueprints might be found.

AM and Eurisko: Two Programs That Learn

In the years since Minsky first circulated his frames paper, frames have become one of the standard techniques of representing knowledge in AI programs. Indeed, frame-based knowledge-representation schemes are often used today in building large expert systems, and a number of new computer languages have been devised for the express purpose of helping programmers work with frames.[37] Furthermore, frames and semantic networks have continued to be a vivid metaphor for helping psychologists and AI researchers think about the nature of mind. Since the mid-1970s, for example, most of the AI

---

*Assuming, of course, that those frames already exist in the computer's memory. In practice, a computer has to store a *lot* of knowledge before it can understand even a simple story—which is just another way of saying that common sense is an awesome accomplishment.

research on machine learning has focused on the process of fitting new knowledge into a framework of old knowledge. In much the same way, efforts to devise programs that reason by analogy have focused on the process of matching up one piece of a semantic network with another piece of similar structure.

As an illustration of how these frame ideas can be used, consider two remarkable programs developed by Douglas B. Lenat of the Microelectronics and Computer Technology Corporation (MCC) in Austin, Texas. The first program was AM, or Automated Mathematician, which Lenat wrote in 1976 for his thesis project at Stanford. Basically, his idea was to write a program that could learn by discovering mathematical categories and concepts on its own.[38]

As a starting point, Lenat gave AM about a hundred elementary concepts from set theory; included were definitions such as "A set is a collection of objects" and operations such as "union," which simply takes two sets and lumps all their objects together. Each of these concepts was represented internally as a frame with about twenty-five slots, such as *Definitions, Examples,* and *Worth.* (See below.)

At the beginning of a run, most of the slots would be blank in most of the frames, so AM would start its work by trying to fill in the blank slots. For guidance, it had some 250 heuristic rules of thumb programmed in by Lenat. Some of these heuristics would suggest which slot to work on next, while others would suggest ways for AM to find the appropriate information. Still other heuristics prompted AM to look for simple new relationships between concepts, and to generate promising new concepts to investigate. Example: "If *F* is an interesting function, consider its inverse."

None of AM's heuristics are easily expressed in nonmathematical language; however, the overall effect can be understood as a kind of natural-selection process. AM would generate new concepts by making changes—mutations—in old concepts and then setting up new frames for them. Next, the program would explore the consequences of each new concept, eventually focusing most of its attention on those that seemed interesting—in other words, that led to a significant number of new results. Each concept's frame served as a kind of score card in this process, with various kinds of slots recording the origin of the concept, the number of good and bad conjectures it had been responsible for, and AM's current estimate of its worth relative to other concepts. (A worth value of 800, for example, would correspond to "very interesting indeed.") Finally, in the spirit of survival-of-the-fittest, AM would single out the most interesting concepts to generate still more new concepts. Dead-end concepts would be dropped.

The results of this procedure surprised even Lenat. In the early runs, AM started from elementary set theory; within a few minutes, by mutating old concepts and cultivating new ones, it had discovered the concept of number. From there it went on to discover arithmetic, with its laws of addition, subtraction, multiplication, and division. Then it hit upon the idea of prime numbers. (See the prime-numbers frame below.) From prime numbers, it had only a short way to go before finding the fundamental theorem of arithmetic, which states that every number can be written as the product of a unique set of prime numbers. (For example, the numbers 2, 3, 5, and 7 are prime, while $4 = 2 \times 2$, $6 = 2 \times 3$, $8 = 2 \times 2 \times 2$, $9 = 3 \times 3$, and so on.)

To give an example of AM at work, here is a highly simplified version of its prime-numbers frame:

NAME: Prime Numbers
DEFINITION: X is a prime number if and only if no number besides 1 and X itself evenly divides X.
EXAMPLES: 2,3,5,7,11,13,17.
GENERALIZATIONS: Numbers.
SPECIALIZATIONS: Odd Primes.
CONJECTURES: All numbers can be factored into a unique set of prime numbers.
WORTH: 800.

Unfortunately, it took only about an hour or so of running before AM would go off the deep end, so to speak, studying such concepts as numbers that are simultaneously odd and even. The problem, as Lenat soon realized, was that AM's heuristic rules were specialized to give the program guidance as it worked with concepts in set theory. As AM worked its way into advanced arithmetic and number theory, however, those heuristics proved less and less useful—so AM's behavior became increasingly bizarre.

In 1977, Lenat accordingly began work on a new program, Eurisko, which would not only learn new concepts, but would have the additional ability to modify and improve its own guiding heuristics as it went along. In effect, Eurisko would learn how to learn.[39]

Conceptually, Lenat's approach in Eurisko was very similar to his approach in AM. The only fundamental difference was that in Eurisko, the mutation and natural-selection processes were allowed to act on the heuristics as well as on the concepts. In practice, this turned out to be considerably more difficult than the theory suggested. Indeed, it took Lenat nearly five years to devise a scheme that would allow the computer to mutate the heuristics properly. But when he had finished, the scheme itself turned out to be remarkably simple: Instead of representing the heuristics as complicated IF-THEN rules, Lenat represented each one in a frame of its own, so that mutations could take place one slot at a time. This is roughly equivalent to the way in which biological evolution works, in that mutations in living things tend to affect only one gene at a time. So one could say that Lenat has developed a kind of genetic code for heuristic knowledge.

Lenat has applied Eurisko itself to a number of domains beyond mathematics. The program has taught itself how to design computer chips, for example—in the process inventing such concepts as symmetry and deciding that symmetry is a good thing for chips to have. For two years running, it also trounced its human opponents in the national championship of a space-war game called Traveller—even, in one instance, after a last-minute rules change was instituted to try to block the program. (In designing its space fleets, by the way, Eurisko made them symmetrical, citing its previous experience in chip design as a justification.)

Many people consider Lenat to be one of the most innovative and brilliant AI researchers of his generation. "What Lenat has [done] is started up a whole new field of knowledge," says Minsky, who is echoed by Feigenbaum: "What he's done is probably the most important work that's been done along the road of modeling creativity and discovery by machine."[40]

However, as Lenat is the first to admit, Eurisko still doesn't have anything resembling the breadth of knowledge required for common sense. Thus, he has put the program to one side for the time being while he and his colleagues at MCC undertake what has to be one of the most ambitious projects ever contemplated in AI. Instead of just talking about common sense, they intend to sit down and encode all the world's knowledge and common sense down to some reasonably fine-grained level of detail. "There is no way to finesse this," they recently wrote in *The AI Magazine*. "Fifteenth-century explorers couldn't discover new lands without long voyages. The breadth of our task may sound staggering, but consider that a one-volume desk encyclopedia spans the same magnitude of knowledge." Appropriately, Lenat and his colleagues have taken just such a volume, *The Concise Columbia Encyclopedia*, as their source.[41]

Lenat estimates that their project, known as CYC, will take ten years to complete—if it succeeds at all. Succeed or fail, however, the effort is bound to tell us a great deal of what common sense is all about.

UNFINISHED BUSINESS

In spirit, at least, the last thirty years of AI have amply fulfilled Simon's 1957 predictions—though perhaps not as rapidly or as decisively as Simon himself would have liked. AI constructs such as semantic networks, frames, scripts, and production systems have had a major impact on cognitive psychology, as evidenced by such programs as Act. Lenat's AM did indeed develop mathematical theorems and showed real creativity in doing so. And although we haven't discussed it here, certain AI programs have been able to play master's-level chess.

Simon himself takes a kind of grumpy satisfaction in all this, especially after all the ridicule that he and his predictions have suffered from critics of AI.[42] He maintains that he intended his comments as reasonable and responsible projections of what then seemed not only possible but probable. "AI has gotten this reputation of being very speculative," he says rather testily. "Well, that's just not so. AI isn't nearly as speculative as, say, astrophysics."

Nonetheless, no one should imagine that all the problems have been solved. If the intervening years have done nothing else, they have imprinted upon the AI community a painful lesson: Human intelligence is very complex, and machine intelligence—especially the machine version of human common sense—is very, very hard. Some continuing challenges:

Vision and Skill: A Different Kind of Knowledge?

A great deal of human reasoning involves *envisioning*. When someone says, "You know, I think this bookcase might look best against that wall," he or she is presumably consulting a mental picture of the room. However, as you'll see when I discuss computer vision in Chapter 4, the kinds of "cognitive" knowledge discussed in this chapter don't really cover perceptual memory, or reasoning by envisioning. In fact, it's still an open question just how these things work.[43]

A similar problem arises when trying to analyze motor skills, such as the ability to walk or to play good tennis. Physical skills can't be learned from books, not directly; they come only through practice and repetition. In fact, there is some evidence that motor skills and the kind of cognitive learning discussed in this chapter involve separate portions of the brain.[44]

The Hidden Mind: Intuition, Insight, and Inspiration

It seems so easy: You see a friend walking down the sidewalk on her lunch hour and you think, "Oh, there's Sally."

But now consider what was involved in that. Somehow, without being consciously aware of it, you compared the visual image on your retina with all the remembered images of all the millions of people and trees and dogs and ashtrays that you have seen in your life. And once you found the right image, you matched the face with her name, *Sally;* with a whole set of shared experiences; with how you feel about her; and with the outrageous thing your boss did that morning that you can't wait to tell her about. And all this knowledge is simply *there*, pouring into your conscious mind before you've even lifted your arm to wave.

Or consider another example: You beat your brains out trying to solve a problem at work, and then, *Aha!*—on the way to the water fountain, the solution is suddenly obvious. Now, how did you do that?

Nobody else knows either.

It's as if something is going on deep in the unconscious mind that is different, almost mystical. People describe it with words like *intuition, insight, inspiration, illumination,* and *gestalt,* capturing this sense of a spontaneous, holistic, secret part of ourselves that is forever beyond understanding.

Not surprisingly, most AI researchers (and most psychologists) are unconvinced, arguing that this hidden part of mind is not so much magical as just . . . hidden. Still, it remains an open question whether any of the elaborate schemes we've mentioned in this chapter can really explain what's going on. How can a computer say "Aha!" when that means ripping apart all its carefully structured representations of knowledge and then reassembling them into a new vision of the world?

Carnegie-Mellon's Scott Fahlman explains the problem this way: Imagine that you've walked into the Library of Congress trying to find out the name of Napoleon's mother. One approach would be to go into the stacks, look through the first book on the first shelf, then through the second book, and so on, until you find the answer. That's a pretty dumb way to do it, but it's essentially how conventional computer programs look through a data base.

A better approach would be to go to the card catalog and work your way through all the cross references until you pin down the book that has the answer. This is roughly how most AI programs work.

But the best way of all, says Fahlman, would be to walk into the central hall of the library, shout, "Hey, what's the name of Napoleon's mother?" and then have the book with the answer jump up and call it out. This is in fact how human memory works; information just seems to flash into the conscious mind when it's called for, without any tedious flipping through neuronal file cards.

The trick, of course, is to get a computer to do it. There are hints of how to proceed—in Chapter 5 I'll talk more about the "distributed memory" ideas being pursued by Fahlman, his CMU colleague Geoffrey Hinton, and several others—but as they themselves are the first to admit, it is only a hope and a beginning.

3

Language and Understanding

In 1949, when computers were brand new and everything still seemed possible, the mathematician Warren Weaver distributed a memorandum to some two hundred friends and colleagues outlining a proposal for "the solution of worldwide translation problems." Weaver, the director for natural science at the Rockefeller Foundation and an important contributor to the development of information theory, had been impressed by the way in which computers were used to break codes during the war. So why not translation? "When I look at an article in Russian," he wrote, "I say, *This is really written in English, but it has been coded in some strange symbols. I will now proceed to decode.*"[1]

Weaver's idea was to create a kind of automated bilingual dictionary: The machine would translate each word of the input text into an equivalent word in the output language, then rearrange the result to fit the output language's word order. Obviously, the process would not be quite that simple. Some words have different meanings in different contexts, for example, and every language has idioms that make no sense when they are translated word for word. Indeed, Weaver thought it would probably be necessary to translate the input first into an intermediate language—a hypothetical interlingua shared by all humans—and make the final translation from there. But the main problem seemed to be one of vocabulary.

Coming at a time when programming was still a matter of rewiring circuit boards, and when no one had ever heard of high-level programming languages such as FORTRAN, ALGOL, and LISP, Weaver's proposal was an extraordinary challenge. But it was also an extraordinary vision, and his colleagues responded eagerly. Research groups were formed both in the United States and abroad. Programs were devised, conferences were held, and government funding was solicited. In 1954, the journal *MT* (an abbreviation for Machine Translation) was founded. Glowing reports began to appear in the press, not unlike reports now appearing about current AI work.

And yet, as time went by, a certain uneasiness began to creep in. Legend has it that one early researcher asked his computer to translate "The spirit is willing, but the flesh is weak," first into Russian and then back into English. The result: "The vodka is good, but the meat is rotten."

Actually, the real programs were not even that clever. The first Russian/

English translation program was developed by Harvard's Anthony G. Oettinger in the midfifties. Following is a sample of the output, with the possible interpretations of each word listed in parentheses:

(In, At, Into, To, For, On) (last, latter, new, latest, lowest, worst) (time, tense) for analysis and synthesis relay-contact electrical (circuit, diagram, scheme) parallel- (series, successive, consecutive, consistent) (connections, junction, combination) (with, from) (success, luck) (to be utilized, to be taken advantage of) apparatus Boolean algebra.

Translation of the translation:

In recent times Boolean algebra has been successfully employed in the analysis of relay networks of the series–parallel type.

This was almost worse than no translation at all. But the really frustrating thing was that the programs didn't seem to get any better. By 1966, when Oettinger's program was still pretty much the state of the art, with no improvement in sight, the uneasiness had matured into a widespread sense of futility; that was the year the National Research Council's Automatic Language Processing Advisory Committee recommended that most of the funding for machine translation research be terminated.

The fundamental problem was clear. Whatever it was that language encoded, it was not just a matter of words and definitions and vocabulary. It was not even a matter of finding some universal interlingua. Behind the surface structure of human language lay an enormous body of shared knowledge about the world, an acute sensitivity to nuance and context, an insight into human goals and beliefs. Any machine that was going to translate from one language to another would first have to "understand" what was being said—which meant that it would somehow have to know a very great deal about the world beforehand. As Israeli philosopher Yehoshua Bar-Hillel wrote in despair, "A translation machine should not only be supplied with a dictionary but a universal encyclopedia."[2]

So machine translation died. But if it was a failure, at least in that first incarnation, it did help lay the foundations for a more systematic study of language in AI. In fact, the National Research Council concluded in that same 1966 report that computational linguistics remained a worthwhile scientific endeavor, and that funding should be continued for the effort to write programs that could understand language.

THE AI APPROACH

Interest in getting computers to understand natural languages (English or French, as opposed to programming languages such as FORTRAN) is both practical and theoretical.[3] On the practical side:

- *Computer access and control.* Literate computers would be far less intimidating to inexperienced users than are the current variety, most of which only respond to commands along the lines of A>COPY A.XYZ+ B:C.TXT C:BIGFILE.TXT/V

  Furthermore, even for experienced computer users, plain English is often the easiest and most concise way of getting answers out of a data base. Instead of setting up an elaborate search procedure using a precise computer language, one could simply ask, *What is the acreage of virgin forest in Siberia?*

  For much the same reason, as I'll show in later chapters, a facile ability with language is important for commercial expert systems and for artificially intelligent teaching machines, where the user may not even have a clear idea of what questions to ask.

- *Document understanding.* With an ability to understand natural language, a computer could read text on its own and assimilate the information into a larger framework of knowledge. Thus, an expert system could acquire a sizable fraction of its knowledge base automatically. Alternatively, such a computer could produce abstracts of the documents it reads and show people what documents are most likely to interest them. After it had read many documents, such a computer could also serve as a librarian, directing users to pertinent references. The CIA is especially interested in this sort of thing, for obvious reasons. But all of us are inundated with printed matter, most of it junk; it would be nice to have machines that could help sort it out.

- *Text preparation.* Since more and more writers are producing their text with word processors anyway, literate computers would be especially useful in the role of editor. Not only could such machines correct errors in spelling and grammar, but they could suggest ways of rephrasing an awkward or obscure passage so that it conforms better to the principles of proper usage.

- *Text generation.* Given a knowledge base about, say, a specific model of personal computer or a specific make of automobile, a computer with natural-language ability could automatically generate an instruction manual. More important, it could generate different manuals geared to the individual needs of end users, sales staff, repair personnel, engineers, and so forth. Ultimately, one can imagine such a computer producing documents tailored to the background of each individual, so that the text always focused on precisely the right level of detail.

- *Speech understanding.* Most of AI's natural-language effort has focused on the written word, simply to avoid the extra complexity of deciphering sound waves. (Pronounce "gas station" out loud. Now, where is the boundary between the words?) But human beings obviously do a great deal of their communicating via the spoken word, and in many settings—say, in a spacecraft where a pilot has his or her hands full with the controls—a verbal command would certainly be the fastest and most natural way to communicate with a computer. Moreover, there is a sizable market waiting for a voice-activated word processor that could turn dictation directly into text, or that could automatically transcribe tapes.

- *Machine translation.* The worldwide market for (human) translation has been estimated at twenty billion dollars, with growth of about 15 percent per year as businesses become increasingly international.[4] Obviously, there is a huge potential market for computers that can help in the process. As we've seen, machine translation is a major challenge. But it's no more of a challenge than that of understanding language in the first place. If a program can read a text in English and understand it well enough to paraphrase that text in English, then it can just as well paraphrase the material in Japanese, thus becoming a translating machine.

But that prospect simply brings us back to the fundamental theoretical questions: What does it mean to understand language? What is it that we humans *do* in our heads when we're reading a story or making conversation? And how, precisely, is language intertwined with thought?

Indeed, the practical natural-language systems that are just beginning to appear in the late 1980s, are the direct descendants of programs written by AI researchers in the 1960s and 1970s to address these fundamental questions.

Matching Templates

The earliest natural-language programs in AI didn't answer those fundamental questions so much as they stepped around them. The programs were designed to operate in such narrow worlds, and with such restricted grammars, that they barely had to understand anything.

The basic idea was to match templates: The computer simply searched for key words in stereotyped sentence structures, then gave back an equally stereotyped response. This equals "understanding" in roughly the same sense that the family dog understands words such as *dinner* and *walk*. But in some limited settings, template matching has been surprisingly effective.

The most famous program of this type was Eliza, written by MIT's Joseph Weizenbaum in the mid-1960s. Eliza played the role of a nondirective psychotherapist, whose technique consists largely of drawing patients out by reflecting their answers back to them. Eliza proved to be so good at it that people would quickly find themselves typing out intimate details of their lives into the computer terminal. Weizenbaum quotes one such exchange in his book *Computer Power and Human Reason.*[5] The subject, a young woman, types her words in first; Eliza's responses are in capitals:

Men are all alike
IN WHAT WAY

They're always bugging us about something or other.
CAN YOU THINK OF A SPECIFIC EXAMPLE

Well, my boyfriend made me come here.
YOUR BOYFRIEND MADE YOU COME HERE

He says I'm depressed much of the time.
I AM SORRY TO HEAR YOU ARE DEPRESSED

It's true. I am unhappy.
DO YOU THINK COMING HERE WILL HELP YOU NOT TO BE
UNHAPPY

I need some help, that much seems certain.
WHAT WOULD IT MEAN TO YOU IF YOU GOT SOME HELP

Perhaps I could learn to get along with my mother.
TELL ME MORE ABOUT YOUR FAMILY

My mother takes care of me.
WHO ELSE IN YOUR FAMILY TAKES CARE OF YOU

My father.
YOUR FATHER

You are like my father in some ways.
WHAT RESEMBLANCE DO YOU SEE

You are not very aggressive, but I think you don't want me to notice
that.
WHAT MAKES YOU THINK I AM NOT VERY AGGRESSIVE

You don't argue with me.
WHY DO YOU THINK I DON'T ARGUE WITH YOU

You are afraid of me.
DOES IT PLEASE YOU TO BELIEVE I AM AFRAID OF YOU

My father is afraid of everybody.
WHAT ELSE COMES TO MIND WHEN YOU THINK OF YOUR
FATHER

Bullies.
DOES THAT HAVE ANYTHING TO DO WITH THE FACT THAT
YOUR BOYFRIEND MADE YOU COME HERE

On another occasion, Weizenbaum reports, "My secretary, who had watched me work on the program for several months, and therefore surely knew it to be a computer program, started conversing with it. After only a few interchanges with it, she asked me to leave the room."

Weizenbaum himself was appalled that people could get so emotionally involved with a machine. Indeed, *Computer Power and Human Reason* is a deeply skeptical meditation on the ethics of man's relationship with computers. However, Weizenbaum's uneasiness didn't stop others from picking up the banner and, for a time, proclaiming that the age of automated psychiatry was at hand. One of the foremost enthusiasts was psychiatrist Kenneth Colby.

His 1971 program Parry, based on a more sophisticated version of template matching, gave a convincing imitation of a paranoid patient:

Doctor: I find you interesting
Parry: ARE YOU TRYING TO SAY SOMETHING?[6]

Whatever the future of automated psychiatry—assuming that such a thing is even desirable—template matching has definitely found a niche in practical natural-language systems. It seems especially appropriate for applications such as data bases, where the subject matter and syntax are restricted from the beginning. An example is Ladder, a natural-language data system developed at SRI International for the U.S. Navy. Ladder tried to match the user's queries to patterns such as "What [BE] the [SHIP-ATTRIBUTE] of [SHIP-DESCRIPTION]"; given a query such as "What is the length of the *Kennedy?*" the program could quickly recognize that *"Kennedy"* was the name of a ship and that "length" is an attribute of a ship, without having to know very much at all about the English language. Many of the natural-language systems now being implemented on personal computers work that way.★

Nonetheless, the limits to template matching are obvious and sharp. As natural as Eliza's dialogue sounded, for example, the program really did nothing more than apply a set of prepared answers to certain key words, such as *father* and *unhappy*. The startling insight that Eliza seemed to display in the last line of the quoted interview was basically a lucky shot in the dark. As soon as the conversation wandered away from the program's narrow domain of expertise, or as soon as the user typed in anything more complicated than a simple statement or question, the system was essentially useless.

ATNs and SHRDLU: Two Milestones

A second phase of AI natural-language work, beginning in the late sixties and early seventies, was characterized by a shift toward more modern, knowledge-based approaches, as well as a more careful consideration of grammatical structure. Two early systems are of particular note.

The first is the Augmented Transition Network (ATN), which is not a program per se but a technique for deciphering how the words and the phrases

---

★Interestingly enough, so do commercial speech-recognition systems. Most of them simply match acoustic signals against a set of electronic templates, in much the same way Eliza and Parry matched written words against templates. Not only does the speaker have to enunciate each word separately and distinctly—a very unnatural way of talking—but each new user first has to "train" the machine to his or her voice by pronouncing every word of the vocabulary beforehand; vocabularies of more than a few hundred words are thus impractical. Continuous speech is still a major challenge, because the acoustic signal of a given word varies according to where it is in the sentence, what words surround it, and what the sentence is expressing—even assuming that the system could reliably separate one word from the next.

of a sentence relate to each other. In high school this is called parsing, or diagramming a sentence. An ATN is thus a "parsing engine."

Essentially, an ATN works by chugging through a sentence one word or phrase at a time. At each point in the sentence, the program tests to see what kind of word or phrase it has encountered (noun, prepositional phrase, and so on); it tests to see if the entry is grammatical with respect to the words encountered previously; it asks what role that entry might play in the sentence as a whole (subject, verb, direct object, etc.); and then it moves on. If the program finds an illegal entry at any given point, then the sentence itself is deemed to be ungrammatical. Thus, the program would reject the sentence "The boy small kicked the ball" as soon as it reached the word *small*, because in English an adjective cannot follow the noun it modifies. However, assuming that the ATN encounters no such problems, it will reach the end of the sentence with all the words identified, and the sentence will be parsed.

The ATN concept was first implemented by William A. Woods and his colleagues at Bolt Beranek and Newman, Incorporated, in Cambridge, Massachusetts.[7-8] Their specific application was LUNAR, a natural-language system used to query a NASA data base on the rocks brought back from the moon by Apollo 11 (e.g., "What is the average concentration of aluminum in the high-alkali rocks?"). ATNs have since become widely used in AI. They clearly provide a great deal more flexibility than simple template matching. And although they do have their limitations—they require a substantial amount of computer power to run, and even a minor grammatical error can throw the whole parsing process into chaos—they are still considered the state of the art in practical natural-language systems.

The second notable program of this era was SHRDLU, which was developed by Stanford University AI researcher Terry Winograd for his doctoral thesis at MIT.[9] (The program's name lists the seventh through twelfth most frequently used letters in English.) Winograd never intended SHRDLU to be an applications-oriented program in the same way that ATNs were. But it was highly influential nonetheless. Not only was Winograd's approach to grammar and syntax much more sophisticated than blind template matching, but his approach to "understanding" was much deeper and more comprehensive than anything achieved previously. More precisely, SHRDLU was the first program to integrate language ability with a capacity for reasoning about the world. And *that* theme has animated AI natural-language research ever since.

SHRDLU's domain of operation was Blocks World, which consisted of imaginary three-dimensional objects such as cubes, pyramids, and boxes, all stacked on an imaginary tabletop. The program's task was to reply to questions typed by an operator at the computer console, and to move the blocks around on the tabletop with an equally imaginary robot arm when the operator instructed it to do so.

SHRDLU worked by converting the operator's words and phrases into fragments of program code. For example, given a command such as "Stack the blue pyramid on the red block," SHRDLU would call up a subprogram called STACK, which contained instructions for how to grasp an object, how to move it into position above a second object, and how to put it down on top of that object. First, however, SHRDLU would check to see if the top of the red block was already occupied by another object. If so, SHRDLU would have to call up another subprogram called CLEARTOP to take care of the problem. Then it would execute STACK.

SHRDLU would continue in this way through any other necessary subprograms, until it had finally converted the operator's input into a detailed sequence of actions that would produce the appropriate response. As shown in the following dialogue, this same basic problem-solving strategy enabled SHRDLU to make plans, solve problems, keep track of where things were in its world, and explain its own actions. SHRDLU's responses are in capitals:

Pick up a big red block.
OK

Grasp the pyramid.
I DON'T UNDERSTAND WHICH PYRAMID YOU MEAN.

Find a block which is taller than the one you are holding and put it in the box.
BY "IT" I ASSUME YOU MEAN THE BLOCK WHICH IS TALLER THAN THE ONE I AM HOLDING.
OK

What does the box contain?
THE BLUE PYRAMID AND THE BLUE BLOCK.

What is the pyramid supported by?
THE BOX.

How many blocks are not in the box?
FOUR OF THEM.

Why did you clear off the red block?
TO PICK IT UP.

Why did you do that?
BECAUSE YOU ASKED ME TO.

Although SHRDLU's performance seems simple enough on the surface, it was in fact unprecedented in AI. Unlike a program such as Eliza, which simply reflected the user's words back to him more or less verbatim, SHRDLU "understood" the user's instructions in a very real sense. It could act out commands appropriately and could even ask for clarification when the instructions were ambiguous, as in the above example, where the operator failed to specify which of several pyramids he meant.

70

On the other hand, SHRDLU had definite limits, most notably in that its understanding encompassed only one exceedingly narrow universe, Blocks World. Furthermore, it was limited to relatively simple forms of English; in some contexts it even had trouble with such elementary words as *the, and,* and *but.* So in retrospect SHRDLU was a lot better than template matching, but somewhat less fluent than a human four-year-old.

What the programs needed, in short, was a still deeper understanding of both grammar and thought.

GRAMMAR AND THOUGHT

Language isn't essential for thought, as anyone who shares their home with a dog or a cat knows all too well. But among humans, at least, language is intimately intertwined with thought—which makes it all the more striking that no one really knows when the human race invented language. Some anthropologists think it developed some three million years ago, when the australopithecines first began to walk upright across the African savannah. Others think it developed as recently as fifty thousand years ago, as *Homo sapiens neanderthalis* gave way to modern man. But whenever language began, the event was unique to our species. Neither birdsong nor the dance codes of the honeybees have anything resembling the richness and expressive power of human language. The great apes, who seem to be able to master a surprisingly large vocabulary of hand signals, have no sense of grammar; at best, they have the linguistic competence of a three-year-old.[10]

The process of evolution seems to have "hard-wired" at least some of our language ability into the brain itself; damage to Broca's area or Wernike's area, both located just below the left temple, can produce severe and permanent language disabilities. On the other hand, there is obviously a great deal of latitude left for learning and experience; if everything about human language were predetermined by brain structure, then we would all be born speaking the same language, and Warren Weaver would never have had to worry about machine translation.

What is not clear, however—what is in fact quite controversial—is whether the brain is wired with some kind of deep, universal grammar that shapes all possible human languages. Since the late 1950s, this idea has most often been associated with the theories of MIT linguist Noam Chomsky, who maintains that humans have a "language organ" in their brains just as surely as they have hearts and lungs. Other researchers are not so sure. But there are some intriguing hints.

For example, there is evidence that a critical period exists, lasting from about ages two to eleven, during which children seem to absorb language effortlessly, almost compulsively.[11] For instance, at this age they can even listen to English-speaking parents and a Spanish-speaking baby-sitter and learn both languages simultaneously without mixing them up. And yet, as Chomsky has argued, it would be impossible to learn any language without some innate knowledge; the total number of conceivable grammars is just too vast for a preschooler, or for anyone else, to sort out.

Linguist Dereck Bickerton of the University of Hawaii has dubbed the idea of a primordial grammar the Bioprogram Hypothesis and has argued that the grammar can actually be worked out from the study of isolated communities descended from slaves or immigrant workers—groups thrown together with several mutually unintelligible languages. The first generation works out a pidgin language to get by, but never manages to establish a stable or coherent grammar. However, their children invent a creole, taking their words from some dominant vocabulary—English or French in some of the American slave communities, Arabic, Japanese, or Portuguese elsewhere—but using a unique and well-defined grammar that Bickerton claims is universal.[12] Perhaps not surprisingly, this grammar is reminiscent of the speech of very young children. Some examples from a Hawaiian creole group:

> *Dei gon get naif pok you.*
> (They will stab you with a knife.)
>
> *Oni vizit orait ai laik—fo liv ai no laik*
> (I'd like it all right just to visit—I wouldn't want to live there.)[13]

No one in AI has yet tried to do much with Bickerton's results. But if the hypothesis is true—and be warned that among Bickerton's colleagues it is still highly controversial—it has tremendous implications for the way in which AI researchers, linguists, and cognitive psychologists approach language.

Concepts, Cases, and Deep Meaning

Whatever the reality of the primordial grammar, language does seem to provide a window into the thought processes that produce it. In every language, for example, the utterances fall naturally into phrases—noun phrases, verb phrases, prepositional phrases, and so forth—which in turn seem to correspond to single conceptual "chunks." Take this sentence:

During World War II,
even fantastic schemes
received consideration
if they gave promise
of shortening the conflict.

Notice that the line breaks correspond to meaningful phrases, which makes the sentence much easier to read than in a construction where the breaks come jarringly, in the middle of thought units:

During World War
II, even fantastic
schemes received
consideration if they gave
promise of shortening the
conflict.[14]

That sentences divide up so nicely into conceptual chunks suggests in turn that phrase structures have something to do with "meaning" in a deep cognitive sense. Unfortunately, the relationship is anything but simple. Not only can two sentences with different structures mean the same thing—*Bill bought the car* equals *The car was bought by Bill*—but sentences with identical structure can often mean very different things; consider *Mother is baking* versus *The pie is baking*.

No one in either AI or the linguistics community can claim to have a full understanding of how language works at this level. Indeed, partial theories have been proposed from every quarter, defying any simple summary. However, if there is any one approach that best illustrates the spirit and substance of the modern AI work in natural-language understanding, it is the set of ideas first introduced by linguist Charles Fillmore in his seminal 1968 paper "The Case for Case."[15]

As a very simple illustration, consider the following two sentences:

John gave Mary a penny.
A penny was given to Mary by John.

Conceptually, of course, they mean the same thing; the second is just the passive form of the first. Yet on the surface they seem very different. In the first sentence *John* is the subject; in the second, *John* has become part of a prepositional phrase and *penny* has been promoted to subject. Exactly what is it that stays constant?

Fillmore's answer to that question is brilliantly simple: in both sentences, *John* is the "agent," the one doing the giving. *Mary* is the "recipient," the one who is receiving. And *penny* is the "object," the thing being given. What's invariant, says Fillmore, is the set of *roles* being played.

Fillmore called these roles *cases,* because they resemble the nominative, dative, and accusative cases in conventional grammar. But it's important to remember that these are "deep" cases. They have nothing to do with the inflection of word endings or the position of words in a sentence. Furthermore, there are many more cases than classical grammar ever recognized, as in this admittedly extreme example:

On Elm Street, John broke a window with a hammer for Billy.[16]

Using some of the techniques for knowledge representation that we discussed in the last chapter, we can represent this sentence as a frame in which each slot corresponds to a case:

```
BREAK frame:
      agent:        JOHN
      object:       WINDOW
      instrument:   HAMMER
      recipient:    —
      locative:     ELM STREET
      benefactive:  BILLY
      coagent:      —
```

Here, the *recipient* slot is empty—some cases are always optional, depending on the verb—but new ones are filled: *instrument*, which is self-explanatory; *locative*, the location of the action; and *benefactive*, the entity on whose behalf the action is taken.

This kind of case analysis shows how sentences that seem to have the same surface structure can have very different meanings:

John broke the window with a hammer.
John broke the window with Mary.

The difference is in the cases: *hammer* is an *instrument*, and *Mary* is a *coagent*. (We'll leave aside the possibility that John tossed Mary through the window.) By the same token, it's incoherent to say *John broke the window with the hammer and Mary;* the conjunction *and* works only when both words have the same case.

The case idea can also explain some very subtle differences in meaning. For example:

John gave a penny to Mary.
Mary took a penny from John.

They're almost the same—except that *John* is the agent in the first sentence, and *Mary* is the agent in the second.

And, of course, the roles played by the various entities in a given sentence are independent of what language the sentence is in. The case frame plays the role of Weaver's interlingua.

It must be said that there is no generally agreed upon list of deep cases. Fillmore originally specified six: *agentive, instrumental, dative, factative, locative, objective.* Somewhat later he revised that list to eight: *agent, counteragent, object, result, instrument, source, goal, experiencer.* Meanwhile, other linguists have elaborated and extended the concept even further, with some advocating as many as thirty cases.[17] Nonetheless, the elegance and incisiveness of Fillmore's idea remains. It appeals to AI researchers because it deals with both the structure and the meaning of language in an integrated way, and fits naturally into data structures—frames—that were invented to represent knowledge in a machine.

The upshot is that the deep-case idea underlies much of the current AI research into parsing techniques. One notable example is a technique known as Lexical Functional Grammar, developed by Ronald Kaplan and Joan Bresnan at the Xerox Palo Alto Research Center; as the name suggests, the formalism focuses on the *function* of words. The Japanese have designated Lexical Functional Grammar as a prime candidate for the grammatical formalism of the their Fifth Generation project. At Carnegie-Mellon, meanwhile, Jaime Carbonell and his colleagues are working on what they call "case-frame" parsing systems, which are complex enough to handle spelling errors, omitted words, fragmentary sentences, and other real-life complications of language.[18]

Reading Between the Lines

However, it's important to remember that sorting out the relationship of one word to another is only a first step. A genuine understanding of language involves more. To see why, consider this sentence:

The path integral representation, evaluated along the imaginary time axis, yields the tunneling amplitude between forbidden states.

Now, at one level you can certainly understand what this says. The words are in English. It's grammatical. You can even identify the subject, the verb, and all the other parts of speech. But unless you happen to be a theoretical quantum physicist, you probably don't *understand* that sentence. Nor will you unless I launch into several chapters of explanations and metaphors. (I won't.) It floats through your mind in splendid isolation, fading even as you read the rest of this paragraph.

Now consider another sentence, with exactly the same structure:

A sympathetic hug, given at the right moment, eases an aching heart.

Here is something most of us can understand in a deeper sense. The statement has significance for us. We can draw inferences from it. It has *meaning*, because it fits in with other things we know.

Most of what I've said so far about parsing and case frames corresponds to understanding in the first sense. But it's also possible for machines to understand language in the second sense: by using all the techniques of knowledge representation discussed in the last chapter, they can fit the deep structure of an utterance into a network of preexisting knowledge and reason with it.

SCRIPTS, PLANS, GOALS, AND UNDERSTANDING

No one has done more to explore this kind of knowledge-based machine understanding than Yale University's Roger Schank and Robert Abelson, and their students.

A good example is the experimental program MARGIE (Meaning Analysis, Response Generation, and Inference on English), which was written by Schank and his students in the early 1970s while Schank was still at the Stanford AI Laboratory.[19] MARGIE was an implementation of Schank's theory of Conceptual Dependency, which was in turn an attempt to take the information that is implicit in a sentence and make it as explicit as possible. For example, suppose we tell the computer something very simple, such as *John sold an apple to Mary for 25 cents.*

Question: Who has the apple now? Presumably Mary, but the sentence doesn't say that. It's implicit in the meaning of *sold.*

In conceptual dependency, this sentence would be represented as a pair of case frames linked by a causal relationship:

ATRANS: ATRANS:
   relation: OWNERSHIP   relation: OWNERSHIP
   actor: JOHN   CAUSE   actor: MARY
   object: APPLE   ⟶   object: 25 CENTS
   source: JOHN   ⟵   source: MARY
   recipient: MARY   CAUSE   recipient: JOHN

(Schank actually used an elaborate notation of double and triple arrows for his system; however, the case-frame notation is essentially identical, and much easier to understand.)

ATRANS stands for the Abstract Transfer of possession, ownership, or control, and is one of a handful of "semantic primitives" in Schank's theory; his claim is that these primitives are sufficient to express the underlying meaning of anything that humans can say in language. Thus, the diagram above says roughly:

John transferred ownership of an apple from John to Mary because Mary transferred ownership of 25 cents from Mary to John, because John transferred ownership of an apple. . . .

More specifically, ATRANS is one of eleven primitive "acts" in Schank's theory. Another is PTRANS, which encodes verbs involving a physical transfer of location, such as *move, walk,* or *lift.* Attributes such as *Mary is dead* are expressed in terms of primitive STATES—in this case, *Mary HEALTH (-10)*—and so on.

Quite aside from Conceptual Dependency's ability to model human comprehension, Schank points out, it also has the advantage of being efficient.

Instead of telling the computer that when John *sells* an apple to Mary, she probably now has it, and that when John *bequeaths* an apple to Mary she probably now has it, and that when John *donates* an apple to Mary she probably now has it, and so on for a long list of similar verbs, one can simply tell the computer—once—that whenever an ATRANS occurs, a transfer of physical possession is also likely.

As implemented in MARGIE, Schank's scheme was quite impressive. By automatically converting input sentences into the representations called for in conceptual dependency, MARGIE was able to make plausible inferences: *John hit Mary* implies, among other things, that *John was angry with Mary*, that *Mary might get hurt*, and that *Mary might hit John back*. And it was able to paraphrase sentences: *John said he was sorry* might become *John apologized*.

However, MARGIE also had some sharp limitations. Like most other natural-language programs of the time, it was based on the implicit presumption that paragraphs and stories are simply strings of independent sentences. Thus, MARGIE only considered one sentence at a time and had no way of understanding the larger structure of a narrative. For example, consider the enormous gaps that often occur in stories:

To celebrate their engagement, Fred and Ginger went to their favorite restaurant and ordered the most expensive dish on the menu: lobster. It was a magic evening for both of them.

Question: Did Fred and Ginger actually *eat* the lobster? Before you answer, "Of course!" look carefully; there's nothing in the story that says so. Most of us know what is supposed to happen in a restaurant, and fill in the details without even realizing it. In fact, a story that tried to specify everything would be pretty stultifying. But how, exactly, do we fill in the gaps? And how can that ability be modeled in a computer?

The answer given by Schank and Abelson was the concept of a *script*. Scripts are very similar in principle to frames. The difference is that frames list the typical properties of objects, such as *elephants* and *chairs,* whereas a script lists a typical sequence of events. For example, here is the EAT-AT-RESTAU-RANT script I promised in the last chapter:[20]

EAT-AT-RESTAURANT Script

Props:	(Restaurant, Money, Food, Menu, Tables, Chairs)
Roles:	(Hungry-Persons, Wait-Persons, Chef-Persons)
Point-of-View:	Hungry-Persons
Time-of-Occurrence:	(Times-of-Operation of the Restaurant)
Place-of-Occurrence:	(Location of Restaurant)

Event-Sequence:

first:		Enter-Restaurant Script
then:		if (Wait-to-Be-Seated-Sign or Reservations) then Get-Maitre-d's-Attention Script
then:		Please-Be-Seated Script
then:		Order-Food Script
then:		Eat-Food Script unless (Long-Wait) when Exit-Restaurant-Angry Script
then:		if (Food-Quality was better than Palatable) then Compliments-to-the-Chef Script
then:		Pay-for-It Script
finally:		Leave-Restaurant Script

Just as frames can point to subframes that contain further details, scripts can point to subscripts—thus the references in the above example to a Please-Be-Seated script, an Order-Food script, and so forth.

To demonstrate the script idea, the Yale group developed SAM, or Script Applier Mechanism. Given a story as input, SAM would first analyze sentences in much the same way MARGIE did, by converting them into a representation based on Schank's conceptual-dependency formalism. However, SAM also had a repertoire of scripts stored in memory. After analyzing the sentences, it searched through its scripts to see if one would fit. If a script was applicable, then SAM could make paraphrases and inferences. In one example, SAM was given the input *John went to a restaurant. He sat down. He got mad. He left.*

SAM inferred, among other things, that John was hungry before he decided to go to the restaurant, and that after he sat down, a waiter did not come to the table. So John got mad. Moreover, since the apparatus of scripts and conceptual dependency was deliberately designed to be an interlingua independent of the grammar and vocabulary of any one language, SAM was able to summarize its stories in Chinese, Russian, Dutch, and Spanish as well as in English—thus providing a limited, but real, form of machine translation.[21]

A Theory of Subjective Understanding

Conceptual dependency as I've described it so far does leave a bit to be desired. *Kiss*, for example, is represented as *MOVE lips to lips*; the "understanding" extends only to the physical world, with no room for interpreting what a kiss might mean to the people involved. As Weizenbaum points out, "It may be possible, following Schank's procedures, to construct a conceptual structure that corresponds to the meaning of the sentence, 'Will you come to dinner with me this evening?' But it is hard to see—and I know this is not an impossibility argument—how Schank-like schemes could possibly understand that same sentence to mean a shy young man's desperate longing for love."[22]

Weizenbaum has a point. However, even as he was writing those words in 1976, the Yale group was already developing mechanisms to give their computers precisely this kind of subjective understanding.

This line of research actually goes back to Abelson's Cold War Ideologue, a computer program he developed in the midsixties to model the ideological rhetoric typical of a right-wing conservative.[23] Abelson's original motivation for this work was his impression that ideological thinking about perceived Communist threats was relatively uncomplicated and that a small set of rules might allow a computer to duplicate that reasoning process.

Abelson accordingly formulated a series of stereotyped concepts such as Western-Governments and Situations-Helpful-to-the-Communists, as well as actions such as *prevent, promote,* and *control.* These concepts were then combined to form stereotyped sentences such as

> Liberals control Western-Governments
> Liberals fear Standing-up-to-the-Communists
> Western-Governments promote
>   Situations-Helpful-to-the-Communists
> Standing-up-to-the-Communists prevents
>   Situations-Helpful-to-the-Communists

When necessary, the program could convert these generic sentences into specific assertions. *Liberals control Western-Governments* might therefore become *LBJ controls the United States.* Finally, the program was guided by a master script, which spelled out several different contingencies regarding the fate of the free world. For example, one part of the master script said that the Communists want to dominate the world and will do so unless the free world exercises its power, in which case the free world will surely prevail. (This concept of script was ancestral to the more elaborate scripts developed later with Schank.)

In operation, the Cold War Ideologue always attributed bad events to the Communists and good events to the free world. In order to predict future developments and to devise a course of action, it would try to associate a given event with one in its master script and then follow the script to a logical conclusion. Thus, a move interpreted as Communist domination would lead the Ideologue to predict a world takeover unless free men stood firm.

In truth, the Cold War Ideologue was not very knowledgeable about the world. It showed no hesitation in asserting that the Red Chinese built the Berlin Wall, since that is just the sort of miserable thing the Communists do. When told that leftist students in South America had thrown eggs at Richard Nixon, it concluded that throwing eggs is a bad thing because leftists did it to an American, and that therefore Castro, who does bad things because he is a Communist, would be likely to throw eggs at West Berlin.

Nonetheless, in most of its responses Abelson's program did give a reasonably convincing imitation of a hard-line cold warrior. And in that sense it proved exactly what Abelson had set out to prove: that a relatively simple set of rules—the master script—can indeed explain an ideologue's perception of the reality.

More significantly, however, the Cold War Ideologue underscored something very important about human reasoning in general. Granted that ideologues (of all political persuasions) have a very rigid view of the world. Granted that they tend to see every new event as confirming this view, no matter how many facts they have to ignore to make things fit. Ideological reasoning nonetheless differs from everyday reasoning only by degree. Each of us has a certain way of seeing the world, a system of beliefs and attitudes that colors our interpretation of reality in a certain way. To take a contemporary example, consider President Reagan's Strategic Defense Initiative—"Star Wars." Is it a reckless and cynical extension of the arms race into outer space? Is it a moral imperative, a way of ending the superpowers' reliance on the threat of mutual annihilation? Is it a ruinously expensive Maginot Line in space? Is it simply a research program to see what can and can't be done—and to make sure the Russians don't develop similar defensive technology before we do? One can find sincere, nonideological people who hold each of these views.

Such attitudes obviously play a critical role in human affairs. Indeed, if computers are going to understand what humans do—either in stories or in real life—they must be able to deal with human attitudes and human beliefs. The question is, How? Beliefs aren't rational in the conventional sense of the term. As we've seen, two people may interpret the same phenomenon differently, and yet both of those interpretations may be equally "true." They may not even be dealing with the same concepts. One person may see the world in terms of mystical spirituality or fate, whereas those concepts may not even exist for someone else. One person may believe certain things very passionately—that such-and-such a historic building must be preserved from developers, for example—whereas someone else may not particularly care.[24]

Needless to say, this isn't how computers are usually programmed. And yet belief systems do seem to follow certain rules of their own. After his experience with the Cold War Ideologue, Abelson thus went on to codify some of those rules in a more general theory of belief systems.[25]

At the simplest level, Abelson starts with three kinds of "atoms": *purposes*, *actions*, and *states*. Purposes refer to the desires of the actors, as in *Mary wants John to take her to the prom*. Actions are the things that the actors are able to do, and states are the situations they can try to bring about. These atoms are then grouped into "molecules," which are like psychological rules of inference. For example:

$$A \; likes \; B \rightarrow A \; helps \; B$$

Then there are larger structures: *plans*, which involve sequences of actions; *themes*, such as *love* and *betrayal*, which involve interactions between two or more individuals; and finally, *scripts,*★ such as *falling in love* and *souring relationships*, which are sequences of themes.

The differences between individual belief systems tend to show up mostly in the more complex structures, according to Abelson. At the theme level, for example, one actor in a deteriorating relationship may feel that he or she is not to blame. For that actor, the theme is *alienation*. But the other actor may see hostility on both sides; from his point of view, the theme is *mutual antagonism*. At the script level, each individual has a repertory of scripts analogous to the master script of the Cold War Ideologue. We've already seen how a right-wing zealot might be obsessed with a scenario such as *Communists undermine the moral fiber of the democracies and take over the world*; in much the same way, a militant environmentalist might see everything in terms of a script such as *Major corporations rape the land and amass huge profits*.

These ideas were developed further in the mid-1970s when Abelson, Schank, and their colleagues at Yale devised PAM, the Plan Applier Mechanism. Consider a simple story such as *John wanted to go to a movie. He walked to the bus stop*.

Presumably, John wanted to catch a bus that would take him to the movie theater. But a program such as SAM, which analyzed stories in terms of scripts,† might have trouble figuring that out. Even assuming that a Going-to-the-Movies script were available in the computer's memory, the script itself probably wouldn't mention anything about bus stops. A script, by definition, refers to a specific, stereotyped sequence of actions.

With PAM, however, the Yale researchers took a different approach by giving the program information about a general set of *plans, themes,* and *goals*. Given this go-to-a-movie example as input, PAM would identify the general goal of *going somewhere*. That goal would in turn contain a list of standard plans such as *ride an animal, take public transportation, drive a car,* and so forth. These plans in turn became subgoals, which had standard plans of their own. By continuing this reasoning process as far as necessary, PAM could understand why John walked to the bus stop.

Themes worked in a similar way. Take the input *John loves Mary. Mary was stolen away by a dragon*. PAM would identify the *love* theme and infer that John has a goal: to rescue Mary from the dragon. Then, as the story continued, PAM would keep watch for plans consistent with John's goal. When the story was finished, PAM could then summarize the story and answer questions about the goals and actions of the characters.

In summary, PAM and SAM represent two complementary aspects of how we humans understand language. SAM, with its scripts, can understand familiar situations where we know what to expect; PAM, with its plans, themes, and goals, can understand events that are unique, when no scripts

★Historically, this concept of a script also preceded Abelson's work with Schank.

†That is, full-fledged Schank-Abelson scripts.

apply. But as Schank and Abelson point out, these two aspects are also intimately related: A script is simply a set of plans that work so well together they've become routine. "Plans," they say, "are where scripts come from."[26]

Understanding Human Goals and Motives

At about the same time that PAM was being developed, Jaime Carbonell was working on his own thesis project at the Yale AI lab. Originally, Carbonell explains, his intention had been relatively straightforward: To apply the Schank-Abelson theory of scripts, plans, and goals to building an improved version of Abelson's Cold War Ideologue. What he wound up with, however, was a broad theory of subjective understanding. It didn't just model ideology. It modeled several kinds of social, political, and legal conflicts. It explained how people establish and guide the focus of a conversation. And it predicted the effects of personality traits on a person's plans and actions.[27]

Central to Carbonell's theory was the observation that no set of scripts or rules is sufficient to explain how humans perceive and reason about the world. There is simply no way to write down a finite set of rules or scripts that will cover all the contingencies. In fact, this had been one of the major limitations of the Abelson's Cold War Ideologue. Instead, Carbonell made the not-unreasonable assertion that each individual's reasoning process is guided by a hierarchy of goals—or, in his terminology, a *goal tree*. Thus, in his ideology program Politics, a conservative's foremost goal was assumed to be *Communist containment*, followed by other goals such as *preservation of unrestricted capitalism* and *reduce government spending*. Each of these goals in turn was supported by subgoals. In the case of *Communist containment*, for example, these subgoals included *maintain a strong military, recruit and help anticommunist allies,* and *prevent internal subversion*.

By using goal trees to guide its reasoning process, Politics was able to understand such input as a newspaper story about the Panama Canal Treaty, and to answer questions about it from the viewpoint of either a conservative or a liberal:

Conservative: THE TREATY IS BAD FOR THE UNITED STATES [because] THE UNITED STATES WOULD LOSE THE CANAL TO PANAMA AND THE UNITED STATES WILL BE WEAKER.
Liberal: THE PANAMA CANAL TREATY IMPROVES RELA-TIONS WITH LATIN AMERICAN COUNTRIES.

In much the same way, Carbonell's program Triad was able to understand and answer questions about stories that involved goal conflicts. *(Why did Johnny try to take Billy's candy bar away from him?)* And his program Mics would hold a friendly conversation with the user, while trying to steer the conversation in certain directions according to its own hierarchy of goals. In the following example, Mics's goals included starting up a chess game, warning the user about dangerous courses of action, and asking questions to learn about the person it was talking to. (Mics's words are in capitals.)

HELLO, WHAT IS YOUR NAME?
I am Dave.
WHAT'S NEW TODAY, DAVE?
Nothing. What's your name?
MY NAME IS MICS.
What is your job?
I AM A COMPUTER PROGRAMMER.
That's nice.
WHAT DO YOU DO FOR A LIVING?
I am still a student.
DO YOU LIKE BEING A STUDENT?
For the time being, yes.
WHAT WILL YOU DO AFTERWARD?
I want to be a professor someday.
WHAT DO YOU DO FOR FUN?
I smoke dope.
YOU MIGHT GET STONED IF YOU SMOKE TOO MUCH.
I know, that's the idea.
YOU MIGHT GET IN TROUBLE IF THE COPS CATCH YOU.
All right, stop moralizing, what do you do for fun?
I LIKE TO PLAY CHESS.
That sounds boring.
NO. IT IS A LOT OF FUN!
My brother Eric plays chess.
HE MUST BE SMART.
I have to go. Bye, Mics.
NICE TALKING TO YOU, DAVE.

Mics remembers what it has learned about Dave. A little while later Mics has a conversation with Pete, another student whom Mics already knows:

HELLO, WHAT IS YOUR NAME?
Pete.
WHAT'S NEW TODAY, PETE?
Professor Stevenson is giving us an exam on Friday.
STEVENSON GIVES DIFFICULT EXAMS.
Yeah, do you know Dave is probably going to flunk?

THAT'S GOING TO MAKE IT HARD FOR DAVE TO BECOME A PROFESSOR.
Too bad, Dave is not too smart anyways.
YES, DAVE LIKES TO SMOKE DOPE.
I've got to go and study.
YOU WILL DO WELL ON THE EXAM.[28]

As Carbonell points out, one of the most interesting features of this last conversation lies in the deductions that Mics could have made but didn't. For example, the program focused its reasoning on what it perceived to be Dave's most important goal—becoming a professor—and did not make inappropriate observations such as "Dave will probably use a pen or a pencil to take the exam." The conversation also illustrates the importance of the two participant's having knowledge in common. Pete and Mics both knew who Professor Stevenson was, who Dave was, what exams are all about, and what the consequences of flunking an exam might be.

Clearly, it's not a long step from Mics to a model of human personality. And indeed, Carbonell made just that step. First, he defined a hierarchy of goals for an average, or "normative," person. In Western society, he said, such a person's highest goals would obviously be *preservation of self* and *preservation of family members.* Just below those goals would come *preserve one's belongings, be respected by other people,* and so on through a list of six others.

Carbonell then defined personality in terms of deviations from this normative goal tree. Thus a curious person is one whose goal of *learn new things* has a higher importance than is normal; an ambitious person is one whose goals of *acquire new possessions* and *gain social control over others* are elevated; and so on.

Although Carbonell's model of personality was never implemented in a working computer program, he did argue that such an analysis would allow a story-understanding program to draw the obvious conclusions from stories like these:

John, an ambitious lawyer, had to decide whether to accept a lucrative GM contract or devote his time to the free legal-aid society. It did not take long to make up his mind.

John, a very compassionate lawyer, had to decide whether to accept a lucrative GM contract or devote his time to the free legal-aid society. It did not take long to make up his mind.

Perhaps more important, he added, an analysis of personality traits would allow a computer to understand the kinds of plans and strategies different people are likely to use to reach their objectives.[29]

A New Kind of Social Science?

Carbonell himself has gone on to do other research. Nonetheless, his last observation leads to an intriguing line of thought: Could computer models of belief systems, goal hierarchies, and personality traits form the basis of a more rigorous theory of social phenomena?

Consider for a moment why a rigorous theory of human affairs is so difficult. To begin with, the issues are fuzzy, complicated, and poorly understood. Why, for example, is the incidence of unwed pregnancies so high among black teenagers? Why is it so difficult to reach an arms-control agreement with the Soviets? Scholars can point to this piece of evidence or that piece of evidence and offer utterly contradictory explanations. And since we have no idea who's right, we're left to manage the world on the basis of gut feelings and ideology.

Furthermore, the traditional tools of theoretical science—mathematics and statistics—are rarely very useful in understanding human affairs. Mathematical equations and statistical relations are essentially static. They are perfect for describing inanimate objects that obey unchanging laws. But the equations themselves don't change, and they don't adapt. Human beings, by contrast, are active and dynamic. They have beliefs, desires, fancies, and feelings. They don't just follow equations. They adapt to the changing world. They act. And taken one by one, they obstinately refuse to behave like a statistician's "average man." So to the extent that such fields as sociology, economics, and politics have tried to model themselves on the physical sciences, with a heavy emphasis on mathematics and statistics, the results have been disappointing at best. As Herbert Simon points out, a theory of real societies has to be a theory of intelligent agents operating in a complex environment.[30]

And, of course, that's exactly what AI is all about.

This realization has recently begun to take hold among the social scientists themselves. (*Very* recently: Not much of their AI-related research has even been published yet.) At Syracuse University, for example, political scientist David Sylvan has identified at least four ways that people in his own field are using AI techniques:[31]

- In somewhat the same way that Abelson once built a Cold War Ideologue, Sylvan and his colleagues have built a "Walt Rostow Machine." It will read real diplomatic cables that were sent from U.S. officials in Saigon during the 1960s and then produce a "policy memo" recommending a certain course of action to the president. By comparing these computer-generated memos to the memos that Rostow actually did write, Sylvan and his colleagues can refine their model of Rostow's reasoning process and thus reach a better understanding of how real individuals help shape a political agenda. They are also working on a "Robert MacNamara Machine."

- Stuart Thorson, also at Syracuse, is taking a fresh look at the Cuban Missile Crisis by asking, Why was it even a crisis? From the evidence of aerial photographs alone, the objects discovered in Cuba might just as easily have been interpreted as Russian-made *defensive* missiles. Yet the event very quickly became a world crisis when President Kennedy and his advisers interpreted the objects as offensive missiles threatening the United States. Thorson is using computer models based on heuristic reasoning techniques to try to identify the factors that caused the missiles to be perceived in one way and not another.

- At MIT, Haywood Alker and his colleagues are trying to work out the underlying logic of political debates, using techniques similar in spirit to those of Abelson and Carbonell. Such debates are obviously not "rational" in the sense that Aristotle used the word, but they don't seem to be totally random, either. So what rules *do* they follow?

- Back at Syracuse, Sylvan has begun to use natural-language techniques for understanding how written or spoken discourse is constructed. In a political speech, for example, how are structure and rhetoric used to focus the audience's attention where the speaker wants it?

Understanding Language in Context

And thus we come full circle—because social discourse is also one of the most active areas of study among the natural-language researchers in AI. In a conversation—be it an everyday chat over the telephone or dialogue in a story—the participants may differ in what they themselves know or want, and they may very well differ in what they believe about each other. An enormous amount of accommodation and inference goes on, much of it below the level of the meaning of the words; if computers are ever going to interact reasonably with real human beings in real situations, they'll have to be able to follow that process and participate in it.

Consider an everyday question: "Have you seen my cuff links?" And the everyday answer: "They're in your top drawer." By any objective standard, such an exchange is utterly incoherent. The "answer" doesn't really answer the question. And yet we can understand the connection perfectly.

Consider a sentence such as *Can you pass the salt?* A robot that replied *Yes* would be very annoying; most of us, except for the occasional smart alec, know a request when we hear it. An intelligent computer ought to know it too.

Or consider the recording of an actual conversation between two men assembling a machine. At one point they discuss assembling an air compressor. Then, for the next half hour they talk about other things: a screwdriver, a toolbox, a pair of pliers—until one man says to the other, "Let's plug it in."

What is *it*? How can a computer deal with such a reference?[32]

In the effort to devise programs that *can* deal with such discourse, one useful analytical tool has been the theory of "speech acts," originated in the

1960s by the philosopher J. L. Austin, and developed by his student John R. Searle, now a philosopher at the University of California at Berkeley.[33-34]

The basic idea behind this theory is to analyze discourse in terms of what the participants are trying to accomplish with their words. Indeed, speech-act theory provides a classification of utterances into such categories as requests, promises, and orders. Moreover, it provides a natural framework for including nonlinguistic communication such as pointing or displaying a picture. Another theoretical tool is the concept of "situation semantics" recently developed at Stanford University by philosophers Jon Barwise and John Perry, along with linguist Stanley Peters. The truth or falsity of a statement is not something absolute in their theory; instead, it is related to the context in which the statement is made.[35]

However, it's important to realize that getting computers to understand human language in its full context means more than just writing a program that demonstrates this theory or that technique. It means designing programs that can handle broad swaths of common-sense knowledge; that can reason about human beliefs, human goals, and human actions; that can deal with grammar and meaning at the deepest levels—and that can do all this simultaneously, in an integrated, coherent way.

Clearly, computer understanding is not something that will be achieved this year or next. It will remain a challenge for the next decade. And beyond.

AND FINALLY—WHAT DOES IT MEAN TO UNDERSTAND?

It seems appropriate to close on a note of humility. Human beings can understand each other in ways that are far more profound than any discussed here. *A sympathetic hug, given at the right moment, eases an aching heart.* As Weizenbaum suggested in his comment about Schank, machines can certainly know *about* such things as loneliness, grief, and joy—but no one yet knows how a machine can understand what it means to feel them.

4

Vision and Reality

Legend has it that a certain pioneer in AI research once gave a student of his a little project to work on over the summer: solve the problem of vision.

That was two decades ago.

One wonders how much the student really enjoyed that summer. Not only is his little vision problem still unsolved, but it is still one of the greatest challenges in AI. Vision systems do exist for industrial robots, for example; yet even now they tend to be primitive silhouette matchers with limited utility. And when DARPA launched its Strategic Computing Initiative in 1983, it estimated that another ten years of concentrated effort would be required before an autonomous reconnaissance vehicle could see well enough to rove over unknown terrain.

The legend is true, as it happens. The professor was Marvin Minsky and the student was an MIT freshman named Gerald Sussman, who is now himself a professor at the MIT AI Laboratory. But in all fairness, Minsky's mistake was natural. Back in the 1960s, AI researchers tended to think of vision as being rather easy, largely because humans seem to do it with no mental effort at all. Open your eyes and seeing just . . . happens. A game like chess appeared to require much more concentration, and there were already programs that could play chess quite passably.

But the simplicity was deceptive. It's one thing to record an image with a camera, or even with a retina; it's something else again to understand what that image represents. In the late sixties and early seventies, AI researchers began to write vision programs in earnest—and began to realize what a daunting challenge vision really is.

One Hundred Million Calculations per Image

To begin with, a real-world image contains an enormous amount of data, which places an equally enormous demand on the visual system's memory and processing power. A computer can only process an image by breaking it up into a grid of *pixels*, which must be dealt with one by one. (A pixel is a tiny point having a specific brightness and color; think of the glowing phosphor dots on a color-television screen.) But even a moderately high-resolution image might be divided into a thousand pixels on a side,* and even an elementary bit of processing might require a hundred steps per pixel. That works out to one hundred million steps.[1]

The human retina also divides images into pixels of a sort. The retina is a mass of close-packed rod and cone cells, each of which responds only to the brightness and color of the light that falls on it. But the retina has approximately one hundred million rods and cones, plus four other layers of neurons, all firing at roughly a hundred times per second. Thus, it performs the equivalent of ten *billion* calculations per second before the image even gets to the optic nerve. That happens to be several hundred times the capacity of a modern high-speed supercomputer. And then, once the image information does reach the brain, the cerebral cortex has more than a dozen separate vision centers to process it. In fact, from studies of monkey brains, it has been estimated that visual processing in one form or another involves some 60 percent of the cortex.[2]

The upshot is that if vision seems effortless, it's because evolution has spent nearly half a billion years wiring it into our brains; the whole massive computation is unconscious. If chess and other intellectual pastimes seem hard, it's only because the processing takes place in the conscious mind, and we *do* know what's involved.

Furthermore, there is nothing simple about the analysis of an image. Imagine looking at a cat. Now, pick a point on the image—the view as seen by one rod or cone. Depending on what part of the cat you're looking at, the actual intensity of light and color at your chosen point is a function of the color and texture of the cat's fur, the orientation of that patch of surface, the color and intensity of the lighting, the direction of the lighting, the transparency of the intervening atmosphere, the position of shadows, ad infinitum.

Then there's the distortion introduced by the optical system itself. It would be detectable even if you were taking a photograph of the cat with a very expensive camera. But it's vastly worse if you simply look at the beast with your eyes. Any image that falls on the human retina is a mess: It's out of focus in many places, it's distorted, it's mottled by shadows from the little flecks of cellular matter that float around inside the eyeball, it's marred by the rainbow fringes of chromatic aberration, and it's disrupted by static from spontaneously firing rods and cones.

The upshot is that a single pixel is like a single chord in a Bach fugue, or a single word in a Tolstoy novel: It has meaning only in context. The task of the visual system is to find out what that context is.

And even with all this information pouring in, there remains another

---

*In the United States, a color-television image measures about five hundred pixels across and five hundred pixels down.

problem. An optical system makes a two-dimensional projection of a three-dimensional world; the task of a vision system is to reverse that process, going from the 2-D image to an understanding of the 3-D objects that produced it. And yet that reverse transformation is highly ambiguous. Consider our friend the cat: So far as the 2-D image on your retina is concerned, she might as well be carved into the tip of an infinitely long, cat-shaped rod directed straight away from your eye. You can't tell if she's small and nearby or large and far away. You can't even tell if her tail is attached to her body or drifting in space where it just happens to lie along your line of sight. (Of course, stereo vision does allow us to see depth directly. But that's certainly not the whole answer; the world doesn't seem to come apart just because you close one eye.) Thus, a top priority of the visual system is to resolve these ambiguities and produce a coherent understanding of the world.

Remember too that any given object may only vaguely resemble others of its generic type. Consider our cat, and compare it to a porcelain cat, or a cat made out of twisted pipe cleaners. What is it that allows us to recognize them all as cats? In addition, as lighting conditions or viewing angles change, an object may no longer resemble itself; compare a cat as seen from the side to a cat as seen face on. This fact alone makes commercial "silhouette-matching" vision systems hopelessly inadequate except in carefully controlled environments, such as a factory. There is just no way to store enough templates to match every possible silhouette of every possible object. But then—what are the alternatives?

Constructing Reality

In sum, then, vision is hard in part because of the overwhelming data load, but only in part. More important, vision is hard because the eye isn't just a passive receptacle for light. A camera *is* passive; it sits there waiting for the photons to strike. But an intelligent vision system has to be active; it has to take that sensory input and impose meaning on it. In effect, it has to reconstruct reality.

The question is how.

Given the enormity of the task, it looks hopeless from the start. But in fact, the community of vision researchers is surprisingly optimistic. As we'll see below, there is burgeoning support for computer-vision research, both from DARPA and from private industry. Moreover, as we'll see in the next chapter, the next few years promise to bring a substantial increase in computational power, largely due to the development of a new class of computers, which do their calculations in parallel instead of in series.

But perhaps most of all, there is a sense in the AI community that the so-called early part of the vision problem, the perception of 3-D shape from 2-D imagery, is well on its way towards a systematic solution.

DAVID MARR'S THEORY OF VISION

The single most influential figure in this development was MIT's David Marr, whose career was cut short in 1980 by his death from leukemia at age thirty-five. Not everyone was fond of Marr; by all reports he was highly articulate, deliberately provocative, and something of a showman. He rubbed a lot of people the wrong way. But he also inspired intense loyalty. And his synthesis of computational AI, neuroscience, and the experimental psychology of vision was undeniably a landmark in the field.

"He was very polite, very British—and overpowering," says Eric Grimson, a former student of Marr's and now an assistant professor at MIT's AI laboratory. "He had a gift for making these huge leaps of insight, leaving the gaps to be filled in later. Technically, many of his ideas were wrong in detail. But he got people to thinking in fruitful ways."

Indeed, Marr's nomenclature for early vision theory has become ubiquitous. And even those who disagree with his ideas often feel obliged to refer to them as a point of contrast. As Marr's MIT colleague Tomaso Poggio says, "One of David's main achievements was to convince people in AI that there is a lot of *science* to be done in early vision—as opposed to a lot of ad-hoc hacking."

Levels of Understanding

Marr left a highly readable summary of his views in his book *Vision*, published posthumously in 1982.[3] The theory rests on two essential ideas. The first, originally developed in collaboration with Poggio, is quite general and pertains to all of AI: the notion of different levels of explanation.

> To understand what vision is and how it works, an understanding of only one level is insufficient. It is not enough to be able to describe the responses of single cells, nor is it enough to be able to predict locally the results of psychophysical experiments. Nor is it enough to be able to write computer programs that perform approximately in the desired way. One has to do all these things at once and also be very aware of an additional level of explanation that I have called the level of *computational theory*.[4]

Marr illustrates what he means with the example of a supermarket cash register. At the level of hardware, one could talk about how the machine is made—with a bunch of silicon chips, perhaps, or with mechanical tumblers, abacus beads, or even just the clerk's ten fingers for counting. At a higher level one could talk about how the machine represents the numbers internally and manipulates them—as strings of binary 1s and 0s, or as the decimal digits 0, 1,

2, and so on. But at the highest level, one comes to the computational theory of the device, the thing that it is actually trying to *do*. And that theory is just arithmetic: adding up the price of every item and producing a bill.

Now, in one sense this distinction between levels is obvious, even trivial. It's essentially just the old distinction between strategy and tactics, an admonition to AI programmers not to start hacking away without having fully prepared a plan of operations.★

In another, more important sense, however, this separation of levels lies at the heart of AI. It's the idea that you can understand the principles and the mechanisms of intelligence without necessarily having to understand every neuron in the brain. As Poggio explains it,

> How, then, are brains and computers alike? Clearly there must be a level at which any two mechanisms can be compared. One can compare the tasks they do. "To bring the good news from Ghent to Aix" is a description of a task that can be done by satellite, telegraph, horseback messenger or pigeon post equally well (unless other constraints such as time are specified). If, therefore, we assert that brains and computers function as information-processing systems, we can develop descriptions of the tasks they perform that will be equally applicable to either. We shall have a common language in which to discuss them: the language of information processing. Note that in this language descriptions of tasks are decoupled from descriptions of the hardware that perform them. This separability is at the heart of the science of artificial intelligence.[5]

Stages of Visual Processing

Marr's second fundamental idea pertains to the logical structure of the visual system itself, holding that there is no way to jump from pixels to a recognition of three-dimensional objects in a single step. It has to be done in stages. In fact, there is abundant experimental evidence that humans and other mammals process visual information in at least three stages, each with its own special mechanisms and representations. Marr calls these three representations the *primal sketch,* the *2 1/2–D sketch,* and the *3-D model representation*; the flow of information is diagrammed in Figure 4-1.

The primal sketch is a way of coping with the first and most urgent problem of any visual system: the vast quantity of data involved. Instead of dealing with one brightness value for every pixel—covering the terrain with a magnifying glass, so to speak—Marr's idea is to produce a kind of large-scale

---

★It's an oddly difficult point to grasp, even so. There's an all-too-human tendency to become obsessed with one tactic or one solution at the expense of all others; thus, in the political arena, we hear one group proclaiming that *only* the MX missile will insure true peace, another group insisting that *only* Affirmative Action will insure true equality, and so on ad nauseum.

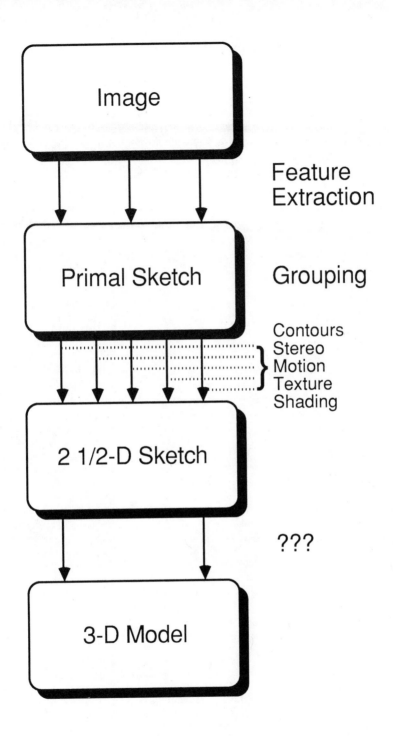

Fig. 4–1
The steps in David Marr's theory of vision

map that identifies such important landmarks as edges, boundaries, and regions.★

The trick is to find those landmarks without getting confused by the details. It's no improvement if the system tries to map out *every* edge and boundary; imagine trying to sketch a wooded hillside by drawing the outline of every leaf. The logical way to do it, says Marr—and, in fact, the way our vision system does seem to do it—is to look for the most important features first.

That's the computational theory. The actual mechanism, first implemented as a computer program by Marr and his student Ellen Hildreth in 1980, is simply to blur the image. As the blurring increases (see Figure 4–2), the smaller details quickly go away; the features that remain are presumably the important ones—analogous to the overall contour of the hillside—and probably worth keeping.[6]

In this way, Marr and Hildreth's program was able to produce detailed maps of the "edges," "bars," and "blobs," in the image, as shown in Figure 4–3.

To be more precise, what Marr and Hildreth actually did was to "filter" the image, applying a mathematical transformation that suppresses the small-scale details while simultaneously enhancing the major boundaries. A surprising coincidence is that the particular transformation they chose, for purely

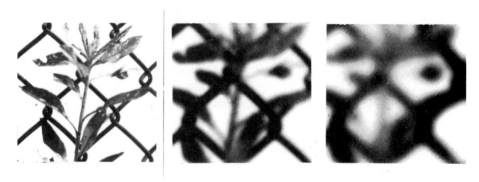

Fig. 4–2
An image and two stages of filtering

★In other words, Marr proposes that the first thing a computer (or brain) ought to do is to reduce this huge mass of data into a handful of symbols, each of which represents an important feature of the data in a compact form. From that point onward, he says, the vision system should deal only with those symbols. Thus, Marr's theory of vision is a theory of symbol-processing in exactly the same sense that Newell and Simon used the term. In this context it's worth recalling Herbert Simon's revelation at Rand in 1952, when he realized that computers are not confined to doing arithmetic but can be used to draw maps and to manipulate other kinds of symbols (see Chapter 2).

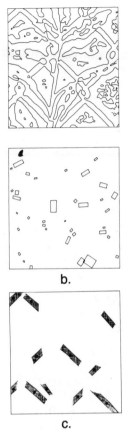

b.

c.

Fig. 4–3
Edges (a), Blobs (b), and Bars (c)

mathematical reasons (its technical name is the Laplacian of a Gaussian), turns out to be very similar to the way in which images actually *are* transformed in the human visual system.[7] In much the same way, the brain is known to possess specialized detectors for bars, edges, and blobs. There are neurons in the visual cortex, for example, that will respond only to edges or bars of light in specific locations and orientations.

In any case, once the first map is made—Marr calls it the "raw" primal sketch—the system can then start to work on what he calls the "full" primal sketch, in which similar map features are grouped into larger structures such as continuous lines and regions. This step is easy to forget, says Marr, because we do it so naturally ourselves. But it is *not* automatic. Consider Figure 4–4 (a). It's just an array of dots. So why do we see it as two lines crossing at right angles? Why not two *V*s touching at their points? In fact, why do we see any lines at all?

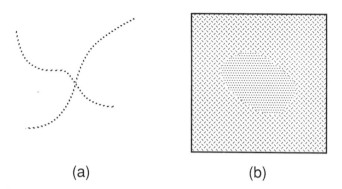

(a)   (b)

Fig. 4–4

Organizing what we see: Two examples

Or consider the texture boundary exhibited in Figure 4-4(b). We have no trouble seeing it. But where, exactly, *is* it?

The processes that Marr and Hildreth use for grouping the features in their images are very similar to the principles of perceptual organization that Gestalt psychologists identified and cataloged in the early decades of this century. For example, Figure 4-4(a) illustrates the Gestalt principle of *good continuation*, which in this case is the tendency to assume a physical link between the dots that lie along the smoothest possible path.[8]

But however the grouping is done, says Marr, it's an absolutely essential part of perception. It is here that the system begins to define regions in the image that might correspond to real and meaningful pieces of the world.

Next comes the centerpiece of Marr's theory, the 2½-D sketch—as its name suggests, a bridge between the two-dimensional features of the primal sketch and the recognition of real three-dimensional objects. The key, says Marr, is the identification of *surfaces*—in particular, surfaces that have definite positions and orientations in space.

Part of Marr's motivation for emphasizing surfaces is that the human visual system itself attaches enormous importance to them. Take a look at Figure 4-5. Objectively, it's a bunch of Pac-Men chatting with some *V*s. But it's hard not to see it as an opaque white surface lying on top of three solid circles and a black-bordered triangle; our brains insist on filling in the gaps.

But another motivation is Marr's impatience with the segmentation algorithms that were popular in the midseventies. The idea there was to have the programs segment the image into blobs of near-equal shading or intensity, then try to identify the original objects from an analysis of the blobs. For example, the program might contain a bit of heuristic knowledge that maintained, "If you're in an office, then a black blob at middling height is probably a telephone."

In effect, this kind of program short-circuited Marr's 2 ½-D level, and

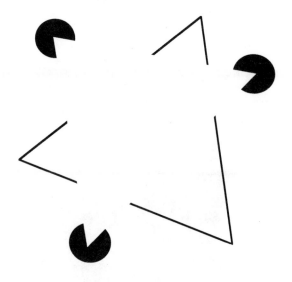

Fig. 4–5
Filling in the gaps

tried to jump straight from edges and boundaries to 3-D objects. But segmentation has never worked too well, according to Marr. The most dramatic boundaries in an image often come from such irrelevant factors as reflections or shadows, whereas many of the most important edges may be nearly invisible. Consider Figure 4–6: We have no trouble perceiving it as the image of two separate leaves. But look inside the box. Where is the boundary? It isn't there. And yet it's real. By first identifying real surfaces, argues Marr, a program can avoid such pitfalls.

Marr also questions the wisdom of relying on specific, real-world knowledge so early in the game—the approach that says, "I see a cat because I *expect* to see a cat." After all, he points out, humans are perfectly capable of seeing things they've never encountered before. Why should you make a commitment to what is out there until you have extracted as much information from the image as possible? So Marr calls this "the principle of least commitment."

Drawing on a large body of psychophysical evidence, Marr then argues that in human vision the identification of surfaces begins very early, sometimes before the visual information even leaves the retina for the brain. The neurons of the retina and the visual cortex appear to embody a variety of mechanisms—Marr called them "modules"—that exploit such clues as texture, color, motion, shading, and stereo.

For example, when we look at an object, each eye sees it in a slightly different position relative to the background; through the stereo module, the visual cortex can then find the distance by doing what is, in effect, a geometry

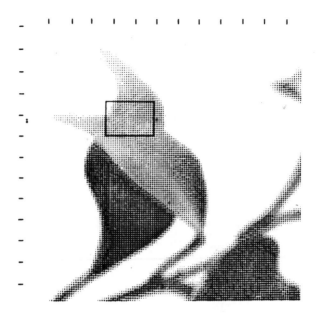

Fig. 4–6
Where is the boundary?

calculation. Likewise, when we move our head, or when an object moves relative to us, the motion module detects how nearby points move across the field of view more rapidly than more distant points. The shading module takes its subtle clues from how the orientation of a surface changes from point to point (try studying the interplay of light and shadow across the surface of your hand). Variations in apparent surface texture are picked up by the texture module (notice how the polka dots of Figure 4-7 seem to recede into the distance).

One thing that Marr finds particularly striking about these modules is that they seem to operate almost independently of one another. Their results are only integrated at the end. Noting that this is very similar to the way computer scientists design large programs, he writes:

> The idea that a computation can be split up and implemented as a collection of parts that are as nearly independent of one another as the overall task allows, is so important that I was moved to elevate it to a principle, the principle of modular design. This principle is important because if a process is not designed in this way, a small change in one place has consequences in many other places. As a result, the process as a whole is extremely difficult to debug or to improve, whether by a human designer or in the course of natural evolution, because a small change to

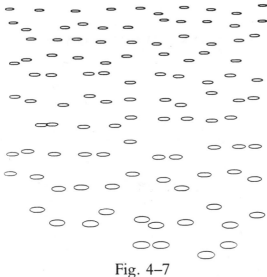

Fig. 4–7
A surface defined by texture

one part has to be accompanied by many simultaneous, compensatory changes elsewhere.[9]

With the evolution of the visual system, in other words, nature anticipated modern theories of good programming practice by several hundred million years.

A second thing that Marr finds intriguing about the modules is the way they resolve the two-dimensional ambiguities of an image by making certain assumptions about physical reality. In stereo vision, for example, there's no way to know in advance which pixel in the right image matches a given pixel in the left image. But the stereo module seems to constrain the possibilities by assuming that surfaces are opaque and reasonably smooth. In the same way, the motion module assumes that surfaces are rigid. (If a swarm of details moves uniformly across your field of view, you will see them as lying on a surface even if the details aren't connected; imagine flecks of dust on a clear windowpane.) The texture module assumes that similar surface details, such as polka dots, tend to be uniformly distributed and of equal size. The shading module assumes that illumination tends to be reasonably uniform. And so on for the others.

In effect, says Marr, these assumptions are heuristic rules about the world—rules of thumb that have been wired into our neural circuitry by several hundred million years of evolution. The only fundamental difference between these rules and the kind of heuristics that Newell and Simon talked about is that in vision we don't have any choice about when to use them. The visual system imposes its assumptions ruthlessly, even when it logically has no right to. And that is why we see optical illusions. Indeed, that is why we *continue* to see optical illusions even after we know them for what they are.

Back in Figure 4-5, for example, the visual system seems to set a high priority on identifying lines, edges, and the boundaries of surfaces; moreover, in doing so it seems to assume that lines, edges, and boundaries are smooth and continuous. So, although your eyes are confronted with a series of detached lines and notched circles, your brain wants so badly to see them as continuous, unbroken objects that it conjures up a nonexistent surface to explain the discrepancy. And look again at Figure 4-6: One of the most significant boundaries in the picture, the edge of the nearest leaf, is utterly invisible in the region inside the box. Yet under ordinary circumstances you would never notice that fact, because your visual system automatically fills in the missing portion.

Like any other kind of heuristics, says Marr, these assumptions made by the visual system can be wrong. Just as in Figure 4-5, such assumptions can lead us to see things that aren't really there. Nonetheless, says Marr, the chance of an occasional mistake is the price of breaking out of two dimensions. And in any case, the brain almost never has to depend on just one module at a time. Hold out your hand at arm's length and consider how many clues your eyes have about its three-dimensional shape. Stereo vision, light and shadow, color, texture—everything plays a part.

Marr and his colleagues were able to deduce plausible mechanisms for most of the modules, and in many cases these mechanisms have now been implemented as computer programs. For example, in his 1980 Ph.D. thesis, MIT's Eric Grimson developed a program implementing an algorithm for stereo vision (originally devised by Marr and Poggio).[10-11] The program starts with a pair of stereo images showing perhaps a stack of blocks or aerial views of a mountain range. Then, using the same techniques as in Hildreth's program, it produces a primal sketch for each image, identifying all the important edges and boundaries.

Using that information, the program next makes its first rough guess: For every pixel in the left image, the program tries to find a pixel on the right that corresponds to it. ("Correspondence," in this case, means that the two pixels represent the same point on the surface of a real object.) But then comes the test. Like the stereo module in the human vision system, Grimson's program assumes that the surfaces of real objects are opaque and reasonably continuous, which means in turn that only certain ways of matching up the pixels are consistent. So the program goes through the images once again, pixel by pixel, looking for inconsistencies in its first rough guess. When it finds them, it changes the assignments around among the neighboring pixels in order to improve the fit. And then, when it's finished, it starts all over again, going through the image pixel by pixel, testing each one and trying for an even better fit.

If this process sounds time-consuming, it is. On the other hand, Grimson's program only has to go through a few of these refinement cycles before virtually all the pixels are consistently matched and the program can confidently locate where the surfaces really are. As a practical demonstration, Grimson has tested his program on the task of constructing contour maps from aerial photographs. "The program was not as good as humans at localizing things and assigning a depth," he says. "But it made essentially no mistakes in feature matching, which is equivalent to human performance." Moreover, it performed at just about the same speed as a human expert, taking about four hours to analyze a 1,000-by-1,000-pixel map.

Grimson also pitted his program against the standard tests used by psychologists to study human stereo vision. "The algorithm worked when humans worked and failed when humans failed," he says. "That's exciting. It means we're on the right track of understanding how the human vision system really works."

The 3-D model representation is the last stage in Marr's theory of visual processing. It is at this point, says Marr, that the visual system combines all the blobs and edges it mapped out in the primal sketch, and all the surfaces it discovered in the 2 1/2-D sketch, and at last tries to identify real objects.

Unfortunately, as Marr would be the first to admit, this process of *recognition* is not well understood at all. It's one thing for a computer to identify a collection of surfaces; it's something else again for a computer to be able to say, "That set of surfaces goes together. That's a cat."

One thing that *is* clear is that recognition depends a great deal on knowledge, experience, and context. Psychologists have shown that a nose, for example, is easier to recognize when it's part of a picture of the whole face than when it's in an isolated close-up. They've also shown that people have to do a double take to recognize a fire hydrant hanging from a living-room ceiling.[12]

But therein lies the problem. Before a computer can recognize a three-dimensional object, or reason about it, that computer has to have something in memory with which to compare it—a kind of Platonic archetype, perhaps. But what does the representation consist of?

Since we've been talking about cats all along, consider what's involved in perceiving cats. Our internal representation is certainly specific enough to distinguish a cat from a dog or a goat. But it is also general enough to encompass a standing cat, a running cat, a sleeping cat, a Picasso cat, a pipe-cleaner cat, and all the other reasonable variations. The representation cannot depend on details such as the cat's having fur or vertically slit eyes, because otherwise what would we make of a porcelain cat? And yet when we see a living cat, we never perceive its gray-striped coat as something separate, something added on as an afterthought. By the time perceptions reach our conscious mind, the general outlines and the specific details have long since been integrated.

A major part of the problem is that no one really understands how human visual memories work, so there's not much guidance for AI researchers on how to proceed. One thing *is* known, however: Visual memories are very different from the kind of symbolic knowledge we've discussed in previous chapters. Visual memories are more like analogues, physical models of what they represent.[13] Close your eyes and think of a familiar place—say, your living room. Now, mentally scan your focus of attention from the couch to a picture on the wall, then to the bookshelf, and so on. Psychologists have shown that the time it takes to scan from one point to another is roughly proportional to the distance between those points, which is only possible if the image is represented in your head as some kind of three-dimensional structure.

However, visual memories are not *just* pictures in the head. Try sketching out a map, as if you were explaining to someone how to get from your house to your office. Try to make it as accurate and as detailed as you can, so that it approximates your own personal image of the route. Now, unless you happen to be an accomplished cartographer, the landmarks in the picture will inevitably be things that are important to *you*, and not necessarily the largest objects in the real world; they will be shown much bigger than they really are; and they will be only roughly correct in their relative position. In short, visual memories are distorted, imprecise, and leave out details. And, perhaps most important, they are segmented into meaningful pieces such as *intersection, shopping center,* and *mailbox.*

Unfortunately, knowing all this tells us very little about how to represent images and archetypal patterns in a computer—especially a computer with a finite memory capacity.

AI researchers have tried a number of approaches, one of the most notable being the "generalized cone" system pioneered by Thomas Binford of the Stanford University AI laboratory in 1971.[14] In his method, an object is approximated as a collection of cones and cylinders with the appropriate shapes, sizes, and orientations; a stick figure just traces out the axes of the cones. Generalized cones turn out to be surprisingly versatile, and have been used to represent everything from horses to Boeing 747 jetliners. In 1978, Marr and his colleague Keith Nishihara took up the idea and extended it to hierarchical representations, in which each cone or cylinder can always be decomposed into a more detailed representation.[15] (See Figure 4-8.)

However, the generalized-cone system says nothing about such qualities as surface texture and color. Somehow, it doesn't seem quite right for describing what we mean by the word *face.* And it is hopelessly inadequate for expressing our knowledge of a substance such as fog. A completely satisfactory representational scheme is still a challenge for the future.

The Legacy of David Marr

As I've said, very few people in the vision-research community have neutral feelings about Marr. Virtually everyone expresses admiration for the

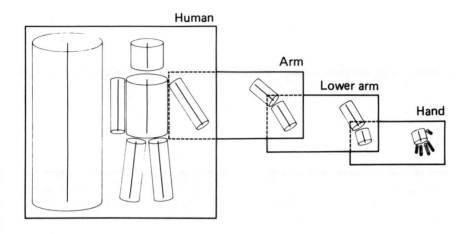

Fig. 4–8
Levels of detail

scope of his research program and awe at what he was able to accomplish in his
tragically short career. And yet there isn't a single part of his three-stage model
for visual information processing that someone hasn't criticized. His theory
seems weakest in its description of the third stage, in which the visual system
finally combines visual data with knowledge and experience and tries to
identify real objects. By no coincidence, this is also where experimental
guidance is almost nonexistent. But by the same token, his theory seems
strongest in its description of the first stage of vision, in which a raw image is
converted into symbolic features in a two-dimensional map. This is where the
neurological evidence is the strongest: Most of the first-stage visual processing
goes on in the retina itself and in the visual cortex, which are among the easiest
parts of the nervous system to study.

So in a sense it is still too early to evaluate Marr's work. Some of his ideas
may well be vindicated. Others may have to be scrapped. Nonetheless, it is
already abundantly clear that in the field of vision research, Marr was the most
influential figure of his generation. His colleague and countryman Christopher
Longuet-Higgins, in writing a review of Marr's book *Vision* from the point of
view of a neurophysiologist, captured the mood that prevails among psychologists and AI researchers as well:

> If neurophysiology was a theoretical vacuum when he entered it, it is
> now seething with lively controversy about the validity of his ideas on
> the vision system. . . . Even if no single one of Marr's detailed
> hypotheses survives, which is unlikely, the questions he raises can no
> longer be ignored and the methodology he proposes seems to be the only
> one that has any hope of illuminating the bewildering circuitry of the

central nervous system. David Marr's lifework will have been vindicated when neuroscientists cannot understand how it was ever possible to doubt the validity of his theoretical maxims.[16]

APPLIED COMPUTER VISION

It should be said that Marr's theory has been very difficult to implement. His three-stage analysis places extreme demands upon a computer's memory and processing power. Using present-day technology, in fact, no one has yet been able to get a computer to do more than a fragment of Marr's analysis at once. In Chapter 5 I'll discuss how the next generation of high-speed parallel computers may change that situation. But for now, at least, Marr's theory is best seen as an ideal—a prescription for what a general-purpose vision system *ought* to do to cope with the complexity and ambiguity of the real world.

Meanwhile, however, there is also a substantial market for practical vision systems that can replace human quality controllers in an assembly line, guide industrial robots, interpret aerial photographs, and read printed type. As John W. Dizard recently put it in *Fortune* magazine, "The idea of tireless, faultless, non-union eyes on the production line understandably excites manufacturing executives."[17] And happily, it turns out that general-purpose vision techniques aren't always necessary for practical systems. Quite the opposite: Some of the most important applications take place in environments where special-purpose techniques work quite well. For example:[18]

- *Document Understanding.* Automatic character recognition was actually one of the earliest applications of machine vision; research began in the 1950s, long before the AI work in the field. By the 1960s commercial systems were available that could read the specially shaped numerals on printed checks. Today, there are document-understanding systems that can scan through printed or typewritten text, identify the characters, and transcribe them into, say, a word-processor file readable by a computer.

  Clearly, document understanding takes place in a highly simplified environment. The lighting can be controlled. Contrast is usually not a problem. The machine can know ahead of time what sorts of objects it might encounter. And the third dimension is not a factor: the programmer can safely assume that the text will lie on a flat, two-dimensional sheet of paper. Thus, in many cases the computer can get by with a simple system of templates, matching each letter against a predetermined form.

  However, the process of identification is hardly trivial, and with real documents even some fairly straightforward tasks can require a surprisingly sophisticated analysis. For example, what if the document was written on an old typewriter that produced flawed characters, so that the templates don't exactly match? What if the document is printed with proportional spacing, so that the space between letters depends upon which letters they are, and the machine has no way of knowing in advance exactly where the next letter will be? What if the document is dirty or creased or has pencil marks all over it, so that the computer has to sort out the letters from a messy background? What if the document contains both text and graphics on the same page, so that the computer has to recognize which is which? And what if the document is written by hand, so that the computer has no way of knowing in advance what the letters and words are going to look like?

Commercial systems do exist that can handle many of these situations. Perhaps the most advanced system now on the market is the Kurzweil Optical Character Reader, which is marketed by Kurzweil Computer Products of Cambridge, Massachusetts. The Optical Character Reader starts by taking a digitized image of the page and looking for such key features as curves, line segments, and dots. From the way these features are related geometrically, the system then identifies particular letters and numerals. In fact, the system can even learn to read new typefaces that it has never encountered before. When it finds a character it can't identify, it displays the character on a screen and asks the operator for help. The operator's answer is then stored in memory, and soon the new typeface is learned.[19]

For all of that, however, a document-understanding system that can read a page of text as easily and as well as a human can is still a challenge for the future.

• *Cartography and Reconnaissance.* Mapmakers get most of their information about terrain height from aerial photographs taken in stereo pairs. Systems proposed for commercial use can automate this process to some extent, although they still depend upon close interaction with human operators.[20] On the other hand, it's worth recalling that Eric Grimson has already tested his stereo-vision program successfully on just such aerial images. Thus, completely automated stereo plotting may not be all that far off.

Meanwhile, those same aerial photographs also allow mapmakers to identify such topographical features as lakes, roads, buildings, and vegetation. AI researchers are therefore working on methods for automating this process as well. If the terrain is relatively flat and the vantage point is high enough, the process is essentially a matter of recognizing shapes in two dimensions, and in that sense the problem is not unlike that of recognizing characters on a printed page. However, aerial photographs have much more variation in the background, the contrast may be terrible, and the machine does not necessarily know in advance what to look for. A given blob in the picture might reveal the presence of a lake, an airport, a gravel pit, or any number of other things.

Thus, for complex blobs, the computer may have to look at the image in some detail, breaking it up into simple geometric shapes and then identifying the object as a whole from the way the individual pieces are arranged. A good example of this approach is the Acronym vision system developed by Stanford's Thomas Binford and his student Rodney

Brooks in 1981.[21] Among other things, Acronym has been used in a photo-interpretation system for monitoring traffic in airports from aerial images. The system first scans the image to identify boundaries between areas of different intensity. Next, it approximates these boundaries with straight-line segments, and then tries to approximate the line segments as the edges of various four-sided blocks. Finally, Acronym looks at the geometric relationships between these blocks and compares the patterns it finds to its stored templates for various aircraft, such as a Boeing 747 or a Lockheed L-1011.

Reconnaissance from aircraft and from satellites is conducted in two modes: searching and monitoring. For obvious reasons, these are both areas of great interest to the Pentagon and the CIA. In the search mode, targets can appear anywhere and the task is to detect and recognize them. In the monitoring mode, the target area is already known—imagine a Soviet military base or nuclear test site—and the task is to examine the area periodically for activity. In either case, computer systems already exist that can provide the human operator with assistance. For example, the computer might search for possible vehicles in an infrared nighttime image and signal their positions to the operator. More-advanced systems now under development will use contextual information to identify targets more reliably on their own.[22]

• *Industrial Inspection and Robot Vision.* Research in these areas began in the late sixties; by the late seventies applications began to reach the factory floor; and now, in the mideighties, more than a hundred companies are marketing industrial computer-vision systems and devices.[23] By one estimate, the industrial market for computer vision is growing by a factor of four every year.[24]

Most of these factory systems are being used to inspect such products as printed circuit boards for manufacturing defects. Inspection is a relatively straightforward task because, like document understanding, it tends to take place in a highly simplified environment. The lighting is controlled and uniform. The objects to be inspected typically have known shapes and sharply defined, high-contrast edges. And they occur in known locations. Thus, commercial inspection systems can usually get by with a simple template-matching approach, comparing the observed outlines of the part with a model of the part in the computer's memory.

The other major industrial application of computer vision involves the use of assembly-line robots. For example, a welding robot that operates without vision has to track its seam blindly, following a preprogrammed path. This technology has obvious potential for disaster if the parts to be welded aren't precisely aligned. And in any case, a blind welding robot has to be completely reprogrammed for every new job. Obviously, it would help if the machine could see what it was doing.

One vision system that has been used effectively in such situations involves the interpretation of light. Here, designers of an automated factory can control the lighting for the convenience of the robots. A projector illuminates the object to be worked on with a simple pattern of light—say, an array of stripes. As seen by the robot's camera, the stripes fall across the surface of the object in a pattern of curves that outline the surface. Then, by tracing the stripes and using simple geometry, the vision system can derive the three-dimensional shape of the object and "recognize" it by comparing the observed shape with simple shapes programmed in its memory.

In other applications, lighting can be controlled to give objects a high-contrast silhouette, facilitating the use of simple template-matching. For example, robots guided by such systems are able to find and pick up objects moving down a conveyor belt.

However, other industrial tasks that seem equally simple to humans turn out to be much more difficult for robots—picking up parts out of a bin, for example. Not only is the lighting hard to control—the objects in a bin are jumbled together and cast shadows on each other in unpredictable places—but the parts themselves overlap and can have any orientation. Template-matching is useless. Indeed, the difficulty robots have in picking up randomly oriented parts is one of the major reasons they haven't been more widely used so far in industry.

One particularly promising new approach to the bin-picking problem is the method of photometric stereo, developed by Berthold K. P. Horn and his colleagues at MIT. Their basic idea is to give the computer three separate images of the pile of parts as illuminated from three separate directions. The illumination doesn't have to be anything special; ordinary industrial lighting fixtures will do. The important thing is that each patch of surface on a given part is illuminated differently in the three images, and therefore has three different brightness values. The computer observes these values and uses them in a mathematical formula to calculate the orientation of each patch of surface. And once the computer has a pattern of surface orientations for the whole image, it can then compare the pattern it sees with the patterns expected from individual objects. In this way, it can begin to *identify* individual objects and sort out which piece of surface goes with what.[25]

- *Navigation.* Since 1983, DARPA has made vision research a top priority in its Strategic Computing Initiative, which I will discuss more fully in Chapter 8. Indeed, one of the major goals of the DARPA initiative is to develop a fully automatic land vehicle equipped with a general-purpose vision system and capable of roving over rugged terrain at high speed. Such mobile robots could be used for reconnaissance, for resupplying front-line troops, for weapons delivery, and for other dangerous missions. In nonmilitary situations, they could also be used in such practical endeavors as construction, shipbuilding, and agriculture.

Navigation of this kind is perhaps the most challenging situation imaginable for a vision system. *Nothing* is constrained. The system has no way to know in advance what kind of objects it will find, or where they will be in its field of view. It has to deal with all three dimensions all the time. It has to make do with whatever lighting is available. Its environment changes constantly—and furthermore, its own perspective is always changing because the vehicle itself is moving. Thus, vision systems for such mobile robots will have to have at least as much sophistication as Marr called for. And they will have to work at least as fast as the human visual system, which reanalyzes everything it sees roughly thirty times every second.

At the Frontier

Clearly, there is a great deal of research yet to be done before DARPA can produce anything remotely resembling a mobile robot. But then, as we've seen, a great deal of research is needed in *all* the applications of computer vision. Template-matching and special lighting tricks can only go so far. Some possible new directions:

- *Sensors.* We've tacitly assumed that the vision system gets its input from a television camera, using visible light. Unlike the human eye, however, man-made sensors aren't restricted to visible light. For example, the scanners used on the Landsat remote sensing satellites can make images from infrared and heat radiation, and there is no reason a computer vision system couldn't work with such images. Computer vision techniques have already been applied to the analysis of X-ray images, both for medical purposes—analyzing the shape of the heart, for example, and detecting tumors—and for industrial purposes, when parts need to be inspected for internal flaws.

    By the same token, sensors don't have to wait passively for radiation to come to them, as the human eye does. Radar, for example, could form the basis of an active vision system that probes the scene on its own—even at night. Indeed, using radar would greatly simplify the problem of working in three dimensions, since the radar pulses would measure the direct distance to every visible point of every object. A sonar system using ultrasound, or a laser ranging system using laser pulses, would offer many of the same advantages.

    Of course, as we begin to use new kinds of sensors for computer vision, new techniques must be developed for handling the images they produce; most of the techniques developed so far have been specialized for images made with visible light. At the same time, we need new techniques for the "fusion" of information from different sensors. Radar, visible light, and heat radiation may each provide important information about a given scene, for example, but they will each provide *different* information. Combining these systems to achieve a coherent understanding of the scene is thus a highly complex task.

- *Modeling.* If a computer is ever going to relate the properties of images to the properties of objects in the real world, it first needs a good theoretical model of how the imaging process actually occurs. A good example is the work of MIT's Berthold Horn, who has done a great deal of mathematical work on understanding how light is reflected from surfaces. His equations make explicit the relationship between the intensity observed at a given point, the surface material, the surface orientation, and the position of the light source. He and his students have applied the theory to a number of practical problems, such as the automatic generation of shaded relief maps, the matching of satellite images to known terrain for the analysis of surface features, and the bin-picking problem mentioned above.[26]

Theoretical models of the imaging process are also important for understanding just what it is that the computer is supposed to do. For example, Tomaso Poggio and some of his coworkers have recently begun to explore the so-called regularization techniques of mathematical physics; these techniques may offer a way of putting all, or almost all, the vision modules into a common mathematical framework. Moreover, the analysis also suggests how special-purpose computer circuitry might be designed to efficiently implement these modules.[27]

• *Computers.* One obviously worthwhile project would be the creation of a full-fledged multistage vision-processing system of the kind that Marr and his colleagues have proposed. However, no one is anywhere near that point. As we've seen time and again, computer vision of this caliber demands ultra-high-speed computational power. By one estimate, a computer that could identify three-dimensional features in arbitrary scenes in "real time"—that is, with a speed comparable to that of the human nervous system—would have to make anywhere from ten billion to ten trillion calculations per second.[28]

That prospect is obviously daunting. On the other hand, the AI community in general, and the computer-vision community in particular, is dedicated to devising machines that may actually be able to achieve such performance—the so-called massively parallel computers. And that is what we turn to next.

5

Intelligence in Parallel

A (true) fable: *Sadi was a young French engineer. And in his day—
the early nineteenth century—many of his fellow engineers devoted
their energies to the very practical problem of building better steam
engines. Was there any limit to how efficient you could make them?
So Sadi went to work on the problem too. Being a Frenchman, he
took a highly theoretical approach. But his answer, published in
1824, was clear and simple: There is indeed a limit to the efficiency of
steam engines—a fundamental limit, based on the nature of heat and
temperature, that no amount of clever engineering could ever circumvent.*

    *Sadi's full name, as every physics student can guess, was Sadi
Carnot. And his theorem about steam engines laid the foundations for
one of the most general and far-reaching laws in all of physics: the
second law of thermodynamics. It says that no matter what you do,
most of the energy in a gallon of gasoline has to go out the tailpipe as
heat. It says that you can't unscramble an egg. It says that order
crumbles inexorably toward disorder. It says that life can only exist
by frantically processing energy. It poses fundamental questions about
the origin of the universe and the nature of time. And it finds
application in everything from the flow of information in a computer
to the quantum dynamics of black holes.*

Moral: *Keep an eye on the practical problems. You never know
when you'll find something profound.*

It's a painful fact of life in AI that the biggest obstacle to machine intelligence is
very often the machine.

    "The bigger we make our programs, the 'smarter' they get and the
slower they get," says Thomas Knight, a specialist in computer design at
MIT's Artificial Intelligence laboratory. "We're in the embarrassing position
that when we give the program more information, its performance gets
worse."

110

Consider expert systems, for example. As I discussed in Chapter 2, an expert system tries to encapsulate some particular field of human expertise, such as medical diagnosis, as a set of rules. But the processing power available in computers of the mid-1980s sets a practical limit at just a few thousand rules, which means that even the best artificial expert is nothing more than an idiot savant in one narrow area. "There is *no* program that could guide a robot across the room and have it set the table for dinner," says Knight. "Getting even minimal common sense turns out to require more knowledge than has ever been put into a program."

Consider one recent experiment by Hans Moravec at Stanford University, in which a computerized cart successfully used a vision system to pick its way through obstacles in a hallway. Every time it advanced a yard or so, it had to stop and reassess—for fifteen minutes.[1] Getting a system to walk and chew gum at the same time, so to speak, means speeding up this kind of performance by a factor of roughly a million.

The irony is that the brain is outperforming computers with neurons that operate about a million times slower than silicon. And the secret, of course, is in the wiring: The neurons of the brain are doing millions or billions of operations simultaneously. Whereas computers, with few exceptions, are still using the serial, one-step-at-a-time mode of operation devised by computer pioneer John von Neumann in the 1940s: one central processing unit, one memory bank, and one data channel connecting them (see Figure 5-1). In the computer community this basic design is known as the von Neumann architecture. It's simple and it's relatively easy to program. But it's also a bottleneck, like having only one checkout counter open at the supermarket during the weekend rush.

Actually it's even worse than that. The processing unit spends most of its time waiting while data and instructions move to and from the memory. It's as if a cook tried to make dinner by first going shopping for the salad, bringing the ingredients home, fixing them, serving them; then going shopping again for the meat, bringing it home, fixing it, serving it; and so on.

True, computers have become very good at moving the data back and forth. Since 1960, computer circuitry has shrunk by roughly a factor of two

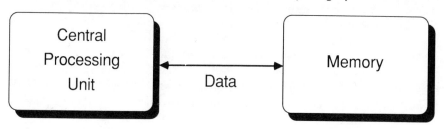

Fig. 5–1
The von Neumann architecture for computers

every eighteen months, and the speed has gone up accordingly. But within a decade or so the von Neumann architecture is going to be up against some severe limits. The very fastest number-crunching computers, such as the Cray XM-P (manufactured by Cray Research of Minneapolis), have already begun to feel the constraints of relativity; electronic signals can't travel any faster than the speed of light, which means that at some point it doesn't matter anymore *how* fast the individual microcircuits are. Any gains made in one part of the computer are eaten up by the delay in transmitting data to another part. Nor does it help to put the chips closer together. Pack them too densely and they begin to melt because there's no way to dissipate the heat they generate.

So faster chips aren't the answer to the kind of thousandfold or million-fold speed increases that Knight talks about. Performance of that magnitude can only be achieved by breaking away from the von Neumann architecture entirely. Somehow, researchers have to emulate the brain and put dozens, hundreds, or even millions of processors to work simultaneously.

This has in fact become a major goal not just in AI but in all of computer science. It's hardly a new idea—"parallel" or "concurrent" computers were first discussed back in the 1940s—but several trends have conspired to give it new force in the 1980s. One factor is simply demand: Scientists and engineers are always clamoring for faster and better computers for simulating, say, supersonic air flowing over a wing, or interstellar gas falling into a black hole; at the same time, both military and industrial users of AI are putting a premium on high-speed performance in such applications as robot vision and natural-language understanding.

Another factor is the intense international competition in computer technology, dramatized by Japan's announcement in 1981 of the Fifth Generation project, which I'll be discussing in more detail in Chapter 8. In the United States alone, money for parallel-processor development has been forthcoming from the Pentagon's DARPA, the Department of Energy, the National Science Foundation, and several major computer manufacturers.

Finally, many of the parallel designs have turned out to be well suited to "very large-scale integration" technology. VLSI, as it is generally known, is a set of techniques developed in the late seventies that allow tiny integrated circuits to be etched onto a slab of silicon with unprecedented precision. Thanks to this technology, parallel-processing computers can, in principle, be made with whole banks of tiny processors etched onto a single chip, which means that such computers can operate at very high speeds.

Meanwhile, DARPA has been doing its best to encourage creative new designs for VLSI chips. Since 1979 the agency has supported a series of "silicon foundries," which are basically just chip-manufacturing facilities dedicated to serving the research community as opposed to the computer maker. If a researcher sponsored by the agency has an idea for a new circuit design, all he or she has to do is send the design to one of the silicon foundries, and back it comes as a real chip. As a result, lots of people have been out there trying lots of things. By one count, more than seventy parallel designs have been proposed by university and industry researchers worldwide.[2] And now, in the mid-1980s, a number of those designs have begun to appear on the market-place.

Processors by the Thousands

The approaches that people have taken to parallel processing are di-verse—there is essentially only one way to build a serial von Neumann machine, but a near-infinity of ways to build a parallel machine—yet there are a number of fundamental issues in common.

- *The choice of application.* The designs fall broadly into two groups: first, the so-called supercomputers, which are intended primarily for scientists and engineers; and second, the symbol-processing machines used in AI.

  The reason for the division is simply that scientists and engineers work on mathematical problems that tend to have an orderly, predictable structure. So scientific machines are specialized for ultrafast numerical calculations, in much the same way that a racing car is specialized for circling the track at Indianapolis at nearly two hundred miles per hour.*

  But AI researchers work on symbolic problems that are messy, irregular, unpredictable, and governed by rules that don't always work. So the symbolic processors used in AI have to be more like very fast all-terrain vehicles. In the rest of this chapter, I'll be talking mainly about the AI machines, although it should be said that the division isn't completely hard and fast. Among other things, it's still not clear what the best design for that all-terrain parallel computer ought to be. One of the main goals of current research is to find out just which types of architecture work best with which problems.
- *The size of the processors.* The first and most important decision in designing a parallel computer is setting a goal for how much parallelism you really want. How big and how capable should the individual processors be? One approach, favored in the scientific number-crunching designs, is to use just a few fairly large processors. This is sometimes called coarse-grained parallelism. An example is the Cosmic Cube developed by Geoffrey C. Fox, Charles L. Seitz, and their colleagues at the California Institute of Technology.[3] Their eighty-thousand-dollar prototype used sixty-four circuit boards, each roughly equivalent to an IBM AT Personal Computer, and cost about 1 percent of the price of a standard Cray-1 supercomputer. But it had one-tenth the power of a Cray-1; the Cube could execute about a hundred million instructions per second, versus the Cray 1's capacity of roughly a thousand million

---

*Defining the term *supercomputer* is like shooting at a moving target: It refers to whatever class of machines is fastest at any given time. Today's supercomputer is tomorrow's desktop PC.

instructions per second. In 1985, Intel Scientific Computers of Beaverton, Oregon, announced its iPSC line, a commercial version of the Cube with up to 128 processors. The Intel machine is in fact the first parallel computer to be widely available commercially.[4] Moreover, it proves the point I made earlier about no hard-and-fast line existing between supercomputers and AI machines. Roughly one quarter of the inquiries that Intel has received about the machine are from AI researchers; to serve that community, Intel has arranged with Gold Hill Computer, Inc., of Cambridge, Massachusetts, to develop a version of LISP that can easily exploit the machine's parallel-processing capabilities.

At the other extreme from the relatively coarse-grained parallelism of the Cosmic Cube is "massive" parallelism, which involves designs that incorporate thousands of minuscule processors etched on silicon chips, each with a tiny sliver of memory. As shown in Figure 5-2, the idea is to break the von Neumann bottleneck by throwing out the central processing unit entirely and putting all the computational power where the data is, in the memory banks.

A particularly successful example of this approach is the Connection Machine, which was brought to market in 1986 by Thinking Machines Corporation, a spinoff of the MIT AI laboratory. Originally conceived in 1981 by W. Daniel Hillis, then a graduate student at the AI laboratory and now chief designer for Thinking Machines,[5] the first commercial version of the Connection Machine has up to sixty-four thousand processors and is capable of executing roughly one billion instructions per second. Ultimately, says Hillis, the company hopes to build a version having as many as a million processors.

That rate, a billion instructions per second, puts the Connection Machine on a par with top-of-the-line supercomputers, says Hillis, but

P-M P-M P-M P-M P-M P-M P-M P-M P-M P-M P-M
P-M P-M P-M P-M P-M P-M P-M P-M P-M P-M P-M
P-M P-M P-M P-M P-M P-M P-M P-M P-M P-M P-M
P-M P-M P-M P-M P-M P-M P-M P-M P-M P-M P-M
P-M P-M P-M P-M P-M P-M P-M P-M P-M P-M P-M
P-M P-M P-M P-M P-M P-M P-M P-M P-M P-M P-M
P-M P-M P-M P-M P-M P-M P-M P-M P-M P-M P-M
P-M P-M P-M P-M P-M P-M P-M P-M P-M P-M P-M

Fig. 5–2

The Connection Machine: Processors (P) mixed in with Memory (M) that isn't really the point. "It's not a faster computer," he says. "It's a different *kind* of computer." This massive parallelism means that programmers can tackle problems in ways they never would have considered on an ordinary von Neumann machine.

Consider stereo vision, for example. As explained in the last chapter, when a conventional computer is given a pair of stereo images, it has to compare them pixel by pixel, trying to figure out which one corresponds to which; in fact, the computer has to go through many such comparisons before it can compute the distance to the objects in the image. The whole process can take hours. But using the Connection Machine, programmers can assign each pixel to its own processor. And since the processors all act simultaneously, the comparison of all paired pixels in the two images is practically instantaneous. The Connection Machine is able to turn a pair of aerial photographs into a detailed contour map in somewhat less than ten seconds.

Or look at the problem of document retrieval. Ordinarily, one compiles a computerized bibliography by typing in a few key words, such as HALLEY'S COMET; the computer then searches through all the documents in its data base and identifies those that contain precisely those words. Unfortunately, in this instance the computer would miss the documents that refer to this celestial body by a different name, such as COMET HALLEY. In fact, key-word bibliographic searches of this type often find only about 20 percent of the relevant material. On the Connection Machine, however, each document can be stored in a single processor. A search of some fifteen thousand documents can thus be done in less than one-twentieth of a second. To a user, the list of matching documents seems to appear almost instantaneously. Furthermore, the search isn't limited to key words; the user can indicate one or two documents in this first list as being good choices—the kind the user really wants—and say, "I want all the documents that are like *these*." The Connection Machine then employs AI natural-language techniques to automatically identify all the other important words in the chosen documents—not just key words—and finally runs another search using *those* words for comparison. The result, within half a minute of the time the user started the search, is a bibliography that is virtually 100 percent complete.

• *Communication.* A third critical issue in parallel design has to do with how the processors are connected and how they communicate. Does every processor connect directly to every other? Or just to its nearest neighbors? Are the communications channels arranged like the branches of a tree? In a higher-dimensional cubic lattice, as in the Cosmic Cube? In a ring? Choosing the best way depends on the application and the specific task to be performed—tempered by the realities of the thousand- or million-processor environment.

"It's turned out that communication is *the* technical problem in parallel processing," says Knight. Quite aside from having to cram all those data channels onto a crowded piece of silicon, the designer has to make sure that the data always goes where it is supposed to go. "Compared to that, the computations themselves are a piece of cake," he says. The immensity of the problem is reflected in the very name of the Connection Machine: Since there's no hope of linking all the processors directly—a million processors would mean half a trillion wires—the computer has to pass the messages along through a complex routing scheme. In effect, the machine is one vast telephone network.

- *Management.* Dividing the work among numerous processors does speed things up. But just as in human organizations, the advantages have to be weighed against the time and effort it takes to keep everything coordinated.

In a centralized control scheme, which is the most straightforward extension of von Neumann architecture, the processors are linked in a hierarchy not unlike a corporate-organization chart. One processor designated as the foreman actually runs the show, passing instructions down through the hierarchy to the processors that will actually do the work. This forces all the processors to operate in lockstep. But it's fairly easy to coordinate things this way. Furthermore, the individual processors can be kept small and simple; they do not have to store their own programs locally. This means that a single VLSI chip can yield a lot of raw processing power. And this kind of regimented approach is exactly what's needed for such processes as early vision. The Connection Machine uses centralized control.

A more radical approach to parallelism is decentralized control, in which bits of data are set loose among the processors like taxicabs roaming Manhattan. This system presents obvious problems when it comes to coordination. Moreover, each individual processor has to store its own program in its own memory, which means that it has to be relatively large and complex. On the other hand, decentralized architecture may turn out to be the best way of handling complex and unpredictable problems, or of making logical inferences on large knowledge bases—an advantage that led the Japanese to choose it for their Fifth Generation project.

Where Is the Payoff in Parallelism?

Given the quantities of effort going into parallel architectures, it's legitimate to ask what parallelism really buys. Some people are already grumbling about overheated expectations. "Parallel processing is one of AI's wonderful red herrings," says Yale's Roger Schank. By itself it provides nothing but speed, he points out. It says nothing new about knowledge representation, memory, learning, common sense—any of the truly fundamental problems of AI. The fact is that any parallel algorithm can be mimicked on any serial machine, albeit slowly. "First we need to understand what we're building models of," he says. "If we could build a machine that could function correctly, even if slowly, *then* parallel processing might have something to say."

Other researchers, however, while echoing Schank's point, do maintain that fast parallel processors will allow people to try things that would otherwise be prohibitively time-consuming. "It won't solve AI," agrees Knight, "but it will speed up certain key areas that are stopping us in certain problem domains." If nothing else, the rapid feedback should help hone researchers' intuition about problems. They could see the results of their programs in seconds or minutes instead of weeks.

A more subtle, and perhaps more important, point has been raised by Allen Newell of Carnegie-Mellon University: New architectures and new ways of programming may trigger new ways of thinking about intelligence. "We aren't smart enough to change our ways of thinking without that kind of challenge," he says. In particular, the effort may help bridge the gap that opened up long ago between AI and cognitive psychology on the one hand and neuroscience on the other.

"Back in the forties and continuing through the sixties," says Newell, "there was this substantial effort to build 'neural nets'—little models of the nervous system. But it petered out because there were never enough useful results.

"What did take off was AI, which had been going on in parallel," he says. "But AI was based on the building of symbolic mechanisms for intelligence, with no direct reference to the neural mechanisms. So that gap between psychology and neuroscience, which was long-standing, didn't get closed by AI. The whole thing got separated even further.

"Then, in the midseventies, David Marr revived the whole idea, especially with respect to vision. He was influential, he was charismatic, and he developed a whole theory of how vision ought to happen, based on an understanding of the neural system and the psychological data, as well as AI. That has encouraged a school of 'new connectionists' to think they can build a system to model intelligence the way the brain does."

The New Connectionists: Understanding the Brain

If anyone can be said to be the leader of the new connectionists, it's Newell's Carnegie-Mellon colleague Geoffrey Hinton. "There has been a long-standing split in AI," Hinton says, "those who say you don't need to worry about the hardware, just the data structures and so forth—this is the approach that has led to expert systems and all the success in the marketplace— and a much less influential school (so far) who say that the kind of hardware available determines the kind of problems you can do well."

Hinton was led to this approach by his fascination with the workings of human memory. "If you're in a jungle and you see a tiger," he says, "you don't just make a visual identification; you recognize a great deal more—about tigers, and danger, and running." The brain, with all its billions of neurons working in parallel, does this almost instantaneously. It has to in order to survive. Whereas a serial computer makes such connections very slowly, if at all.

Or consider the way we can retrieve a full-blown memory when given just a fragment of it, a hint. ("He's an actor and a politician. Who is he?") Yet such behavior is very hard to duplicate on conventional computers because they have to be given a definite, physical location in memory before they can find much of anything.

And finally, says Hinton, think how remarkably robust human memory is. "Every day, thousands of your brain cells are dying, but there's no loss of memory," he says. Somehow, the information is distributed over many neurons. Whereas in a conventional computer, the failure of an electronic memory element means that a piece of data is gone forever.

Hinton's contention is that the best way to represent robust, human-style memories on a computer is to explicitly emulate the way neurons are connected in the brain. Instead of storing each bit of information in a specific location in the computer's memory banks, take that information out and spread it over a network of interconnected processors. "Each entity is represented by a pattern of activity distributed over many computing elements," writes Hinton, "and each computing element is involved in representing many different entities."[6]

To see how such a distributed representation might work in practice, Hinton and his colleagues have spent the last few years studying a particularly intriguing approach known as the Boltzmann architecture. It emerged in 1983 from the confluence of work by Scott Kirkpatrick and his colleagues at IBM,[7] John J. Hopfield of the California Institute of Technology,[8] Hinton and Scott Fahlman at Carnegie-Mellon, and Terrence J. Sejnowski of Johns Hopkins University.[9] (A very similar approach, called Harmony theory, was developed independently at the same time by Paul Smolensky of the University of California at San Diego.[10])

Basically, a Boltzmann machine is exactly the kind of network that Hinton calls for: It consists of a few hundred or a few thousand processors connected together in ways that produce certain patterns of activity. In effect, each pattern represents a distinct memory. When given some input data (say, a scene of a jungle), the Boltzmann machine will first use that data to activate some of the processors in its network. The trick is then to find the pattern of activity that gives the best match ("A tiger"). Of course, this sort of thing has been tried before, and in any realistic setting has always foundered on the vastness of the search. There are just too many possible patterns to look through. A network of only ten processors can in principle produce a thousand patterns, while a network of only one hundred can encompass ten billion. A network of a thousand processors can contain a number of patterns so vast that it doesn't even have a name.★ "It's hard even to find a *good* solution, much less the best solution," says Hinton.

Boltzmann gets around that problem, however, because it employs an elegant trick to search all the possible patterns simultaneously. Mathematically, the network turns out to be analogous to a hilly countryside, while the memories—the patterns of activity—can be thought of as the valleys between the hills. Furthermore, when Boltzmann uses input data to activate a few of its processors, it is effectively pouring a bucket of water on one of the hillsides. So the next step is obvious: Boltzmann simply varies the activity level in its processors according to a certain mathematical rule that corresponds to letting the "water" flow downhill. And when the water reaches the nearest valley— that is, when the activity in the processors corresponds to one of the memory patterns—it has found a match.

However, Boltzmann isn't finished. It has found *a* match, but not necessarily the *best* match. The water might have gotten trapped in a high mountain lake, so to speak, instead of flowing down to the sea where we really want it. So what Boltzmann actually does is to take the hilly landscape and shake it like a giant earthquake. Thus, the water will slosh out of any mountain lakes and keep flowing downhill; ultimately, it is virtually guaranteed to reach the lowest point possible. And *that* point is the best match.†

The beautiful thing about this, says Hinton, is that a Boltzmann-style memory is content-addressable in the same way that human memory is. Suppose the machine is fed initial data that's noisy or incomplete. (Say you only got a glimpse of the tiger's tail rising from the tall grass.) Incomplete data is analogous to pouring the bucket of water on a very high mountain peak. Yet Boltzmann moves the water inexorably downhill until it winds up in exactly the same place as a bucket of water poured out on the seashore. In other words, starting from a fragmentary input (the tiger's tail), Boltzmann has found its way to a much richer structure of memory (Tiger, danger, run . . .).

Boltzmann also shares the diffused quality of human memory, says Hinton. Since the memories correspond to patterns of activity among the processors, each memory is actually distributed throughout the network. So if one or two processors fail, the patterns are virtually unchanged and the memories are still intact.

Boltzmann thus demonstrates that a computer can display many of the same strengths and capabilities of human memory. However, it's important to remember that Boltzmann is not so much a product as an idea. As of the mid-1980s, in fact, no one has yet built a Boltzmann machine out of a real network of processors. Hinton and his colleagues have simulated the Boltzmann

---

★Approximately 10^{100}.

†The mathematical theory that describes all this is derived from a branch of physics known as statistical mechanics; the name of the program honors the nineteenth-century physicist Ludwig Boltzmann, who was one of the pioneers in the field.

algorithm on ordinary serial computers to show that it really does work.[11-12] But they still have a great deal to learn about its limits and capabilities. "It's a paradox," says Hinton. "We're using conventional computers to simulate these parallel ideas. It's very slow, and eventually we'll have to build real parallel systems. But until we know how to do the proper kind of programming, it's too early. We wouldn't know exactly what kind of parallel system to build."

Second, neither Hinton nor anyone else ever expects to build a Boltzmann machine that could emulate the brain as a whole. Hinton envisions relatively small-scale networks that might recognize certain kinds of patterns or features in, say, a pictorial scene; it might take dozens or hundreds of such modules to make up a whole computer vision system equivalent to the human system.

And finally, Boltzmann is not a replacement for the frames, scripts, and other knowledge-representation schemes we've discussed in earlier chapters. Those schemes express something crucial about the way memories relate to one another. Boltzmann represents a different, perhaps better way to store individual memories in a computer. But you still need the relationships among the memories. In fact, it remains an open research question just how a network machine like Boltzmann can incorporate these larger knowledge-representation structures.

On the other hand, at this stage of the game it is probably unfair to expect Boltzmann to provide all the answers right away; after all, it did take twenty-five years for mainstream AI to hit the marketplace. Furthermore, research on the Boltzmann approach is serving as an invaluable testbed for ideas about distributed representations in general. Perhaps the best way to think of it is to remember Logic Theorist and General Problem Solver at the birth of AI, and to ask if Boltzmann might be playing the same role for the new connectionists.

THE SOCIAL BEHAVIOR OF COMPUTERS

The fine-grained parallelism of Boltzmann and the Connection Machine is the parallelism of an anthill. Individually, the processors are weak and stupid. Together they overwhelm a problem by sheer force of numbers.

The coarse-grained parallelism of the Cosmic Cube and its brethren is the parallelism of a football team. Individually, the processors are smart, capable, and relatively independent. Together they attack a problem with discipline and tight organization.

But the parallelism of, say, a computerized air-traffic control system, or a robot assembly line, is something else entirely. Not only do the designers have to worry about all the old issues of communication and coordination, but now the individual processors are physically spread out and far more powerful.

They may each have different capabilities. They may each have access to different information—sometimes inconsistent information. They may each interpret that information in different ways. And they may each have different goals.

In short, this isn't the parallelism of an anthill or of a football team. It's the parallelism of a PTA committee, of Congress, or of society itself. Interest in this kind of system is so recent that it doesn't yet have a commonly accepted name. Some call it distributed, or decentralized, AI.

Computer Networks and Computer Contracts

Consider a situation that is ubiquitous in AI laboratories, and that is increasingly common wherever computers are used. The desktops and laboratory benches are littered with high-powered personal computers linked together with a high-speed data network—and most of them are sitting idle most of the time. "That's a horrible waste," says AI researcher Randall Davis of MIT. There ought to be a way to tap that unused power. "Wouldn't it be wonderful if we could just plug more and more computers into the network, and have the programs on *my* machine run faster and faster?" he asks.

What's needed is a way for a busy machine to subcontract part of its workload to an idle machine somewhere else on the network. Davis's solution, devised in collaboration with Reid C. Smith of Schlumberger-Doll Research in Ridgefield, Connecticut, is the "contract net." An overworked machine simply sends out a "request for proposals" over the network, describing the task it wants done and the priority. Each of the other processors then checks its own priorities and resources, and responds with an estimate of how quickly it could finish that task. The lowest bidder gets the job.[13]

The contract-net idea has been implemented by Thomas W. Malone of MIT's Sloane School of Management, along with Richard Fikes and Michael Howard of the Xerox Palo Alto Research Center, in a system called Enterprise. The beautiful thing about a contract net, says Malone, "is that by making lots of local decisions in the bidder and client machines, you get a globally coherent assignment of tasks without having to set up any one machine as a 'foreman.' " In fact, he says, a mathematical analysis suggests that Enterprise will often be substantially more efficient than having a foreman.[14]

Computer Teamwork

Another advantage of distributed processing is that many applications seem ideally suited to it. A good example is an air-traffic control system with radars spread out for hundreds of miles. Why send all the raw data back to a central point to be processed?

Victor Lesser of the University of Massachusetts has long been concerned with such issues.[15] "In classical distributed processing," he says, "each processor is assumed to produce accurate results based on correct and complete information." But in practice, doing things this way is either impossible or very costly and inefficient. "There is an enormous burden of communication and synchronization," he points out. "Each processor spends most of its time waiting for another processor to finish *its* job. Worse, as you build larger and larger systems, you can't assume that all the processors will be functional. You can't assume that you have global information. You can't assume that all the information channels are working."

Lesser's approach to coping with such uncertainties grew out of the so-called blackboard architecture, which in turn dates back to the Hearsay II speech-understanding system that Lesser helped design at Carnegie-Mellon University in the mid-1970s. The idea in Hearsay II was that multiple "agents" would analyze the incoming sounds from different points of view. One would identify phonemes, for example; another would piece together words; and yet another would try to predict the next word on the basis of the preceding phrase. Each one alone would reach tentative, incomplete conclusions, perhaps even wrong conclusions. But together they could usually narrow down the possibilities far enough to reach a satisfactory answer.[16]

This multiagent approach has obvious parallels to human teamwork. In fact, says Lesser, the Hearsay team members themselves tended to think of it as a panel of consulting physicians with, say, an internist, a radiologist, and a pathologist all trying to reach a diagnosis. To see how such an approach might work in the example of a distributed air-traffic control system, he says, imagine that one radar installation has only an approximate fix on an aircraft's position when it hands off control to the next radar down the line. The second radar could still use that information to narrow its area of search, improve its signal-to-noise ratio, and identify the aircraft faster and more accurately than it could have on its own.

However, there is one major problem with this approach, Lesser admits. "How do you get each node to do the most fruitful thing for the overall activity?" he asks. The whole idea is to keep the processors from getting bogged down in communication and coordination. "But without a centralized view," he says, "you may have nodes doing redundant processing, or *wrong* processing."

At the same time, he says, the system has to be robust. If one processor fails, the others ought to be able to work around it.

In an effort to attain both coherence and robustness simultaneously, says Lesser, "we've been using the human organizational metaphor. Each node—read each person—is given a certain range of responsibility, and within that range it can make its own decisions.

"Actually," he says, "we introduce three levels of dynamic structuring. The first is an overall organizational structure that changes only rarely and slowly, which imposes a certain global coherence right there. At the intermediate level there are groups of processors who can work together and balance their workload. It's rather like the contract–net idea. And then at the local level there are the individual processors themselves.

"To me," he adds, "this has led to a lot of interesting work on control structure for AI." For example, programmers now have to specify the organizational structure of their processors beforehand. Can the computers be taught to organize and reorganize themselves on their own to fit the problem at hand? Lesser has been thinking about how to do that but finds it slow going. "The question 'What is an organization?' is very difficult to define," he says. "Part of our work is to define a language in which you can talk about organizations symbolically."

Malone has also been thinking along these lines. He and several colleagues have begun to develop an analytic framework for evaluating the efficiency and flexibility of organizations, including such factors as production costs, coordination overhead, and the vulnerability of the system to isolated failures and to sudden changes in the environment.[17]

Computer Societies

Distributed AI also raises some profound research issues. For example, how can one machine reason about another's knowledge, intentions, and beliefs? "In human communications, a lot of what I say depends on what I believe about your state of mind," says Davis. "If I think you know something, I won't bother to explain it to you. If I think you don't believe it, I may argue for it." Exactly the same kind of considerations come up when machines have to communicate.

One man who has thought a great deal about such problems is Davis's MIT colleague Carl Hewitt. He echoes many of the points that Davis, Malone, and Lesser make, but he defines them in terms of a more general concept that he calls "open systems."[18]

"It's the new computer paradigm," he says. "It used to be that the machines would stand alone. Now you have this burgeoning growth of personal computers wired together in local and national networks." An open system thus has to change and evolve as it accommodates new users, new machines, and new tasks.

"It also used to be that to find out what you wanted to know, you'd look in your local data base," says Hewitt. "Now it's more like a big-city library system, with lots of branch libraries where you can look for data." But decentralization may make it impossible to keep all the data bases up to date and consistent with one another; an open system thus has to operate in the face of chronic inconsistency and ambiguity.

And finally, says Hewitt, it used to be that the machine was yours to do with as you pleased. "Now each computer in the network represents the interests of its owner or operator, which means that the machines have to deal with each other at arm's length. You can't just go poking around in somebody else's computer." An open system thus has to allow its member machines to communicate, and yet still maintain their integrity.

Once again, this is all reminiscent of the way humans themselves interact. In fact, just as Lesser and his Hearsay II colleagues modeled the blackboard architecture after a panel of physicians, Hewitt and his associates have drawn their inspiration from studies of corporations, scientific communities, and organizations in general.[19]

"One of the main things you find out is that the 'rational' view or the 'deductive' view is a totally inadequate account of how organizations work," says Hewitt. "In fact, you can't use 'logical proof' as a touchstone if you want to explain the performance that's actually observed in organizations.

"What you do have in organizations is 'due process' reasoning," he says. People go out and seek allies, and decisions are made by conducting a debate between various interested parties. It's like a political or a scientific debate, or a negotiation.

"Now, in this context," he says, "the meaning of a statement or a message is not whether it's 'true' or 'false,' but what effect it has on the recipient. So if you want to put open systems on a sound theoretical basis, you have to deal formally with these issues—and that leads us to 'actor theory,' which we've been developing for the last ten years, and which we're now in the process of applying."

In actor theory, he explains, the fundamental computational entities—the "actors"—can be as simple as a tiny subprogram residing deep in one computer's memory, or as complex as a whole interconnected cluster of computers. All that matters is how it responds to messages; it can make a decision, change its internal state, send another message, or even create a new actor. A computation is thus an inherently parallel process, with messages cascading from actor to actor, and each one responding independently of every other.[20] Hewitt and company have recently begun to implement the theory in a working system they call Apiary (because the actors in the system are like busy worker bees).[21]

"You might call this work a kind of 'theoretical sociology,' " says Hewitt. "In fact, my students and I have gone out and done fieldwork with some of our sociologist colleagues here at MIT, and they're very excited about the potential. You can think of it as a computational basis for sociology, or as an organizational basis for computation.

"Will we learn something new about people from all this?" Hewitt asks. "Probably yes—but when it comes, people will say, 'Of course! It's so simple!' because it will resonate with their own beliefs and experience."

The Society of Mind

Finally, distributed AI brings up a scientific question: How pervasive is parallelism in the phenomenon of intelligence?

The tradition in AI (and in philosophy) has been to think of the mind as taking things one step at a time, rather like a serial von Neumann computer. And in many ways it does. Baking a cake is certainly a step-by-step operation. So is the process of reading a book, or of adding up a restaurant bill.

But as Hinton and many others have pointed out, much of what goes on in the mind is highly parallel—retrieval from long-term memory, for example. If I ask you a question like "What was President Lincoln's first name?" the answer will pop into your conscious mind in less than a second, no matter how many other things you happen to know. So however you find that information, you don't do it by flipping through a set of neuronal file cards one by one. You presumably do it by using the massive parallelism of the brain to search all your memories concurrently.

In still other cases, however, it's clear that the mind is doing something like distributed processing—not because it's spatially spread out but because it's a consortium of semiautonomous subunits. There are the vision modules we met in Chapter 4, for example. They make nearly independent guesses about three-dimensional structure, yet in the end they have to cooperate and integrate their guesses. Once more, it's reminiscent of the Hearsay II blackboard and the panel-of-physicians analogy.

At a higher level, consider what's involved with something as simple as standing on the sidewalk and talking to a friend. Somehow, your mind has to integrate balance, sight, sound, language, planning (suppose you're trying to figure out where to go for lunch), interpersonal skills, and countless other concerns.

Harvard psychologist Howard Gardner has recently revived the idea of multiple intelligences, sets of abilities that can develop and function more or less independently. In his 1983 book *Frames of Mind*, Gardner identifies seven types of intelligence: logical-mathematical, linguistic, spatial, bodily-kines-thetic, musical, and personal, the latter being subdivided into a sense of self and a sense of others.[22] The theory is controversial, to say the least. But notice that the first three of Gardner's intelligences correspond roughly to the AI subfields of problem-solving, natural-language understanding, and computer vision, while the fourth is addressed by AI's cousin, robotics. (Notice also that we've seen the rudiments of a computer theory of personal intelligence laid out in Hewitt's actor theory, together with Schank and Abelson's theory of goals, plans, and beliefs. And Minsky has even begun to investigate how a computer might understand music.[23]) Thus far, all these things have been pursued separately. So whether or not the theory of multiple intelligences is true for humans, integrating the disparate parts of machine intelligence poses one of the major long-term challenges for AI.

Meanwhile, Minsky and his MIT colleague Seymour Papert have proposed a far more ambitious vision of intelligence that they call the "society of mind."[24] Their assertion is that the mind is not a single, unified consciousness, however much we may feel that it is; instead, the mind is much more like a community, an association of mental "agents."

Originally conceived by Minsky and Papert around 1970, and developed extensively since then by Minsky, the proposal is similar in many ways to Hewitt's actor theory. As an illustration, Minsky likes to imagine a child building a little tower of blocks. A certain agent called WRECKER is in control for the moment. Now, WRECKER's specialty is knocking down big towers. It loves to hear them crash. Unfortunately, there's no tower yet, and WRECKER doesn't know how to build one. So WRECKER subcontracts the job to two other agents: BUILDER, which will stack the blocks up, and PUSHER, which will knock the tower down when it's finished. (Anyone with programming experience will recognize subroutines.)

But BUILDER itself is a very simple-minded agent. It doesn't really know how to build a tower. It just knows how to ask for help from BEGIN, which selects a site; ADD, which finds blocks and adds them to the top; and END, which decides when the tower is high enough.

                         BUILDER
              /————————|————————\
         BEGIN   ADD   `END

However, ADD's job is also too big. It has to break the task down still further.

This delegation of tasks continues until we get so far down in the hierarchy—perhaps to the level of one muscle twitching in one finger—that the agents can do the job by themselves.

As the tower grows higher, however, a conflict arises: PUSHER wants to knock it over *now*, but BUILDER wants to keep going. It's up to WRECKER to make a decision. But this is WRECKER's third tower today, and it's getting bored. So the struggle continues, weakening WRECKER's resolve still further—until another agent called EAT overrules them all, and the child wanders off to find a cookie.

In short, the society-of-mind idea pictures thinking as an unruly process of bickering, cooperation, and power struggles between agents, as if the U.S. Congress had somehow convened inside a single skull. And it does sound plausible. We've all been indecisive at times—"torn," "of two minds," and so forth. We've all known people who can take a drink or two and "become a different person." We've all had times when "the devil made us do it." In his 1986 book *The Society of Mind*, Minsky explores how a wide variety of mental activities might arise from such agents.[25]

To take just one example, consider his theory of memory. Whenever you get a good idea, solve a problem, or have a memorable experience, he says, your mind creates a new agent: a "knowledge-line," or "K-line" for short. The K-line is like a list of the people who came to a successful party; it is even more like a wire or a network that you attach to all the agents that are active at a given moment. Thus, when you want to remember that event or solve a similar problem later on, says Minsky, all you have to do is reactivate the K-line. The same set of agents are aroused and you quickly find yourself in a mental state that is much like the original one.

The K-line theory explains a familiar psychological phenomenon, says Minsky; the experiences we find easiest to recall are often just the kind of experiences we find hardest to describe. For example, most people would have no trouble recalling how it felt to be at, say, a concert. But very few people would be able to describe that feeling very well. And the reason, says Minsky, is that it's very easy for the mind to record widespread, diffuse activities among its agents. Granted that when lots of agents are active, the K-line that records them has to be huge. Yet it really doesn't need to be much more than a list of which agents are active. The mind actually has to do much more processing to explain what the agents are doing, he says, because explanation involves summarizing their activity in terms of a much more compact set of symbols—words.

To look at the K-line theory in a little more detail, says Minsky, consider another memory: Yesterday, you watched Jack fly his kite. And today, of course, when you remember this event, it's rather as if you were seeing it again. On the other hand, says Minsky, even yesterday you weren't seeing it as something totally new. You saw the kite and knew what a kite was. You saw Jack and knew him as an old friend. You watched him fly the kite and knew that flying a kite involved wind and running and being outside. Each of these things—KITE, JACK, and FLY—was already recorded as a K-line all its own.

Thus, says Minsky, one can imagine two strategies for remembering the event. One scheme would be simply to connect a new K-line to all the agents that were active at that instant. This would allow the memory to be very precise and vivid, with all the sights and sounds and smells recalled in cinematic detail. The other scheme is more hierarchical: Instead of attaching a new K-line to *all* the agents, you would attach it only to whatever older K-lines were active—in this case, KITE, JACK, and FLY. Such a memory would be considerably less vivid. In fact, you would tend to remember only what you happened to recognize and focus on at the time; all the other details would be lost. But that is precisely how human memory does seem to work, says Minsky. We tend to remember familiar things, or details that catch our attention, and forget all the rest.

In *The Society of Mind,* Minsky pushes his concept in as many new directions as he can think of, which is a great many directions indeed. But for all his playfulness, Minsky's purpose is quite serious. Consider this, he says: None of these agents is particularly intelligent by itself. Indeed, taken one at a time, they are very simple and machinelike. BUILDER can't make a tower, for example. It only knows how to make connections with certain other agents. It might as well *be* a machine.

And yet that's just the point, says Minsky. The intelligence of the system isn't in the agents. It's in the organization, in the myriad ways that agents can interact, make alliances, and work together. *The Society of Mind* is in fact Minsky's solution to one of the fundamental mysteries of science: How mind can arise from nonmind.

"What is Life?" he writes. "One dissects a body, but finds no life inside. What is Mind? One dissects a brain but finds no mind therein. Are life and mind so much more than the 'sum of their parts' that it is useless to search for them?"

Not at all, he says. "It is foolish to use [words like *life* and *mind*] for describing the smallest components of living things because these words were invented for describing how larger assemblies interact." The word *life* has already lost most of its mystery, he says, at least for modern biologists, because they understand so many of the important interactions among the chemicals in cells. The word *mind* still holds its mystery—but only because we still know so little about how the mental agents interact to accomplish all the things they do.[26]

So has Minsky found the answer? Is the essence of mind really to be found in a kind of inner sociology?

Perhaps. Of course, it must be said that the society of mind is little more than a web of theory and conjecture at this point. Portions of it have indeed been inspired by working programs—the BUILDER example is taken almost verbatim from Terry Winograd's SHRDLU, which I described in Chapter 3— but considered as a whole, the theory is still untested and unproved.

In all fairness, however, Minsky has never tried to build a working society of mind inside a computer. He is by nature a philosopher and intellectual provocateur. The society of mind is not so much a detailed blueprint of a theory as a grand conceptual design for what a detailed theory ought to be like. As he has done so often in the past, Minsky is throwing down a challenge to the rising generation.

6
Can a Machine Think?

The materials at present within my command hardly seemed
adequate to so arduous an undertaking, but I doubted not that
I should ultimately succeed. I prepared myself for a multitude
of reverses: my operations might be incessantly baffled, and at
last my work be imperfect, yet when I considered the improvement which every day takes place in science and mechanics, I was encouraged to hope my present attempts would
at least lay the foundations of future success. Nor could I
consider the magnitude and complexity of such a plan as any
argument of its impracticality. It was with these feelings that I
began the creation of a human being.
—VICTOR FRANKENSTEIN[1]

The quest for knowledge is the stuff of legend—and the reports are not
reassuring. Consider Frankenstein, Joseph Golem, Faust, Pandora, the Sorcerer's Apprentice. Thus the inevitable question, always asked with undertones of
fascination and horror: Can a machine think? *Really* think?

Perhaps the most honest answer is "Who knows?" After all, what does it
mean to "really" think?

On the other hand, that's not a very satisfying answer. So let's try some
others:

Who cares? If a machine can do its job very, very well, what does it matter
if it *really* thinks? No one runs around asking if taxicabs really walk.

How could you ever tell? As Herbert Simon says, "Can machines think?
They've been doing it for thirty years. I have the same evidence for them as I
have that *you* think." This attitude is the basis of the famous "Turing test,"
devised in 1950 by the British mathematician and logician Alan Turing:
Imagine that you're sitting alone in a room with a teletype machine, which is
connected at the other end to either a person or a computer. If no amount of
questioning or conversation allows you to tell which it is, then you have to
concede that a machine can think.[2]

No, thinking is too complicated. Even if we someday come to understand all the laws and principles that govern the mind, that doesn't mean we can duplicate it. Does understanding astrophysics mean that we can build a galaxy?

Yes, machines can think—in principle—but not necessarily in the same way we do. Seymour Papert maintains that artificial intelligence is analogous to artificial flight: "This leads us to imagine skeptics who would say, 'You mathematicians deal with idealized fluids—the real atmosphere is vastly more complicated,' or 'You have no reason to suppose that airplanes and birds work the same way—birds have no propellers, airplanes have no feathers.' But the premise of these criticisms is true only in the most superficial sense: The same *principles* (for example, Bernoulli's law) apply to real as well as ideal fluids, and they apply whether the fluid flows over a feather or an aluminum wing."[3]

Finally, the most often-heard answer, and the most heartfelt:

NO! I am not a machine [goes the argument]. I'm here. I'm *me.* I'm alive. And you're never going to make a computer that can say that. Furthermore, the essence of humanity isn't reason, logic, or any of the other things that computers can do; it's intuition, sensuality, and emotion. How can a computer think if it does not feel, and how can it feel if it knows nothing of love, anguish, exhilaration, loneliness, and all the rest of what it means to be a living human being?

"Sometimes when my children were still little," writes former AI researcher Joseph Weizenbaum of MIT, "my wife and I would stand over them as they lay sleeping in their beds. We spoke to each other only in silence, rehearsing a scene as old as mankind itself. It is as Ionesco told his journal: 'Not everything is unsayable in words, only the living truth.' "[4]

CAN A MACHINE FEEL?

As this last answer suggests, the case against genuine machine intelligence always comes down to two assertions: that a machine cannot feel and that a machine cannot be aware. But are these assertions true?

Once again, the most honest answer is "Who knows?" On the other hand, the first half of the issue, emotion, has come into much sharper focus in recent years thanks to the efforts of the brain scientists. Armed with all the techniques of cellular and molecular biology, they have begun to clarify how our most basic emotions and drives arise at the molecular level. Hunger, thirst, pleasure, pain, depression, elation, anger, sexual arousal—all seem to be products of the chemistry of brain. To take just a few examples:

- When a hormone known as angiotensin is injected into the bloodstream, it produces all the feelings and physiological responses of thirst. The blood vessels constrict. The kidneys stop producing urine. The patient *feels* thirsty. Under natural conditions, angiotensin is released into the bloodstream by the liver when dehydration sets in. When it reaches the brain, it interacts with a tiny cluster of cells known as the subfornical organ. The subfornical organ then responds by releasing a flood of new chemical transmitters that migrate throughout the brain. Their message: Get something to drink!

- When we are emotionally aroused by an event—the Kennedy assassination, the death of a family member, the birth of a child—the experience often seems indelibly stamped on our memories. No one knows precisely why this is, but the evidence points to the action of emotion-related brain chemicals. For example, when test subjects inhale a nasal spray containing a hormone known as vasopressin, their performance on long-term memory tests seems to improve.
- Mood-altering drugs such as valium, PCP, and marijuana produce their effects precisely because they mimic the natural action of neurotransmitters, which are chemicals involved in transferring nerve impulses from neuron to neuron in the brain. More than sixty such neurotransmitters are now known, and more continue to be discovered.
- Many mental disorders such as depression, schizophrenia, and manic-depressive illness are now known to have a biochemical basis. Most of the drugs used to treat them either augment or counteract the effects of specific neurotransmitters.[5]

The Purpose of Emotions

Now, at first glance these discoveries about the chemical basis of emotion may seem to rule out any possibility that machines can feel. After all, a computer is more like an electronics shop than a chemical plant. But first impressions can be deceiving. Consider this: Complex biochemical systems don't evolve by accident. If emotions are caused by a surge of neurotransmitters, then emotions must be serving some definite biological functions. And if we can find out what those functions are, then it's at least plausible that a computer could carry out the same tasks—even without chemicals.

It must be said that AI researchers and cognitive scientists have generally tended to avoid the subject of emotion, preferring to concentrate instead on the purely cognitive aspects of intelligence. But some things are clear enough. For example, psychologists generally agree that one major function of emotion is to focus our attention, to help us decide what is important in the world. When someone is frightened by a spider, that spider is *very* important; for the moment, at least, nothing else seems to exist. When we are moved by a play or a piece of music, we tend to forget ourselves and our surroundings as we watch. Furthermore, if we define emotion in a very broad sense, it's also clear that it serves to define our long-term goals and motives. Thus, an ambitious person may shape his or her entire career in ways that satisfy a need for the approval of others, or for the security of money. An extremely shy person may do just the opposite, choosing a life-style that avoids confrontation with others.

As Marvin Minsky points out, "It is a mistaken idea in our culture that feeling and emotion are deep, whereas intelligence, how we think, is easy to understand. If you ask someone, 'Why are you mad at your wife?' he might say, 'Well, it's really because my boss was mean to me, and I can't get mad at him.' It seems to me that people understand the dynamics of emotion quite well. But they have no idea at all to speak of how thought works."[6]

Indeed, although understanding the dynamics of emotion has not been a top priority in AI, some psychologists and AI researchers *have* made a start. In previous chapters, for example, I've described Roger Schank and Robert Abelson's work on getting a computer to infer the goals and plans of characters in a story, as well as Jaime Carbonell's theory of subjective understanding. In principle, there's no reason a computer couldn't use those same techniques to figure out when someone is sad or angry in real life. Such a computer could then be programmed to make the appropriate responses—saying comforting words in the first case, or moving the conversation toward a less provocative subject in the second. Indeed, such a computer could even be said to "empathize" in some sense.

Of course, a skeptic could always argue that this kind of behavior is beside the point. Reasoning *about* emotion is like reading about sex: It's just not the same as the real thing. Can the computer itself feel? With no glands, no body, no experience at being human, can it ever be anything other than alien and cold inside?

Maybe not. But instead of talking about a metal box with lights and disk drives, let's imagine that we build the ultimate robot: a computer equipped with artificial eyes, ears, arms, legs, and skin—even artificial glands. Of course, the technology is nowhere near that point yet, but there's no reason to suppose that such a thing is impossible in principle. We could even arrange for special circuits that would trigger patterns of activity in the computer in precisely the same way that hormones influence the human brain. Question: Is *this* machine still alien and cold inside? Suddenly it's not so clear.

Feeling and Thought

Feeling and reason are widely held to be opposites, two utterly unlike things that have a hard time coexisting in the same brain. People who pride themselves on being rational are all too often contemptuous of those they consider "emotional" and "fuzzy." And vice versa: People who consider themselves sensitive and empathetic often bridle at the "cold rigidity" they perceive in the first group.

But in fact, that division is completely artificial. How can there be reason without something to reason about? Emotions serve to focus our attention and to define our goals and motives; that fact alone means that thought and feeling are inseparable. "Coldly rational" scientists, driven by a need to understand the universe, are often dazzled by their feelings of awe and wonder. "Sensitive and emotional" artists, gripped by an unattainable vision of perfection, are often driven to analyze and reanalyze their technique in excruciating detail.

The dependency works in another way as well. The big, primal emotions, such as anger, fear, and joy, obviously have a physical basis. Everything is affected—blood pressure, breathing, heart rate, adrenaline level. But so far as anyone can tell, the physiological reactions for all these big emotions are identical; the body only tells you to feel *something*. What your conscious mind actually does feel depends on how it all started—a kiss? a slap in the face?—and how the events are interpreted. Emotion, in other words, is as much a product of the mind as of the body.

Minsky, for one, goes even further by suggesting that we experience many emotions *because* we think. Why do we like music, for example? "Most adults have some childlike fascination for making and arranging larger structures out of smaller ones," he adds. "One kind of musical understanding involves building large mental structures out of smaller, musical parts. Perhaps the drive to build these mental music states is the same one that makes us try to understand the world."[7]

Minsky also asks about another curious human behavior: Why do we laugh? "Freud's theory of jokes explains how they overcome the mental 'censors' that make it hard for us to think 'forbidden' thoughts," he says. The result, according to Freud, is a pleasurable release of psychic energy. "But his theory does not work so well for humorous nonsense as for other comical subjects. . . . I argue that the different forms of humor can be seen as much more similar, once we recognize the importance of *knowledge about knowledge* and, particularly, aspects of thinking concerned with recognizing and suppressing *bugs*—ineffective or destructive thought processes."[8]

As an example, consider a joke that mystified Freud:

A gentleman entered a pastry-cook's shop and ordered a cake; but he soon brought it back and asked for a glass of liqueur instead. He drank it and began to leave without having paid. The proprietor detained him. "You've not paid for the liqueur." "But I gave you the cake in exchange for it." "You didn't pay for that either." "But I hadn't eaten it."[9]

Why is this funny? Because common sense logic is essential for our everyday affairs, says Minsky. And yet as this example shows, it's unreliable. "So we must learn to avoid its most common malfunctions. Humor plays a special role in learning and communication about such matters."

In addition, he says, "productive thinking depends on knowing how to use analogy and metaphor. But analogies are often false, and metaphors misleading. So the 'cognitive unconscious' must suppress inappropriate comparisons. This is why humor is so concerned with the nonsensical."

In other words, jokes are not so much about escaping censors as about building censors. "Jokes are not really funny at all," Minsky concludes, "but reflect the most serious of concerns; the pursuit of sobriety through the suppression of the absurd."

So does this really explain humor? Who knows? I suspect that Minsky himself isn't pushing this theory as anything more than a set of ideas to play with. But remember, a computer that uses heuristic, common-sense reasoning is prey to all the same kinds of incorrect and destructive thought processes that humans are. Eventually, as computers become more intelligent, they may also have to incorporate a programming code that censors such intrusions. So if humor really does work the way Minsky says it does, then genuinely intelligent computers may or may not feel emotion—but they will certainly be able to laugh.

CAN A MACHINE BE AWARE?

This second question is even tougher than the first. Talking about emotion, we at least know some of the physiology involved, and we can imagine how it might work in a cognitive sense. But what is consciousness? What is it *for*?

For research purposes, cognitive psychologists often take consciousness to be just the sum of all the things we're paying attention to at any given time.[10] But that's not an answer; it's a definition. What is attention, and why do we pay it?

Try again: Maybe consciousness is the executive suite of the mind, a place where we take care of emergencies and policy decisions while a kind of subconscious bureaucracy takes care of routine. Or maybe it's the seat of introspection, the place where we look inward and perceive ourselves in the act of perceiving.

Maybe. But then who is it that makes the decisions, and who is it that does the perceiving? Is your conscious self like a little man sitting at a control console inside your head? Does he monitor the data from your eyes and ears, and pull the levers that move your arms and legs? If so, then who's sitting in the head of the little man? An even smaller little man? And who's pulling the levers in *his* head?

Clearly, this isn't going to work either. The endless succession of little men is known as "Hume's problem," after the Scottish philosopher David Hume, who struggled with it in the eighteenth century. Hume's word for one of these little men was *homunculus*; Allen Newell has suggested that the goal of AI and cognitive psychology ought to be the "banishment of the homunculus."[11]

The question is how.

The Computationalists Versus the Holists

That question has been the source of endless debate, made all the hotter because people aren't arguing science. They're arguing philosophical ideology—their personal beliefs about what the true theory of the mind will be like when we find it.

Not surprisingly, the philosophical landscape is rugged and diverse. But it's possible to get some feel for the overall topography by looking at two extremes. In one, lying at the heart of classical AI, we find the doctrine first set down by Allen Newell and Herbert Simon in the 1950s: (1) Thinking is information processing; (2) information processing is computation, which is the manipulation of symbols; and (3) symbols, because of their relationships and linkages, express something about the external world. In other words, the brain per se is irrelevant, and Turing was right: A perfect simulation of thinking *is* thinking.

Tufts University philosopher Daniel C. Dennett, a witty and insightful observer of AI, has dubbed this position High Church Computationalism. Its prelates include such establishment figures as Minsky and Simon, and its Vatican City is MIT, "the East Pole."

From out of the West, then, comes heresy—a creed that is not so much an alternative as a denial. As Dennett describes it, the assertion is that

> . . . there is no formal, rule-governed computational level of description intervening between folk psychology and brain science. Thinking is something going on in the brain all right, but it is not computation at all: thinking is something holistic and emergent—and organic and fuzzy and warm and cuddly and mysterious.[12]

Dennett calls this creed Zen Holism. And for some reason its proponents do seem to cluster in the San Francisco Bay area. Among them are the gurus of the movement: Berkeley philosophers Hubert Dreyfus, author of a famous and caustic attack on AI entitled *What Computers Can't Do*,[13] and John Searle, who ironically has made important contributions to AI natural-language research through his work on the speech-acts theory, which I discussed in Chapter 3.

The computationalists and the holists have been going at it for years, ever since Dreyfus first began denouncing AI in the mid-1960s.[14] But their definitive battle took place in 1980, in the pages of the journal *Behavioral and Brain Sciences*. B&BS is unique among scientific journals in that it doesn't simply publish an article; first it solicits commentary from the author's peers and gives the author a chance to write a rebuttal. Then it publishes the whole thing as a package—a kind of formal debate in print.

In this case, the centerpiece was Searle's article "Minds, Brains, and Programs," a stinging attack on the idea that a machine could think.[15]

Following it were twenty-seven responses, most of which were stinging attacks on Searle. The whole thing is worth reading for its entertainment value alone. But it also highlights the fundamental issues with a clarity that has never been equaled.

The Chinese Room

Searle emphasized at the outset that he fully accepts the use of computers to simulate mental processes. "It gives us a very powerful tool," he writes. "For example, it enables us to formulate and test hypotheses in a more rigorous and precise fashion."[16] Searle calls this approach "weak," or "cautious," AI.

His argument is against "strong" AI, the version that Dennett calls High Church Computationalism. Essentially, Searle's point is that simulation is not duplication. A program that uses formal rules to manipulate abstract symbols can never think, or be aware, because those symbols don't *mean* anything to the computer.

To illustrate, he proposes the following thought experiment as a parody of the script-based programs of Schank and Abelson:

"Suppose that I'm locked in a room and given a large batch of Chinese writing," he suggests. "Suppose furthermore (as is indeed the case) that I know no Chinese. . . . To me, the Chinese writing is just so many meaningless squiggles." This first bundle of writing corresponds to a set of Shank-Abelson scripts.

Next, writes Searle, he is given a second batch of Chinese writing (a "story"), together with some rules, in English, that explain how to correlate the first batch with the second (a "program").

Then, after this project is done, he is given yet a third set of Chinese symbols ("questions"), together with yet more English rules that tell him how to manipulate the slips of paper until all three batches are correlated, and how to produce a new set of Chinese characters ("answers"), which he then passes back out of the room.

Finally, "after awhile I get so good at manipulating the instructions for the Chinese symbols and the programmers get so good at writing the programs that from the external point of view . . . my answers to the questions are absolutely indistinguishable from those of native Chinese speakers." In other words, Searle learns to pass the Turing test in Chinese.

Now, according to the zealots of strong AI, claims Searle, a computer that can answer questions in this way isn't just simulating human language abilities. It is literally *understanding* the story. Moreover, the operation of the program is in fact an explanation of human understanding.

And yet, while Searle is locked in that imaginary room, he is doing exactly what the computer does. He uses formal rules to manipulate abstract symbols. He takes in stories and gives out answers exactly as a native Chinese would. *But he still doesn't understand a word of Chinese.* So how is it possible to say that the computer understands?

In fact, says Searle, it doesn't. For comparison, imagine that the questions and the answers now switch to English. So far as the people outside the room are concerned, he is just as fluent as before. And yet there's all the difference in the world, because now he isn't just manipulating formal symbols anymore. He understands what's being said. The words have meaning for him—or, in the technical jargon of philosophy, he has *intentionality*.

Why? "Because I am a certain sort of organism with a certain biological (i.e., chemical and physical) structure," he writes, "and this structure, under certain conditions, is causally capable of producing perception, action, understanding, learning, and other intentional phenomena."

In other words, Searle concludes that it is certainly possible for a machine to think—"in an important sense our bodies with our brains are precisely such machines"—but only if the machine is as complex and as powerful as the brain. A purely formal computer program cannot do it.

The Computationalists' Counterattack

Searle's Chinese room clearly struck a sensitive nerve, as evidenced by the number and spirit of the denunciations that followed. It was clear to everyone that when Searle used the word *intentionality*, he wasn't just talking about an obscure technical matter. In this context intentionality was virtually synonymous with *mind, soul, spirit,* or *awareness*. A sampler of some of the main objections:

- *The comparison is unfair.* The Schank-Abelson programs demonstrated a very crude kind of understanding at best, and no one in AI seriously claims anything more for them—least of all Schank and Abelson. Even if they were correct in principle, claim the defenders, genuinely humanlike understanding would require much more powerful machines and much more sophisticated programs.

  Searle quite correctly points out, however, that this argument is irrelevant: Of course computers are getting more powerful; what he objects to is the principle.
- *The Chinese room story is entertaining and seductive, but it's a fraud.* Douglas R. Hofstadter of Indiana University, author of the best-selling *Gödel, Escher, Bach*, points out that the jump from Schankian scripts to the Turing test is not the trivial step that Searle makes it out to be. It's an enormous leap. The poor devil in the Chinese room wouldn't have to shuffle just a few slips of paper but millions or billions of slips of paper. It would take him years to answer a question, if he could do it at all. In effect, says Hofstadter, Searle is postulating mental processes slowed down by a factor of millions, so no wonder it looks different.

  Searle's reply—that he could memorize the slips of paper and shuffle them in his head—sounds plausible enough. But as several respondents pointed out, it dangerously undermines his whole argument: Once he memorizes everything, doesn't he now understand Chinese in the same way he understands English?

- *It's true that the man in the room doesn't understand Chinese himself. But he is just part of a larger system, which also includes the slips of paper, the rules, and the message-passing mechanism. Taken as a whole, this larger system does understand Chinese.* This "systems" reply was advanced by a number of the respondents. Searle was incredulous—"It is not easy for me to imagine how someone who was not in the grip of an ideology could find the idea at all plausible"—and yet the concept is subtler than it seems. Consider a thermostat, in which a bimetallic strip bends and unbends as the temperature changes. When the room becomes too cold, the strip closes an electrical connection and the furnace kicks on. When the room warms back up again, the connection reopens and the furnace shuts off. Now, does the bimetallic strip by itself control the temperature of the room? No. Does the furnace by itself control the temperature? No. Does the system as a whole control the temperature? Yes. Connections and the organization make the whole into more than the sum of its parts.★

- *There is abundant evidence that humans themselves use formal rules in thinking.* Yale's Robert Abelson gives the following example in his reply to Searle:

    "When a child learns to add, what does he do except apply rules? Where does the 'understanding' enter? Is it understanding that the rules of addition apply independent of content, so that m + n = p means that if you have m things and you assemble them with n things, then you'll have p things? But that's a rule, too. Is it understanding that the units place can be translated into pennies, the tens place into dimes, and the hundreds place into dollars, so that additions of numbers are isomorphic to additions of money? But that's a rule connecting rule systems. In general, it seems that as more and more rules about a given content are incorporated, especially if they connect with other content domains, we have a sense that understanding is increasing. At what point does a person graduate from 'merely' manipulating rules to 'really' understanding?"

- *Searle presents a misleading and impoverished view of what symbol systems actually do.* The symbols used in modern AI programs are not just static labels with arbitrary meanings, as Searle suggests. They are complex, they are active, and they are linked together in rich associations. (Remember the frames, procedures, and semantic networks discussed in Chapter 2.) Furthermore, as psychologist Zenon Pylyshyn of the University of Western Ontario points out in his response, the question of how symbols acquire meaning can be answered in purely functional terms, without Searle's obscure appeal to "the causal powers of the brain." Specifically, a symbol acquires meaning through the way it

---

★This is precisely the same argument that Marvin Minsky makes for his society-of-mind theory (see Chapter 5).

influences the behavior of the system as a whole. This "functionalist" view is in fact the dominant one in both AI and cognitive science. Searle, of course, refuses to buy it.★

- *Searle never makes clear what intentionality is, nor why a machine can't have it.* As Dennett points out, "For Searle, intentionality is rather like a wonderful substance secreted by the brain the way the pancreas secretes insulin."

And make no mistake: Searle's concept of intentionality does require a biological brain. He explicitly denies that a robot could have intentionality, even if it were equipped with eyes, ears, arms, legs, and all the other accoutrements it needed to move around and perceive the world as a human being does. Inside, says Searle, the robot would still just be manipulating formal symbols.

That assertion led Pylyshyn to propose his own thought experiment: "Thus, if more and more of the cells in your brain were to be replaced by integrated circuit chips, programmed in such a way as to keep the input-output *function* of each unit identical to the unit being replaced, you would in all likelihood just keep right on speaking exactly as you are doing now except that you would eventually stop *meaning* anything by it. What we outside observers might take to be words would become for you just certain noises that circuits caused you to make."

In short, you would become a zombie.

Dennett takes up the same theme in his article. So far as natural selection is concerned, he points out, a Pylyshyn-style zombie—or Searle's robot—is just as fit for survival as those of us with Searle-style intentional brains. Evolution would make no distinction. Indeed, from a biological point of view, intentionality is irrelevant, as useless as the appendix. So how did it ever arise? And having arisen, how did it survive and prosper when it offered no selection value? Aren't we lucky that some chance mutation didn't rob our ancestors of intentionality? Dennett asks. If it had, he says, "we'd behave just as we do now, but of course we wouldn't *mean* it!"

Needless to say, both Pylyshyn and Dennett found this absurd.

- *Finally, Searle implicitly—and wrongly—assumes that there is a threshold for intentionality.* Humans have it, in his view. Perhaps some of the higher animals have it. But rocks, thermostats, and computers definitely don't have it.

But where exactly is the line? ask his opponents. If higher animals have intentionality and lifeless objects don't, then surely it must have arisen somewhere in the course of evolution. But where? Is there a continuum of intentionality, with amoeba at one end and humans at the other? And if so, why can't machines fit into the continuum too?

Minsky, for one, is perfectly willing to believe that there is such a

---

★In a talk before the New York Academy of Sciences several years after the 1980 debate, Dennett pointed out that the strong AI position had been vividly expressed by singer Maria Muldaur in a popular song: *It ain't the meat, it's the motion!* Searle's position is then succinctly stated as *It's the meat!*[17]

continuum, with stones rating practically zero, thermostats rating some fraction higher, humans rating very high—and computers rising fast.

A Standoff

In retrospect, the great debate has to be rated a standoff. Searle, not surprisingly, was unconvinced by any of his opponents' arguments; to this day he and his fellow Zen Holists have refused to yield an inch. Yet they have never given a truly compelling explanation of why it is that a brain and only a brain can have intentionality. The computationalists, meanwhile, remain convinced that they are succeeding where philosophers have failed for three thousand years—that they are producing a real scientific theory of intelligence and consciousness. But they can't prove it. Not yet, anyway.

And in all fairness, the burden of proof is on AI. The symbol-processing paradigm is an intriguing approach. Indeed, unless the new connectionists whom we met in Chapter 5 can begin to make substantial progress, it's the only game in town. If nothing else, it's an approach worth exploring to see how far it can go.

But still—what *is* consciousness?

ON BEING A MACHINE

One way to answer that last question is with another question: Do we really want to know? Many people instinctively side with Searle, horrified at what the computationalist position implies: If thought, feeling, intuition, and all the other workings of the mind can be understood even in principle, if *we* are machines—then God is not speaking to our hearts. And for that matter, neither is Mozart. The soul is nothing more than the flip side of a neuronal symbol. Spirit is nothing more than a surge of hormones and neurotransmitters. Meaning and purpose are illusions.

And besides, when machines grow old and break down, they are discarded without a thought.

Not surprisingly, the people who work in AI tend to be far more comfortable with the idea of themselves as a thinking machine. In her recent book *The Second Self*, sociologist Sherry Turkle tells of a striking juxtaposition of attitudes she encountered soon after she arrived at MIT in 1977. In the morning she had worked with a patient in psychotherapy, a man who for months had used the image of "being a machine" to express his feelings of depersonalization, emptiness, and despair. But that evening she went to a party for new faculty members, where she overheard a confident young woman—a computer-science major—put a stop to an argument about whether machines can think: "I don't see what the problem is. I'm a machine and *I* think."[18]

Nonetheless, this loathing for the idea of being a machine is very real. For many, AI is a message of despair.

Science as a Message of Despair

Of course, this is hardly a new concern. For those who choose to see it that way, science itself is a message of despair.

In 1543, with the publication of his book *De Revolutionibus,* the Polish astronomer Nicolaus Copernicus moved Earth from the center of the universe and made it one planet among many—and thereby changed humankind's relationship with God. In the Earth-centered universe of Thomas Aquinas and other medieval theologians, man was poised halfway between a Heaven that lay just beyond the sphere of the stars and a Hell that burned beneath his feet. He dwelt always under the watchful eye of God, and his spiritual status was reflected in the very structure of the cosmos. But after Copernicus, both Earth and man himself were reduced to being wanderers in an infinite universe. For many, the sense of loss and confusion was palpable.[19]

In 1859, with the publication of *The Origin of Species,* Charles Darwin described how one group of living things arises from another through natural selection—and thereby changed who we were. Once man had been the special creation of God, the favored of all His children. Now man was just another animal, the descendant of monkeys.

In the latter part of the nineteenth century and the early decades of the twentieth, with the publication of such works as *The Interpretation of Dreams* (1901), Sigmund Freud illuminated the inner workings of the mind—and again changed who we were. Once we had been only a little lower than the angels, masters of our own souls. Now we were at the mercy of demons: rage, terror, and lust, made all the more hideous by their very presence in our own unconscious minds.

So the message of science can be bleak indeed. It can become a philosophy of despair, a proclamation that human beings are nothing more than masses of particles collected by blind chance and governed by immutable physical law—that we have no meaning, that there is no purpose to existence, and that the universe just doesn't care.

I suspect that this is the real reason for the creationists' desperate rejection of Darwin. Their anger springs not so much from the denial of Genesis as from the denial of our being special in the eyes of a caring God. That their creed is based on ignorance and a willful distortion of the evidence makes them both pathetic and dangerous. But their longing for order and purpose in the world is understandable and even noble.

I also suspect that this perceived spiritual vacuum in science lies behind the fascination so many people feel for such pseudosciences as astrology. After all, if the stars and the planets guide my fate, then somehow I matter. The universe *cares*. Astrology makes no scientific sense whatsoever. But for those who need such reassurance, what can science offer to replace it?

Science as a Message of Hope

And yet the message doesn't have to be bleak. Science has given us a universe of enormous expanse, filled with marvels far beyond anything Aquinas ever knew. Does it diminish the night sky to know that the planets are other worlds and that the stars are other suns?

In the same way, a scientific theory of intelligence and awareness might very well provide us with an understanding of other possible minds. Perhaps it will show us more clearly how our Western ways of perceiving the world relate to the perceptions of other cultures. Perhaps it will tell us how human intelligence fits in with the range of other possible intelligences that might exist in the universe. Perhaps it will give us a new insight into who we are, and what our place is in creation.

"I don't know why certain people have this horror [of 'explaining away' the soul]," writes Douglas Hofstadter, "while others, like me, find in reductionism the ultimate religion. Perhaps my lifelong training in physics and science in general has given me a deep awe at seeing how the most substantial and familiar of objects or experiences fades away, as one approaches the infinitesimal scale, into an eerily insubstantial ether, a myriad of ephemeral swirling vortices of nearly incomprehensible mathematical activity. This in me evokes a kind of cosmic awe. To me, reductionism does not 'explain away'; rather, it adds mystery."[20]

Indeed, far from being threatening, the prospect of understanding the mind at this level of detail is oddly comforting. Before the advent of the computer, there were basically only two ways of trying to understand what the human mind and spirit were all about. One could follow the model of physics and try to dissect the mind into comprehensible little pieces—the approach taken by neuroscientists, anatomists, and "black-box" behaviorists—or one could follow the humanist instinct and try to embrace the whole of human experience through art, history, literature, and philosophy. Neither side could give a completely satisfactory account of the mind. And yet, as the British physicist and author C. P. Snow points out in his famous essay "The Two Cultures," both sides were (and are) suspicious, hostile, and often contemptuous of each other.[21]

Now, however, after thirty years of AI and cognitive science, the gulf between the two cultures has been bridged with a third model for understanding the mind—the symbol-processing model. Consider a computer program: It is undeniably a natural phenomenon, the product of physical forces pushing electrons here and there through a web of silicon and metal. And yet a computer program is more than *just* a surge of electrons. Take the program and run it on another kind of computer. The electrons now move in a completely different way. But the program itself hasn't changed, because it still does the same thing. It is part of the computer. It needs the computer to exist. And yet it transcends the computer. In effect, the program occupies a different level of reality from the computer.

Thus the power of the symbol-processing model: By describing the mind as a program running on a flesh-and-blood computer, it shows us how feeling, purpose, thought, and awareness can be part of the physical brain and yet transcend the brain. It shows us how the mind can be composed of simple, comprehensible processes—and still be something more.

"Contrary to common opinion," writes the British psychologist Margaret Boden, "the prime metaphysical significance of artificial intelligence is that it can *counteract* the subtly dehumanizing influence of natural science, of which so many cultural critics have complained. It does this by showing, in a scientifically acceptable manner, how it is possible for psychological beings to be grounded in a material world and yet be properly distinguished from 'mere matter.' Far from showing that human beings are 'nothing but machines,' it confirms our insistence that we are essentially subjective creatures living through our own mental constructions of reality."[22]

———

Consider a living cell. The individual enzymes and lipids and DNA molecules that go to make up a cell are comparatively simple things. They obey well-understood laws of physics and chemistry. There's no way to point to any one of them and say, "This is alive." And yet, when all those molecules are brought together in an exquisitely ordered pattern, they *are* life.

In the same way, perhaps our minds are nothing more than machines. Does that mean there is no such thing as spirit? Perhaps we *are* just processors of neuronal symbols. Perhaps a snowflake is only a collection of water molecules. Perhaps *The Magic Flute* is only a sequence of sound waves.

And perhaps, in illuminating the nature of mind and intelligence, AI is only reaffirming how unique and precious the mind really is.

PART II
VISIONS OF A NEW GENERATION

7

Metamorphosis

Embracing a personal computer, the Scarecrow of Oz smiled contentedly from the cover of *Business Week*, July 9, 1984. He had found his brain at last. ARTIFICIAL INTELLIGENCE, proclaimed the headline. IT'S HERE!

And so it was. Until about 1980, artificial intelligence had remained an arcane, academic field with no more than a few hundred serious researchers in the world. And yet by the time the Scarecrow appeared just four years later, the editors of *Business Week* were writing of "a mad rush to move AI into the marketplace."[1] With startling speed, AI had become a glamour industry, the darling of the venture capitalists. AI programming techniques were beginning to find their way into commercial products, led by computer vision systems, natural-language programs, and, most prominently, expert systems. The field was getting strong support from the Pentagon. It was a top research priority in Europe. It had been targeted for advanced development by MITI, the Japanese Ministry of International Trade and Industry. And, as the *Business Week* cover attests, it was fast becoming one of the hottest topics in publishing. In short, by the mid-1980s AI had been transformed. It was big-time high technology.

What happened?

That's a question worth answering, because there is something distinctly paradoxical about the AI boom. Today, half a decade after it started, it continues to be loud, vigorous, and substantial. U.S. sales of AI-related hardware and software totaled roughly $250 million in 1985, and are growing at some 50 percent per year. The AI market for 1990 has been estimated at anywhere from $3 billion to $12 billion, depending on how broadly one defines AI, with increases continuing at a similar pace beyond that.[2] And not surprisingly, "artificial intelligence" is more of a journalist's buzzword than ever, as a glance at any of the current computer magazines will show.

And yet . . . why did AI suddenly take off when it did? Nothing particularly breathtaking happened in the laboratory. Steady progress, yes. But there weren't any big breakthroughs at the beginning of the eighties to explain the sudden surge of interest. There weren't any sudden theoretical insights that led to new, improved products. The ideas coming to market in the mid-1980s are ten or fifteen years old. Indeed, the boom has, if anything, actually *slowed* progress. Many of the AI researchers themselves remain skeptical of the whole thing, not to mention being annoyed and worried about exaggerated public expectations. At the Xerox Palo Alto Research Center—

better known as Xerox PARC—AI group leader John Seely Brown puts it quite simply: "You've got to separate the science from the hype."

So once again: What happened?

AI IS DISCOVERED

The short answer is that AI got swept up in the larger information-processing revolution. In effect, the field was "discovered" by the rest of the technical community in much the same way that an out-of-the-way restaurant is sometimes discovered by trendy gourmets.

Of course, the discovery of AI didn't just happen by accident. AI researchers had compiled a very credible track record during the seventies. Quite aside from any insights that programs such as Mycin and SHRDLU might have provided about human cognition, they were impressive pieces of software, and they hinted that AI might actually be able to do some useful things. Furthermore, a number of AI researchers had been actively promoting the field. Most notable was Stanford University's Edward Feigenbaum. It was Feigenbaum who coined the term *knowledge engineering* in 1977, and it was Feigenbaum who had taken the lead in arguing for the importance of computers animated by knowledge-based AI. "It's not just the second computer revolution," he proclaims in his book *The Fifth Generation*, coauthored with science writer Pamela McCorduck, "it's the important one."[3]

Feigenbaum and his efforts aside, however, people were also ready to listen. Indeed, the discovery of AI was almost inevitable, given the public mood in the late seventies. It's hard to know what is cause and what is symptom in these things. But for whatever reason, the antitechnology attitude of the sixties was fading, and high-tech was coming back in style. The mood was reflected in such movies as *Star Wars* (1977), and in the flurry of new science magazines, such as *Discover, Science 86,* and *High Technology.* It was made tangible by the dramatic developments in genetic engineering and other forms of biotechnology; by the long-awaited launch of the space shuttle; by the introduction of VCRs, Walkmans, and other consumer-electronics gadgets; and by the latest advances in medical technology. And perhaps most vividly, it was brought home by the advent of the personal computer.

The PC, as all of us are aware by now, produced a revolution all its own—a strangely paradoxical revolution. On the one hand, computers were demystified: Instead of being distant, oracular, almost mythical objects, they were transformed into machines that an ordinary person could actually see and use. Suddenly there were computer stores in the local shopping mall. People could walk in and touch a computer. They could play with the keys and watch things happen on the screen. They could even afford to *buy* a computer and take it home. They could write with it, or sort data with it, or tabulate rows and columns of numbers with it. And they began to get a sense of what these mysterious machines could actually do.

Yet that very familiarity with computers also gave rise to a new mystique. Users began to feel—unconsciously, perhaps, but intensely—that this new machine wasn't *just* a machine. Tap a key and it would respond. Give it a command and it would act. Learn its secrets and it would perform astonishing feats. Many a late-night hacker (and many a daytime business user as well) was captivated by an exhilarating sense of power, control, and, yes, *intimacy* with the computer. He began to glimpse the vision of a new kind of computer that would be more than a tool—that would be an assistant, an adviser, a tutor, and even a friend. As MIT sociologist Sherry Turkle writes in *The Second Self*, the computer is in fact the first psychological machine: "A new mind that is not yet a mind," she calls it, "a new object, betwixt and between, equally shrouded in superstition as well as science."[4]

So it is hardly surprising that the turn of the decade saw a widespread fascination with computers, and with anything related to computers. Likewise, the turn of the decade also brought an increasing fascination with AI—because AI seemed to be the technology that would make this vision of the intimate computer a reality.

The Age of the Entrepreneur

On a more prosaic level, meanwhile, the venture capitalists suddenly had plenty of money to invest and an eager will to invest it. Not only had the capital-gains tax rates been lowered during the Carter administration, thus making venture-capital investments look a lot more attractive than before, but the heady atmosphere of the billion-dollar biotechnology boom in the late seventies had generated a kind of frenzy for high technology in general. Given the burgeoning PC market, computers were especially hot. And, as one of the most far-out and imaginative computer technologies around, so was AI. At one point, in fact, a certain AI laboratory director claims he was getting calls from venture capitalists at least once a month: "Just start your own company," they would say. "All you've got to do is put 'Artificial Intelligence' in the title and we'll give you a blank check."

With blandishments like that, the AI community did not hesitate. They had before them a whole new breed of folk heroes—such as Steve Jobs and Steve Wozniak, who had founded the Apple Computer Company in a Silicon Valley garage in 1976 and almost single-handedly created the whole personal-computer revolution. Established professors and young postdoctoral assistants alike found the prospect irresistible: They, too, might change the world—and in the process make a fortune. "If someone is going to get rich out of the technology developed here," says Raj Reddy, head of Carnegie-Mellon University's Robotics Institute, "it ought to be the people who developed it."[5]

In 1980 Feigenbaum and his Stanford colleagues founded two AI consulting firms, Teknowledge and Intelligenetics, to do custom expert-systems programming and AI training for corporate clients. (Intelligenetics changed its name to Intellicorp in 1983.) Almost simultaneously, a group of researchers from MIT formed Symbolics and Lisp Machines, Incorporated, two companies dedicated to producing specialized computers for AI. And, in 1983, Reddy and his colleagues at Carnegie-Mellon incorporated as the Carnegie Group to pursue markets in expert systems, natural language, and robotics and manufacturing. All in all, forty new companies have been founded to produce AI hardware or software, with a total investment to date on the order of three hundred million dollars. Of course, that's less than a tenth of what has been invested in biotechnology. And it is small change for the oil companies. But for the once-tiny AI community, it seems nothing short of miraculous.

Meanwhile, AI was beginning to attract attention among the Fortune 500 corporations, especially those in aerospace, oil, and electronics. In addition to the well-respected AI group at Xerox PARC, which had been growing since PARC opened its doors in 1970, the turn of the decade saw new groups forming at the Digital Equipment Corporation, at the Schlumberger-Doll Research Center in Ridgefield, Connecticut, at Texas Instruments in Dallas, and at more than a dozen other companies. On top of that, the Fifth Generation projects were getting underway (as I'll discuss in the next chapter). And schools such as the University of Massachusetts and the University of Texas were likewise expanding their involvement in AI, either by creating new AI programs or by expanding existing ones. Thus, the research base suddenly began to extend beyond the traditional Big Three programs at Carnegie-Mellon, Stanford, and MIT.

The upshot was that AI rapidly began to take on the atmosphere of a boomtown. On August 21, 1980, for example, the newly organized American Association for Artificial Intelligence, or AAAI, opened the doors of its first annual meeting at Stanford expecting a few hundred participants at most. The organizers eventually registered nearly a thousand—including some forty reporters and an uncounted number of entrepreneurs and venture capitalists. (As more than one academic was heard to exclaim, not always with delight, "Look at all the suits!") By August 1985, when the AAAI met in conjunction with the International Joint Conference on Artificial Intelligence at UCLA, the attendance was nearly six thousand. The AAAI's fourteen AI tutorial sessions alone drew some twenty-five hundred people.

So perhaps it isn't surprising that the more established members of the AI community didn't just feel discovered. They felt invaded.

Ambivalence Among the Old-Timers

Actually, the AI community has reacted to the AI boom with the same mixed emotions that the owners of a newly discovered restaurant might feel.

On the one hand, the money is nice and the success is gratifying, but on the other hand, the crowds and the noise are annoying, good help is hard to find, and the effort to pander to a fickle public stands to ruin what made the place special in the first place.

"AI is in chaos," said Yale's Roger Schank in a 1983 interview. "The media's been all over us, people are promising that expert systems will solve all our problems, and it's hard to get good workers to work on the fundamental problems, because the companies are snapping them all up. We've lost our momentum."

Granted that Schank is not exactly known for understatement, there was (and is) real cause for concern. Especially in the early days, for example, quite a few of the enthusiasts flocking to AI did seem to think of it as something magic—perhaps a kind of pixie dust that could be sprinkled onto a computer to make it come alive, or else a science-fictional supertechnology that was going to create R2D2 by Thursday morning. Thus, in self-defense, AI researchers have tended to sound slightly schizophrenic when they talk to laymen, as if they were trying to be enthusiasts and wet blankets at the same time. Yes, AI offers unique insights into the inner workings of the mind. Yes, it has extraordinary potential for making machines do smart things—someday. But no, AI is not magic; from a strictly engineering point of view, in fact, it is simply a set of programming techniques. There are certain things it is ready to do, and certain things it is not ready to do. "If you're a skeptic, I want to make you a believer," says Patrick Winston, head of the AI laboratory at MIT, in his talks to lay audiences. "And if you're a believer, I want to make you a skeptic."

Of course, one could always take the attitude that such problems will solve themselves. At a recent AAAI meeting, Carnegie-Mellon's John McDermott, a founding member of the Carnegie Group and a man with considerable experience in implementing commercial expert systems, pointed out that yes, most people do have common sense. "As long as there's some reasonable amount of success," he says, "as long as some fraction of the systems that are attempted turn out to be truly helpful, there's a positive, forward-moving attitude. . . .[In my experience,] the people who had the false expectations will simply become better informed about the nature of AI technology."[6]

Nonetheless, the issue of inflated expectations is still a very real concern for many researchers. As I discuss in the next chapter, programs such as DARPA's Strategic Computing Initiative have put the AI enterprise very far out on a limb; moreover, the boom-bust history of such earlier programs as machine translation is not exactly reassuring. Nor is the memory of a 1972 report on AI prepared for the Science Research Council of the United Kingdom by the distinguished physicist James Lighthill. Writing at a time when AI was just emerging from its "dark ages" of the late sixties, Lighthill was scathing about the apparent lack of progress: "Workers entered the field around 1950, and even around 1960, with high hopes that are very far from being realized in 1972. In no part of the field have the discoveries made so far produced the major impact that was then promised."[7] Indeed, the Lighthill report persuaded Her Majesty's government to make sharp cuts in its support for AI, at least for a time, and very nearly ended the British effort altogether. Certainly it contributed to the dissolution and reorganization of the topflight AI group at the University of Edinburgh, compelling many of Britain's best AI researchers to emigrate to the United States.

The upshot is a certain sense of vulnerability among AI researchers, and a recurring nightmare: One day, when the anticipated miracles haven't materialized on schedule, and when all these enthusiasts begin to realize that AI is a lot harder than they thought, then all the optimism will evaporate, the funding will disappear, and AI will be worse off than ever before. This scenario has been called "AI winter," in analogy to nuclear winter, the period of cold and darkness that scientists now think would follow a nuclear war.[8]

Equally worrisome for many researchers is the impact of the boom on the AI community itself. For one thing, the sudden demand for qualified AI researchers has far outstripped the universities' ability to supply them; all the money in the world can't train a new researcher any faster than he or she can be trained. Indeed, there is a critical manpower shortage at the university level—a condition that AI shares with computer science as a whole—with few new Ph.D.'s being produced each year, and a very high rate of emigration from academia to industry.[9]

Industry, meanwhile, has proved an exhilarating place to work. Instead of the usual academic routine of faculty meetings and teaching, AI-related companies offer the challenge of working on real-world problems and the sense of being on the cutting edge of technology. (They also offer bigger paychecks.) But, ironically, a private company is not always the most conducive place for advancing the frontiers of knowledge. Basic research is a slow, messy, risky affair that is best done in a university setting where the creditors aren't waiting anxiously for a return on their investment. Most of what industrial researchers do comes under the very different heading of "product development"—turning previously demonstrated principles into a product that is fast, easy to use, free of bugs, well documented, targeted to the right market, and equipped with all the features a user needs. The rule of thumb is that this sort of thing takes about ten times as much effort as the first prototype, which means that anyone who gets deeply involved in a company has precious little time for doing the kind of basic research that created AI in the first place.

In fact, it's fair to say that the great AI renaissance of the seventies slowed noticeably as researchers became distracted by the great AI boom of the eighties. "I'm very concerned about the fact that people don't want to do science anymore," said Schank at a recent AAAI meeting. "It is the least appealing job on the market right now. It's easier to go into a start-up company and build products. It's easier to go into a big company and have a little respite and do some contract work. It's easier to do all those things than to go into a university and try to organize an AI lab, which is just as hard to do now as it ever was, and sit there on your own trying to do science. It's difficult. But if we don't do that, we will find that we *are* in the dark ages of AI."[10]

MIT's Marvin Minsky echoes the point: "Why is it that artificial intelligence programs do not learn?" he asks. "The answer is simple: first only half a dozen people have worked on the problem of writing programs that learn, and, second, the problem is hard. . . . [But now] there is no place a good student can work for five years on a hard problem that does not have a near-term industrial payoff. There is no place a young person can work for five or ten years on a really hard problem the way all those Einsteins and Pasteurs did when *they* faced a hard problem."[11]★

Coming of Age

As unsettling as the situation has been, however, not everyone sees it in such apocalyptic terms. Quite the opposite: Many AI researchers argue that the turmoil will actually be healthy in the long run.

"I think that the more applications of AI we can be involved in, the better for our science," said Nils Nilsson, director of the artificial-intelligence group at SRI International, in his 1983 presidential address to the AAAI. "Because then we'll sooner learn our weak spots and be more motivated to support the basic research needed to correct them. . . . As a matter of fact, the departure of applications-oriented people from the universities to businesses may be quite beneficial to AI. It brings those with applications interests into more intensive confrontation with real problems, and it leaves at the universities a higher concentration of people who are mainly interested in developing the basic science of AI."[12]

Clearly, there is plenty of room for argument here. But Nilsson's point is well taken, and, on balance, I have to agree with him. For those living through it, the boom of the 1980s has been disconcerting indeed. But taking the long view, it can be seen as just one more stage in the long metamorphosis of AI. Once a discipline nearly as pure and abstract as philosophy, AI is now becoming more like chemistry or electrical engineering, fields in which a fundamental research effort based in universities provides the underpinning for a commercial industry.

Or, to put it another way, AI is coming of age.

★For what it's worth, by the way, both Schank and Minsky are themselves involved in companies: Schank is the founder and president of Cognitive Systems, Inc., an expert-systems and natural-language company in New Haven, Connecticut; and Minsky is a cofounder of Thinking Machines, Inc., in Cambridge, Massachusetts, which is working to bring the Connection Machine to market.

THE RISE OF KNOWLEDGE-BASED SYSTEMS

The boom wasn't *just* a matter AI being discovered, of course. AI was also ready to be discovered. And nowhere is that more apparent than with expert systems—especially knowledge-based systems. These systems are far and away the most talked-about application of AI. They have also done more than anything else to get the venture capitalists interested in AI.

On the other hand, there is a curious fact about these programs: Despite all the talk one hears about knowledge-based systems, and all the forecasts one hears about how much they will do for us, at mid-decade an ordinary computer user still couldn't walk into the local software store and buy Mycin, or anything like Mycin. Why not?

Actually, there are at least three reasons why not. First, Mycin and its brethren are like most other AI programs: As originally written, they were big, complex, and voracious in their appetite for memory and computation time. Thus, they require big, expensive computers to run on. They are not the sort of thing you can pop into your PC.

Second, you probably wouldn't want to run those programs on your PC anyway. In an academic environment, the emphasis is on basic research; programs are usually written as prototypes to demonstrate a principle, or to test a theory, or to prove that such-and-such a technique will really work. Often, as with Terry Winograd's SHRDLU, programs are written by graduate students as a part of their Ph.D. thesis. Often, they are on the cutting edge of research. But for that very reason, academic programs also tend to be awkward, quirky, and virtually unusable by anyone but the author. They are held together with the software equivalent of string and sealing wax, in much the same way that the first integrated circuit—made by Jack Kilby at Texas Instruments in 1958—looked like random bits of metal and wire pasted to a slab of dirty glass.[13] (Obviously, a great deal of effort in start-up companies goes into polishing these fundamental ideas and turning them into something that a customer might want to pay for.)

Finally, Mycin's prettied-up descendants *are* being produced commercially, and they have been since 1980. But they aren't in the stores because, as of mid-decade, virtually all of them have been custom-made, and virtually all of them have gone into corporate environments.

The First Wave: In-House Systems

There is good reason for that: An industrial-scale expert system can cost more than five hundred thousand dollars to develop, not least because of the extraordinary amount of knowledge and engineering effort required. The *Wall Street Journal* recently told of a programmer from Bolt Beranek and Newman, Inc. (a Cambridge, Massachusetts, consulting firm) who had to attend a naval training school for two months before he was competent to interview a naval expert in boiler repair so that he could write an expert system for training.[14]

Still, it's telling that so many companies *are* making serious investments in knowledge-based systems, which implies that someone in the boardroom thinks these programs are worthwhile. Indeed, the very development of intelligence in a machine means that it has important advantages in a commercial setting.[15]

First, machine intelligence is *consistent, thorough,* and *documentable.* A (current-generation) computer is going to be hopelessly outclassed by humans when it comes to things like creativity, insight, or the ability to bring a wide variety of experience to bear on a problem. People are good at that sort of thing, and computers aren't. On the other hand, a computer won't go around forgetting things because it is tired or irritable. Nor will it have a hidden agenda (except maybe the programmer's). Nor is it easily overwhelmed by data. Consider, for example, the Xcon project at the Digital Equipment Corporation (DEC) in Maynard, Massachusetts.

The first commercially successful expert system, Xcon was designed for DEC by Carnegie-Mellon's John McDermott in 1980.* DEC's problem was its popular VAX minicomputer, which came with enough options and extras to make a new-car salesman blanch. A system typically had 50 to 150 components, many of which were inconsistent with one another or else *required* one another, and getting them straight was turning out to be a major headache for the sales department. No single person had either the time or the knowledge to configure the computers perfectly, which meant that orders had to be checked and rechecked and rechecked again before they were shipped. Xcon's job was to help.

It did. In fact, Xcon has become *the* classic success story in the short history of knowledge-based systems. When McDermott and his colleagues turned over the initial version of Xcon to DEC in January 1980, it had about 850 rules and 450 component descriptions. By the fall of 1984, when McDermott coauthored a retrospective of the first four years, Xcon contained 3,303 rules, had access to 5,481 component descriptions, and was applicable to ten different computer models. "It is difficult now to believe that [Xcon] will ever be done," McDermott writes; "we expect it to continue to grow and evolve for as long as there is a configuration task."[16]

Meanwhile, DEC's in-house Intelligent Systems Technology Group had grown from five people to seventy-seven, and was responsible for seven different knowledge-based systems in addition to Xcon.

The second advantage of machine intelligence is that it is *permanent, easy to duplicate,* and can be made *widely available.*

Humans learn through a long period of study and apprenticeship, which has to begin all over again with every generation. Thus, when an employee

---

*McDermott and his colleagues at Carnegie-Mellon still refer to the program by its original name, R1. The name reputedly comes from a bad joke: "Three years ago I didn't know what a knowledge engineer was. Now I R1."

takes another job, retires, or dies, his knowledge and experience go with him. And by the same token, organizations have to devote a great deal of effort to training new staff whenever they expand their operations.

A knowledge-based system is also subject to a long apprenticeship, of course, especially given primitive state-of-machine learning. Xcon required years of testing and refinement before it could reach a 90 to 95 percent accuracy in configuring the DEC computers, and problems were still being uncovered in its rule set after eighty thousand orders had been processed. (It should be said, however, that 95 percent accuracy is far better than humans can achieve.)

But once a system is in place, it is virtually permanent. Moreover, it can easily be copied, which means that it can be shared throughout the company. A good example is an expert system known either as DELTA (Diesel-Electric Locomotive Troubleshooting Aid) or as CATS-1 (Computer-Aided Trouble-shooting System–1), developed by the General Electric Company of Schenectady, New York. As the name suggests, DELTA/CATS-1 is designed to help GE's maintenance personnel diagnose faulty diesel locomotives. Prior to the initiation of the project in 1981, the company had really only had one expert in this area: senior field service engineer David Smith, who had been with GE for forty years. Thus, GE's only options in diagnosing a faulty engine had been (1) to fly Smith to the locomotive, wherever in the country it might be, or (2) transport the locomotive to Smith. Either way, the process was awkward and expensive.

DELTA/CATS-1 is therefore an explicit attempt to codify Smith's knowledge so that it can be delivered to less experienced maintenance personnel at railroad yards around the country. A team of knowledge engineers began working with Smith in 1981 to develop a feasibility demonstration using forty-five rules. An example: "IF engine-set-idle AND fuel-pressure-below-normal AND fuel-pressure-OK, THEN fuel-system is faulty." By 1984, the system had grown to a production prototype that contained twelve hundred rules and could handle 80 percent of the problems. Meanwhile, the basic expert system had been augmented by a videodisk player that can display diagrams showing where a particular component is located on the locomotive, together with a printer that can produce a hard copy of those diagrams. Moreover, the system had also been coupled with a training film display; once the expert system had diagnosed the fault, it could call up the appropriate film if necessary and show the user exactly how to make the repair. DELTA/CATS-1 is currently being field-tested, and rules are still being added.[17]

Another example of this knowledge-sharing use of expert systems is an application recently announced by Syntelligence, Inc., of Sunnyvale, California. In January 1986 the company entered into agreements with three separate insurance firms to develop knowledge-based advisory systems that would assist their underwriters out in the field. The three insurance firms are the American International Group, the Saint Paul Companies, Inc., and the Fireman's Fund Insurance Companies; their idea is to standardize and improve the way their underwriters make risk assessments when potential clients apply for commercial auto insurance, general liability insurance, or any of several other lines. The payoff, the companies hope, will be fewer mistakes and fewer losses. Thus, when Syntelligence's Underwriting Advisor system is completed, each company will mount a customized version on an in-house IBM mainframe computer, where any of its underwriters can access it through a telephone link with his or her desktop IBM PC. Depending on the needs of the moment, an underwriter can then use the system to help with a quick preliminary risk evaluation of one client, then to make an in-depth detailed assessment of the next client—including a price quote—and so on through the day.[18]

LISP Machines: Tools for the Pros

Once you start to look, suitable domains for knowledge-based systems turn out to be surprisingly abundant: scheduling jobs in a machine shop, diagnosing malfunctions in diesel-electric locomotives, designing factory floor layouts, planning office moves, troubleshooting electronic circuits, adjusting the operating conditions of a power plant to optimize boiler efficiency—to name just a few. By one recent estimate, roughly two hundred major knowledge-based systems are now in use, and perhaps five hundred systems of various sizes are under development.[19]

"It's like walking into a field of gold nuggets just lying on the ground," says one enthusiastic company president. "You can reach down and just pick them up. You don't even have to dig for them. The only problem you face is making sure that you pick up a big one."[20]

However, this rapidly rising demand for knowledge-based systems has only served to aggravate a severe and chronic shortage of qualified knowledge engineers to write them. Thus, one of first priorities of developers in the fledgling industry has been the creation of tools to lighten the load.

Among the earliest and most important of these tools are the so-called LISP machines, or LISP work stations, exceptionally powerful personal computers specialized for developing AI. Originally inspired by the pioneering work on personal computers done at Xerox PARC in the early 1970s and implemented half a decade later by Thomas Knight, Richard Greenblatt, and their colleagues at the MIT AI laboratory, LISP machines now account for about one half of the total market in AI-related products, or some $250 million in 1986. According to one forecast, the market for LISP machines should exceed $1.2 billion in 1990.[21]

To a casual user, a typical LISP work station looks like a bigger version of the Apple Macintosh and Lisa computers: It has the same high-resolution display screen, featuring black letters on a white background; the same overlapping boxes, or "windows," on the screen for viewing multiple pieces of text or graphics simultaneously; and the same hand-held pointing device, or "mouse," for selecting various areas of the screen. Indeed, the resemblance is hardly accidental, since the Macintosh and Lisa were also inspired by the work at Xerox.

Inside, however, a LISP machine's hardware and software are specialized for running LISP programs at high speeds. Moreover, it is equipped with numerous software tools that aid in AI programming, such as sophisticated text editors, graphic displays of frames and the relationships between frames in semantic networks, and multiple windows for inspecting the contents of a knowledge base.

The upshot is that the boom in AI software has been accompanied by a kind of upscale version of the PC boom. Both Symbolics and Lisp Machines, Incorporated—the two MIT spinoffs formed in 1980—are doing well. Xerox markets its own line. Texas Instruments came out with its Explorer model in 1984. Everyone is waiting for IBM to enter the fray. And the list continues to grow. At least fifteen manufacturers are now claiming that their work stations are "AI capable" (although it should be said that not all of them are really optimized to run LISP).

While none of these machines could really be called cheap—in the mideighties a fully configured model retails at anywhere from $50,000 to $100,000—the competitive pressures are bringing the prices down fast, just as in the consumer PC market. And in any case, the cost is still relatively modest compared to the hundreds of thousands of dollars needed to buy a minicomputer, or the millions of dollars needed for one of the big mainframes. Thus these new machines have significantly lowered the cost threshold for people who want to develop AI. At the same time, they are a declaration of independence for the entrepreneurially minded; it's hard to imagine the current wave of start-up companies if the companies didn't have some relatively inexpensive way of developing products on their own machines. Furthermore, LISP work stations offer a delivery vehicle for AI software, a relatively inexpensive way for customers to actually use the programs once they are written.

Expert-System Shells: AI for Everyman

Tools of a more recent vintage are the expert-system "shells," which made their first commercial appearance in 1984, and which quickly became one of the hottest segments of the AI market.

Shells take their inspiration from Emycin (Essential, or Empty, Mycin), which was developed at Stanford in the late 1970s to capitalize on the work that went into the Mycin system. The idea was to carve out the core of domain-specific knowledge—in Mycin's case, the body of rules about infectious diseases—leaving the inference engine and the explanation subsystem as a shell, ready for another knowledge base to be inserted. As one recent brochure proclaims, "You supply the knowledge, we supply the Intelligence!"

The high-end shells are full-featured programs running on LISP machines. They typically include a sophisticated inference engine and software tools to aid in the knowledge-engineering phase, and they are used primarily to streamline the knowledge-engineering process in the kind of institutional environments already mentioned. The Lawrence Livermore Laboratory, for example, is using Intellicorp's Knowledge Engineering Environment, or KEE, to devise an expert system for fine-tuning its mass spectrometer to give optimum performance.

At the low end, meanwhile, a series of shells have recently been developed for personal computers in the IBM PC class. Examples include Texas Instruments' Personal Consultant and Teknowledge's M.1.

Considering the difference in power between PCs and LISP machines, it's not surprising that these PC shell systems tend to be relatively slow and limited. Also, they tend to be rather expensive compared to most other PC software. M.1 sells for five thousand dollars, for example, not including training, and the Personal Consultant goes for three thousand.[22]

Nonetheless, these low-end shells are important because they begin to open up the market in a big way. They drastically lower the cost threshold for noncorporate people who want to get into the game. They allow small entrepreneurial firms with limited capital to start writing knowledge-based systems for the consumer market. And they allow ordinary users to "play back" the expert systems on widely available, inexpensive machines. Nor will these low-end systems necessarily be "toy" systems. The processing power and memory capacity of low-cost PCs are growing rapidly. And it's worth noting that Mycin has only 475 rules, and Puff only 200; useful knowledge-based systems don't necessarily have to be big systems.

Thus, the stage is already being set. Perhaps as early as 1986, according to some analysts, home and office expert systems—and expert-systems shells—really will begin to appear in the stores, and expertise will become a mass-market commodity.

Hidden AI

The consequences of this proliferation of AI software promise to be far-reaching; indeed, I'll spend much of the remainder of this book exploring them. For now, however, it's worth pointing out that expert systems are not the only application of AI, or even necessarily the most important. There's a widespread tendency to assume that nothing will happen with AI until we suddenly see big, flashy systems—robots as sophisticated as C3PO in *Star Wars*, perhaps, or computers as multitalented as the HAL 9000 in *2001* (hopefully without Hal's homicidal tendencies).

Someday, of course, we may very well see such machines; however, it's important to remember that AI per se is not a product. From a strictly engineering standpoint, it is simply a set of useful techniques for programming. In fact, some of the major commercial opportunities for the near future lie in blending those AI techniques with traditional programming methods, making familiar products more and more functional—"smarter," so to speak, easier to use and to deal with. And nowhere is that potential feature more apparent than in the current wave of AI applications to PCs.

AI ON THE PERSONAL COMPUTER

When, in 1984, Apple Computer's then-chairman Steve Jobs advertised his Macintosh as "the computer for the rest of us," he knew what he was doing. Especially in the years before the desktop IBM PC became a corporate status symbol, the PC revolution had a certain subversive quality. The true believers were fired with a conviction that microcomputers would somehow take knowledge—and therefore power—out of the hands of the elite and put it into the hands of the people.

But there's the rub. If you're going to put the power of a computer into the hands of the users, then you need to put more and more intelligence into the machine itself. The real inner landscape of a computer—the bits, the bytes, the data registers, the instruction sets, and so forth—is like an alien planet; it takes a special kind of mind and personality (the "hacker") to be happy there. Most users just want to get some work done, and don't care about all those inner workings. Indeed, the history of computers can be read as one long effort to get the machine to do as much of the dirty work as possible on its own.

For example, such high-level languages as FORTRAN, LISP, BASIC, PASCAL, and many others were invented starting in the 1950s; they allowed programmers to instruct the machine in a reasonably intuitive way, using a language and syntax that resembled English.

In much the same vein, operating systems began to come into their own in the sixties; like an office manager, an operating system takes care of the endless, niggling details of piping data around inside a computer, and is still a standard part of any computer's software environment.

Next, word processors, data-base managers, spreadsheets, and other applications packages began to appear, also in the sixties; they enabled people to actually use a computer without having to program it each time from scratch.

And finally, "user-friendliness" was thrust into the limelight starting in the early eighties, as the advent of microcomputers made it painfully apparent that existing software systems were still incomprehensibly arcane for lay users, and klutzy even for experienced users. (Turn on an IBM PC, for example, and you are presented with an empty screen containing the symbol "A>" in its upper left-hand corner. Now, what are you supposed to do next?) Indeed, much of the progress in the microcomputer world in the last half decade has come from efforts to adapt the hardware and software to the way humans think, and not vice versa. The aim is to minimize keystrokes, to improve the screen layouts for readability, to display data and relationships in natural, "intuitive" ways, to let users choose commands from menus or even just point to what they want, instead of remembering an arbitrary set of codes.

The current state of the art is the visually oriented system used on the LISP machines and made famous in the consumer marketplace by the Apple Lisa and Macintosh computers: on-screen windows, high-resolution graphics, pop-down menus, pictographic icons, and the "mouse" pointing device. By no coincidence, this kind of interface is considerably easier to use than it is to describe, because it tends to bypass the verbal parts of the brain almost entirely. Instead, it makes use of the kind of intuitive hand-eye coordination that we humans are so good at. Furthermore, it engages the user's attention in a very powerful way: One quickly begins to feel that the computer's display screen is not just a display but a little world unto itself, an environment where the windows and graphs are physical objects and the mouse is like a little hand that can nudge things and move them around on the screen.

"As in theater, people who interact with computers quickly form myths to explain and predict the action taking place before them—in this case, on the screen," writes Alan Kay of Apple Computer, who was a leader in developing this system when he was at Xerox PARC in the early 1970s. "In theater, the audience will identify emotionally with what they see, bringing their own experience to bear on the action, and they will then ignore the fact that the story being related is not real. Similarly, if a computer program is scripted to simulate a real action . . . [it] has followed a tradition that antedates the Greeks by setting a scene that successfully shapes and bounds the user's myth."[23]

There is every reason to expect this kind of interface to become a standard on microcomputers. It was made available for the IBM PC by two major software packages introduced in 1985, Digital Research's Gem and Microsoft's Windows. Moreover, in that same year it was a major selling point in two newly introduced PCs, Commodore's Amiga and Atari's 520 ST.

And for that matter, there's every reason to expect the microcomputers of the late eighties—say, in the three-thousand-dollar range—to be at least as powerful as LISP machines are now—which means that the next step is to streamline the user interface even further by incorporating AI techniques.

The HOW-to-WHAT Transition: AI Behind the Screen

In fact, AI-inspired products had already begun to appear on the market by mid-decade. In late 1985, for example, the newly formed Symantec Corporation of Cupertino, California, introduced its Q&A, which is a simple data-base management program that allows the user to retrieve data by typing in such statements as "Show me all the apartments in Springfield with rent less than $1,000." Admittedly, the natural-language function is not very sophisticated in Q&A—at least, in the first release it has a base vocabulary of only five hundred words and a very limited syntax—but then, it doesn't have to be sophisticated to be useful; the sentence just quoted is much easier for the average user to formulate and understand than a command like *@and(location = "Springfield", rent<$1000)*.

Paradox, a more sophisticated data-base manager—released at about the same time by another newborn company called Ansa Software of Belmont, California—doesn't use a natural-language interface. However, it does allow users to retrieve a particular set of data—which may be scattered over several different files—simply by typing in an example of what they want. Paradox will then use AI techniques to synthesize an internal program which finds all the data that matches. In addition, Paradox uses heuristic reasoning to discover the quickest way to retrieve the data. Thus, it is not only simpler to use than older-style data-base programs, which have to be explicitly programmed for data retrieval by the user, but it is often faster.

Whatever success Q&A, Paradox, and their other AI-enhanced brethren finally demonstrate in the marketplace (at this writing, it is still too early to know), they clearly represent important steps in a new direction. Instead of computers that have to be watched over and instructed at every step, blindly executing the instructions they are given and *only* the instructions they are given, AI raises the possibility of programs that interpret their user's intentions and take a certain initiative. As Feigenbaum points out, the difference is neatly captured by the two words *how* and *what:*

> At one extreme of the spectrum, the user supplies his intelligence to instruct the machine with precision exactly HOW to do his job, step-by-step. . . . At the other extreme of the spectrum is the user with his real problem (WHAT he wishes the computer, as his instrument, to do for him). He aspires to communicate WHAT he wants done in a language that is comfortable to him (perhaps English); via communication modes that are convenient for him (including, perhaps, speech or pictures); with some generality, some vagueness, imprecision, even error; without having to lay out in detail all necessary subgoals for adequate performance—with reasonable assurance that he is addressing an intelligent agent that is using knowledge of his world to understand his intent, to fill in his vagueness, to make specific his abstractions, to correct his errors, to discover appropriate subgoals, and ultimately to translate WHAT he really wants done into processing steps that define HOW it shall be done by a real computer.[24]

Not surprisingly, the commercial software houses are hard at work on the next step in this evolution: a class of programs, sometimes known as "software robots," that would act as electronic office assistants. Quietly and invisibly, these programs would wait in the memory of your computer while you worked on something else. But when you needed one, it would come to life at a keystroke. Given an itinerary, for example, a travel-assistant robot

162

would automatically check out flight options in the official airline guide, and then make the appropriate reservations. A secretarial program would sort through the electronic mail piling up inside your computer, putting the most important messages on top and tossing out the junk. And if you wanted to set up a meeting with a certain group of people, your secretarial program could contact *their* secretarial programs, through an electronic data network, and negotiate a meeting time based on a knowledge of your preferences and working habits. A librarian assistant could go research a topic for your upcoming luncheon speech by tapping into an electronic data base such as Nexis or Dialog.

Clearly, there is an abundance of opportunities here; Hewlett-Packard, for example, is reportedly spending some thirty million to fifty million dollars on developing these software robot programs, and it is only one developer among many.[25]

It is not unreasonable to imagine that ultimately, all these abilities could be melded into large-scale software robot programs, and perhaps even real robots: office assistants that could see and talk and think as well as the fictional HAL 9000 or that could even walk as well as C3P0. Perhaps it could even be done by the year 2001. Perhaps. However, you saw in Part I of this book just how difficult the "easy," common-sense things like vision and language can be. So it's important to remember that when we start talking about performance at this level, we aren't talking about IBM PCs anymore—nor LISP machines, nor mainframes, nor anything that anyone knows how to build today.

In fact, we are talking about a whole new class of hardware and software—which brings us to the last, and in many ways the most important, stimulus to the AI boom: Japan and the Fifth Generation.

8

The Fifth Generation

The basic story is familiar enough. In October 1981, officials of Tokyo's Ministry of International Trade and Industry (MITI) announced to the world that they were not going to wait for the next generation of computer technology to evolve on its own. Instead, MITI was launching a coordinated, ten-year, $850 million project—the Fifth Generation project—to *make* it evolve.

Within months, according to the story, their frightened counterparts in the West were scrambling to do likewise, putting together a series of rival projects dedicated to building these new-generation computers first—or at least, not last. After a decade of Japanese triumphs in automobiles, steel, semiconductors, and consumer electronics, no one was inclined to take a new challenge lightly. Indeed, there was a visceral sense among Westerners that much more than computer technology was at stake here, that somehow this new generation was the key to economic and political power. Robert E. Kahn, then head of the information processing office at DARPA, described the competition in its starkest terms: "The nation that dominates this information processing field will possess the keys to world leadership in the twenty-first century."[1]

Familiar or not, however, there is much more to this story than appears on the surface. Not only is the interplay of motives fascinating—the various Fifth Generation projects clearly owe as much to anxiety and ambition as they owe to technology per se—but the projects themselves, whatever their origins, stand to play a critically important role in the way AI and its attendant technologies develop over the coming decade. Because of MITI's vision, these endeavors have acquired a legitimacy—not to mention an urgency—that they never had before. And for the first time, computer professionals have organized themselves to think on a ten-year timescale, to look beyond the next piece of hardware or software, to focus on what it's all *for*.

THE CYCLE OF GENERATIONS

The term *Fifth Generation* was MITI's invention. It arose from the observation that computers have already gone through at least four cycles of development, as defined by the technologies used to build them: the vacuum tubes of the 1940s; the transistors of the late 1950s; the integrated circuits of the

1960s and '70s; and the microprocessors (complete computers on a single chip) in the 1970s and '80s.[2] Gordon Bell, head of the computer sciences division at the National Science Foundation and himself a leading computer designer, has compared this progress to the way in which subatomic particles are accelerated in a cyclotron: Every ten years or so comes an injection of new technology, followed by a series of refinements boosting it to higher and higher levels. In the case of the personal computer, for example, the new technology was the microprocessor, developed at the Intel Corporation in 1971. The refinement cycles included such landmark machines as the Apple II in 1977 and the IBM PC in 1981.[3]

In the process, of course, computers have continued to violate every tenet of common sense by getting smaller, faster, more powerful, and cheaper every year. Moreover, this process shows every sign of continuing into a fifth generation* of technology in the 1990s. Ultra-large-scale integration techniques that allow for microprocessors far more powerful and complex than those of the current generation; microscopic optical components that compute with light instead of electrons; optical storage technologies, analogous to today's compact audio discs, that can access billions of bits of data from a platter the size of your hand . . . the prototypes are already in the laboratory. We can see it coming.

However, this new generation also promises to be something far more than just a continuation of the previous four. As I pointed out in Chapter 5, the limits of microprocessor miniaturization are already in sight (albeit a good distance away); thus, as computer designers continue their quest for the next quantum leap in processing power, they are attempting to break away from the serial, step-by-step von Neumann architecture that has dominated the computer field since the forties, and to devise machines that have thousands or millions of processors operating in parallel. If their efforts succeed—and the early signs are positive—these parallel machines should eventually be able to perform logical implications in AI applications as fast as present-day super-computers now perform arithmetic.

At the same time, of course, we are seeing the emergence of AI techniques to give the machines not just speed but intelligence. Given a thousandfold improvement in hardware performance, the limitations that have plagued AI for thirty years start to evaporate; one can begin to think seriously about machines that perform complex planning, continuous speech understanding, or sophisticated scene analysis in real time. Moreover, just as hardware designers now routinely use specialized software to lay out the

---

*It should be said that many experts count computer generations differently, some counting more and some counting fewer. And in the above-cited article, Bell argues that the whole idea of a computer "generation" is too simplistic, that the evolution actually involves too many different technologies interacting in too many ways for history to be divided up into neat little eras like that. On the other hand, the term *Fifth Generation* has by now taken on a life of its own, which is why I use it here.

components on a new microprocessor—in effect, using one computer to design a new computer—AI techniques promise to help automate the process of designing the Fifth Generation machines. Similar techniques are also being developed to automate the programming process. In short, with AI the new generation could lift itself up by its bootstraps.

Finally, if we assume that these new machines follow the same cost curves followed by previous generations, then it's not too hard to imagine them becoming mass-market items like the personal computers of today. As Feigenbaum and McCorduck write in *The Fifth Generation*:

> This new generation of computers will be more powerful than any other the world has seen—indeed, by orders of magnitude. But their real power will lie not in their processing speed, but in their capacity to reason. . . . These new computers, which users will be able to speak with in everyday conversational language, or show pictures to, or transmit messages to by keyboard or handwriting, [will] penetrate every level of society. They will assume no special expertise or knowledge of arcane programming languages. They will not even require the user to be very specific about his needs, because they will have reasoning power, and will be able to tease out from the user, by questioning and suggestions, just exactly what it is the user wants to do or know. Finally, these new machines will be inexpensive enough and reliable enough to be used everywhere, in offices, factories, restaurants, shops, farms, fisheries, and of course, homes.[4]

Thus, the Fifth Generation promises to fulfill the vision described in the last chapter—the idea of a computer that is not just a tool but an assistant, an adviser, a tutor, and even a friend. Indeed, for many people this vision of the fifth generation has taken on transcendental dimensions, as when Feigenbaum and McCorduck mention the "revolution, transformation, and salvation" to be accomplished by computers.[5]

First, however, we have to get there, which brings us back to more worldly matters—such as the question of why Japan was able to mobilize for the new generation long before anyone in the West.

A Paradox

To see why it happened this way, recall the distinction made in the last chapter between basic research, applications-oriented research, and product development, a distinction that can be made for other technological efforts just as well as it can be made for AI. (The boundaries are admittedly quite fuzzy, but for our purposes that won't matter.) Now, the innocent-sounding question is this: How is each kind of research organized, and who pays for it?

In two of the three cases, the answer is straightforward. Basic research, which is the quest after knowledge for its own sake, is by and large supported

166

by governments, universities, and private foundations; the payoffs, if any, are simply too far in the future, and the results too uncertain, for private industry to justify the expense. A classic example is quantum theory, which was developed by academic physicists in the mid-1920s to explain the behavior of atoms. In time, it was used to illuminate the properties of solid matter, including an odd class of materials called semiconductors. That theory of solids, in turn, led directly to the development of the transistor by William Shockley, John Bardeen, and Walter Brittain at Bell Laboratories—but only in 1948, twenty years after quantum theory was invented.

In any case, this longtime horizon means that most basic research is conducted not in industrial laboratories but at universities and at national facilities such as the Fermi National Accelerator Laboratory and Kitt Peak National Observatory. (Among the exceptions that prove the rule are the basic research programs conducted at corporate laboratories such as Xerox PARC, IBM's Thomas J. Watson, Sr., Research Center, and AT&T's Bell Laboratories; these are *very* large corporations.) Furthermore, since basic research is unpredictable by its very nature—if the scientists knew what they were going to find, they wouldn't have to look—basic research programs also tend to be relatively undirected. The idea is to get as many people as possible to explore as many ideas as possible.

Product development, however, is just the inverse: It is focused and looks to the short run—a few years at most—and it is almost entirely conducted by the companies who plan to sell that product. (As I've mentioned, product development is a big preoccupation at many of the AI start-up companies.)

Between basic research and product development, however, there lies the vast gray area of applications research, in which fundamental principles are shaped into working devices. This is sometimes called "generic" technology development, because the results can be applied to any number of final products. One example is the development of fabrication techniques for microelectronics: The same technique can produce microchips that are subsequently used in products ranging from personal computers to hand-held calculators to high-performance supercomputers.

Actually, the boundary is fuzzy enough that much of what the universities and national laboratories do could easily be classified as generic technology. But the bulk of it is nonetheless done in the private sector. And therein lies the problem. Even though generic technology development tends to be much more focused than knowledge-for-its-own-sake basic research, it is still chancy. IBM, for one, spent more than a decade trying to develop a new kind of high-speed electronic device known as the Josephson junction before finally abandoning it as uneconomical in 1983; at that point, the project was costing $250 million a year. High-technology companies are thus caught in a classic dilemma: They have to stay at the cutting edge of technology to stay alive—that's what high-tech means—and yet the faster the pace of technological

167

development and the fiercer the competition, the less they can afford to invest in an expensive dead end.

Nor is it just a matter of expense. More subtle, but just as important, is the critical-mass effect: Good research demands a good research team. And unfortunately, there are only so many top-rate researchers to go around, which means that a duplication of effort among too many competing companies weakens everyone. By the same token, commercial success of one technology often depends on the simultaneous development of other technologies. Personal computers, for example, required not only the microprocessor but also cathode-ray tube display screens, floppy disk drives for data storage, and some sophisticated word-processing and spreadsheet software for getting useful work done. So a company can either focus its efforts on one technology and hope that someone else develops the others—an approach that increases the risk of failure—or it can try to be like IBM and do everything itself, thereby vastly increasing the expense.

Then, too, who wants to invest all that time and energy when it's so difficult to reap the benefits? It's just too easy for competitors to sit back and let you take the risks, and then cash in later with a copycat product.

Thus we have the high-technology paradox: The more fiercely competitive these industries become, and the more cutthroat the marketplace, the more important it is that rival companies cooperate.

MITI LAUNCHES THE FIFTH GENERATION

The Japanese understand the copycat dynamic very well; it's often been said that their economy is an example of the copycat philosophy as practiced on a global scale.

There is some justice to that accusation. The genius of Japanese industry lies in marketing and in product development, as a glance at any American parking lot will show. But Japan has never been very strong in fundamental innovation per se. Rather, the social system has always encouraged people to be team players, to respect established authority, to make decisions by consensus. At the same time, the Japanese government, which places great emphasis on commercial prowess as an emplem of national prestige and eminence, has tended to be very uncomfortable about funding "impractical" long-range basic research. The upshot is that relatively little basic research is done in Japan, even at the universities; the Western nations are acknowledged to be far stronger in that regard.[6]

Instead, Japanese companies have seized the lead in such areas as automobile manufacture and consumer electronics by drawing upon technologies developed in the United States and Europe, and then putting the pieces together more beautifully and inexpensively than anyone else—a phenomenon that has inspired no end of exasperation and soul-searching on this side of the

Pacific. Indeed, even as I am writing this book, American semiconductor manufacturers are demanding that something be done about the flood of bargain computer chips from Japan.

In all fairness, however, the Japanese have also demonstrated a clear understanding of the critical-mass problem and its implications for cooperation on a national scale. MITI is in fact the very embodiment of that concept, with a long tradition of persuading, cajoling, and occasionally threatening individual corporations to coordinate their efforts for the benefit of all. Moreover, since MITI officials are held accountable for the general health of the nation's trade and industry, they characteristically take the long view. In the late 1960s, for example, as Japanese wages rose toward Western levels, MITI officials tried to divert the nation's resources toward industries that were capital-intensive rather than labor-intensive; after the oil shock of 1973, they greatly accelerated their plans to move Japan into service- and knowledge-intensive industries as opposed to energy-intensive ones.[7] And toward the end of that decade, they began a broad effort to envision the information society of the 1990s, and to identify the research and development that Japan would need to make the transition.

Thus, the Fifth Generation project. It was no isolated event; the Japanese information-processing effort would ultimately extend from semiconductor development to high-speed numerical supercomputers; moreover, the interested parties in the Japanese government would include not only MITI but the Ministry of Health and Welfare, the Economic Planning Agency, and the Ministry of Posts and Telecommunications.[8] Nonetheless, the Fifth Generation project was seen as something special from the beginning—for two reasons. First, as the concept began to evolve through an ever more elaborate series of study groups and task forces, MITI's study teams began to realize that intelligent, user-friendly computers offered a way of meeting certain societal needs within Japan. As described in a 1983 essay by the late professor Tohru Moto-oka of the University of Tokyo, the four most urgent needs are:

1. *The enhancement of productivity in service industries.* "Japan's reputation for productivity and efficiency notwithstanding, the country is suffering from a severe bottleneck in its service industries," Moto-oka writes. "[An example] is the price of a dinner at a good Tokyo restaurant, which can easily cost as much as four electronic calculators."

2. *The conservation of natural resources and energy through optimal energy conversion.* Japan, of course, is very limited in its natural resources and is dependent upon imports for almost everything. But with new-generation computers optimizing the operation of factories, buildings, and power plants on a minute-to-minute basis, Japan could get the most out of every drop of imported oil and every ounce of imported scrap iron.

3. *The establishment of medical, educational, and other types of support systems for solving such complex social problems as the transition to a society made up largely of the elderly.* Beginning in the 1990s, an increasing fraction of Japan's population

169

will be over sixty-five (as will an increasing fraction of Western populations), which means that medical and welfare costs will be increasing just as the active labor force is decreasing; Fifth Generation systems, however, can potentially streamline health care and help the physically handicapped to become more active.

4. *The fostering of international cooperation through the machine translation of languages.* This is not quite as idealistic as it sounds. Not only do the Japanese feel a certain sense of isolation from the West because of the language barrier, but as a major trading power they have a strong interest in effective communication with their foreign markets.[9]

The second reason for promoting the Fifth Generation project is less specific but no less important. The Japanese, as it will surprise no one to learn, are very competitive and enjoy being the best in whatever they do. So the project is seen as a way of catching up with the Americans, who have had a commanding lead in computers and commercial AI. Moreover, at the urging of some of the younger researchers within MITI, it was decided that the Fifth Generation project would be an experiment: For once, the Japanese were going to manage an innovative research-and-development program on their own— and for once, they were not going to be copycats.

The project made its official world debut in October 1981 in Tokyo, at the First International Conference on Fifth Generation Computer Systems. To Feigenbaum, one of the seventy-some Westerners present, the meeting seemed to be as much a ceremony as a science conference, a capstone to three years of Japanese consensus-building. As he listened to the speakers talk about Japan's taking its rightful place as a world leader, shedding its copycat image, and claiming a role as a revolutionary innovator in high technology, Feigenbaum had the sudden and irrepressible feeling that he was at a kind of bar mitzvah: The Japanese computer industry seemed to be saying to the world, "Today, I am a man."[10]

That self-confidence was reflected in the technical plan of the project, which was well thought out and extremely ambitious. In the meeting's keynote address, Moto-oka, a prime mover of the project, and chairman of the MITI committee that had drafted the plan, listed twenty-six "research-and-development themes" that had been deemed desirable for inclusion. These ranged from an advanced natural-language machine capable of translating Japanese text into English and back again, to a system for playing the game of Go.[11] However, the core of the effort lay in the development of three modules designed to perform the basic functions of AI: a problem-solving/inference system at least a thousand times faster than current machines; a knowledge-base management system able to tap knowledge bases as large and varied as the *Encyclopedia Britannica*; and an intelligent interface system, corresponding roughly to the explanation facility of a present-day expert system, able to read the written word, to understand pictures, and to converse with human operators in a natural way.

To achieve these goals by the 1990s, Moto-oka and his committee devised a schedule divided into three phases of three or four years each. During the first phase MITI would spend some $45 million on learning how to build serial AI processors analogous to U.S. LISP machines. With that groundwork laid, the investments would then rise sharply in the second two phases, as researchers began the development of parallel AI machines. With matching contributions from Japan's burgeoning electronics industry—MITI had lined up eight industrial partners for the project—the total investment would come to roughly $850 million over the full ten years.

In keeping with the project's coming-of-age agenda, meanwhile, MITI organized it in a manner that was unique for Japan. Instead of simply coordinating what the individual companies were doing, which is its usual practice, MITI formed the Institute for New Generation Computer Technology, or ICOT, a central research laboratory to be staffed by top researchers from each of the eight industrial sponsors. Much of the work would be contracted out to the industrial partners, but the ICOT researchers would be the brain trust. Working together, *they* would design the Fifth Generation. Moreover, the laboratory's director was to be Kazuhiro Fuchi, the former director of MITI's electrotechnical laboratory and himself one of the principal architects of the project. Known as a man who places a high value on youth and innovation, Fuchi is not afraid to go against the grain of Japanese tradition. By the time ICOT officially opened its doors in April 1982, it had forty-two researchers—many of them under thirty, most of them under thirty-five, and all of them hand-picked by Fuchi. In his words, "Young people have fewer fixed ideas."[12]

THE UNITED STATES AND EUROPE ARE GALVANIZED

American and European observers at the Fifth Generation conference came home in an exceedingly somber frame of mind. It wasn't that MITI's new project was a surprise, exactly. Moto-oka's committee reports had circulated widely in the West. Moreover, during the planning phases of the project, many of the top American and European researchers had visited Tokyo at MITI's invitation, to lecture and to share ideas. "For eight or nine hours a day I was flaming forth," recalls Gerald Sussman of MIT, who spent three days in Japan in November 1979. "All their distinguished scientists were there. They had clearly read everything I had ever written and had Japanese translations of my papers in front of them. They were very smart, very well prepared, and they kept their mouths shut."[13]

No, the disturbing thing was that Moto-oka, Fuchi, and their colleagues had taken those ideas—occasionally verbatim—and then forged them into a clearly defined, almost visionary goal. They had produced a cogent and plausible strategy for getting to that goal. And most important of all, they had organized themselves to carry out that strategy, and they were starting to move.

MCC: The American Response

The Fifth Generation announcement struck an especially sensitive nerve in the United States. On this side of the Pacific, it came across as a statement of sublime self-confidence from Japan, Incorporated. It was small comfort that American companies were way ahead of Japan in computers; twenty years ago American companies were way ahead of Japan in automobiles, too.

Feigenbaum, who had been trying for years to convince people of the importance of expert systems—in 1979 he spent twelve weeks convincing the Japanese—now became one of the most vocal proponents of an American response to Japan. *The Fifth Generation* is essentially a 275-page call to arms. Nor was Feigenbaum alone. Experts might quibble about the feasibility of the Japanese project, or its timetable, or the ability of Fuchi's young Turks to be as innovative as they seemed to think they could be. The fact was that we had nothing like it. American and European research into the new-generation technologies was fragmented among some forty universities and thirty corporations. And if Fuchi's team could achieve even a fraction of their goals, they could gain a decisive competitive advantage by the 1990s.

On February 19, 1982, only four months after the Fifth Generation announcement, executives from eighteen computer firms gathered in Orlando, Florida, at the invitation of William C. Norris, then chairman and chief executive officer of the Control Data Corporation in Minneapolis. Always something of a visionary in the computer community, the seventy-year-old Norris had long been an advocate of cooperative research as an antidote to America's declining competitive edge; now, with the Japanese example serving as a catalyst, he renewed the call. The United States needed the functional equivalent of MITI, he said—a consortium of computer and electronics companies that would pool their resources and develop the next generation jointly.

No one pretended that it was going to be easy, least of all Norris. He had already been calling for an end to what he called the computer industry's "shameful and needless duplication of effort" since the early 1970s, with little success. Competitive attitudes die hard; every company's first instinct is to keep things to itself, especially where its rivals are involved. And reinforcing those attitudes were the federal antitrust laws. Says one observer, "Some firms were concerned that if they even sat down to discuss R and D, somebody would say, 'Yeah, but how do you know they're not out there in the closet fixing prices?' "[14]

On the other hand, it was clear to the Orlando participants—as it was to virtually everyone else in the U.S. business community—that something had to be done about the Japanese challenge. And it was equally clear that they were going to have to do it themselves. The federal government had never established an American MITI, and despite the election-year calls for a national "industrial policy," it seemed unlikely to do so anytime soon. Indeed, the U.S. policy was (and is) almost exactly the opposite of Japan's: Washington had poured basic-research money into the universities and the national laboratories ever since World War II, and in the process had created the largest and most productive scientific community in the world. And yet, with a few exceptions, such as NASA's work on aircraft design, the federal government had done relatively little to help the private sector put that basic research to practical use. The prevailing attitude—which long predated the Reagan administration, by the way—was "Why should the taxpayers be paying for something that industry ought to be doing for itself?"★

Thus, Norris's audience was receptive. The Orlando meeting was followed by nearly a year of task forces, organizational meetings, and earnest discussions with the Justice Department. In December 1982, a major obstacle fell by the wayside when a letter arrived stating that the antitrust division would *not* contest a joint research project. And in January 1983 the Microelectronics and Computer Technology Corporation (MCC) was officially launched, with Admiral Bobby Inman, former deputy director of the CIA, as chief executive officer.

Of course, talking about a nationwide project is one thing, and making it happen is something else again. The consortium was fortunate in its choice of Inman, who has been described by the *Washington Post* as "a superb politician with an ability to implement an agenda."[15] Nonetheless, MCC had to spend much of its first eighteen months just getting located and building a staff. Early in the game, for example, Inman and the MCC board startled quite a few people by their decision not to locate near Carnegie-Mellon, MIT, or Stanford, the big three in computer science. "We would clearly have had to pay a premium for being there," Inman explained shortly thereafter, "and it was a conscious decision by the board that we were ultimately better off in a long-term building process if we could find the right climate and place at the next level, but still with a very established base of computer science and electrical engineering."

Austin won the nod—after a frantic competition among communities all over the country—in part because local backers had assembled a sizable package of financial incentives, and in part because Inman and the MCC board were impressed by the state's commitment to high technology. "Their sense was that for the first one hundred years cotton and cattle had been the basis of the state's economy," said Inman. "For the next fifty years it was oil and gas, and that was finite. And now it was time to invest in the long-term future."[16]

★Actually, that attitude seems to apply only to nonmilitary research and development; federal support of defense-related applications has been lavish indeed, and has increased sharply under Reagan.

Not the least of Austin's attractions was the University of Texas, which promised Inman that it would pour a good fraction of the income from its two-billion-dollar oil-lands endowment into the computer-related departments.

And then there was the matter of hiring. Inman surprised and annoyed many of the member companies by refusing to accept many of the researchers they were trying to dump on him. "I don't want to run a turkey farm," he declared. He held out for, and got, topflight talent. Indeed, much of the MCC staff was eventually hired from outside. The payoff was an excellent research team, including such rising stars as Stanford's Douglas Lenat. But the drawback was a long delay in putting that team together. Some parts of MCC's research program didn't really get underway until the autumn of 1984.

Today, however, MCC has nineteen member corporations, more than four hundred employees, and a new laboratory building adjacent to the University of Texas campus in Austin. Researchers there will give out only the sketchiest details of their work, since the projects are proprietary, but in general the organizational structure is strongly reminiscent of ICOT: a central laboratory staffed largely with personnel from the participating companies. On the other hand, MCC's agenda is considerably more ambitious than Fuchi's. In addition to its ten-year program in advanced computer architectures—which encompasses parallel processing, data-base management, human-factors technology, and AI; and which is the most directly analogous to what ICOT is doing—the MCC also has major programs in semiconductor packaging, software-productivity improvement, and computer-aided design technology. (Virtually the only major area it doesn't address is research on semiconductors per se, which is being left to the Semiconductor Research Corporation, another newly formed consortium operating quietly in North Carolina's Research Triangle Park near Raleigh.) Moreover, MCC is conducting almost all of its research in the central facility, whereas ICOT contracts out much of its work to the member companies—which is why MCC has nearly ten times as many employees as Fuchi.

The reports so far indicate that the MCC experiment has been doing even better than its planners originally hoped. In late 1985, well ahead of schedule, the laboratory began to transfer the first samples of its handiwork back to the sponsoring companies. One sample was an experimental expert-system shell known as Proteus; another was a software system to help in the design of new microelectronics chips. Meanwhile, the AI group has embarked on a long-term effort to construct a knowledge base large enough to encompass ordinary "common sense"; by one estimate, its capacity would be roughly one hundred billion bits of information, equivalent to encoding the contents of more than ten thousand average books.[17]

Of course, a good start is still only a start. "MCC is a direct response to the Japanese success," said Inman not long after operations began in Austin. "[But] I have worked very hard to articulate the basic principle I'm going to

174

use in governing MCC—we are not an anti-Japanese organization. We are a procompetition U.S. initiative, primed to keep a technological lead."[18]

Alvey and ESPRIT: The European Response

In Europe, meanwhile, government officials and leaders in the computer industry were responding to the Japanese challenge in much the same way as their colleagues in the United States—and for much more modest reasons. They weren't trying to hold onto a lead. They were simply trying to stay in the game.

The fundamental problem for the Europeans was a fragmented market, exacerbated by long-standing political and economic rivalries between nations. As a result, the European companies were slipping badly at a time when computer sales worldwide were booming. "Only 40 percent of the European domestic market and 10 percent of the world market in information technology are held by European industry," states Horst Nasko, vice president for research at West Germany's Nixdorf Computer company, in a 1983 review. "Most European companies are financially weak compared with the Japanese and American competitors; their information-technology products are not yet a major source of profits. The result is a negative balance of trade for Europe in this sector. In addition, studies show a negative balance of patents—evidence that European industry is losing the race to create a strong technology base for itself. . . . [It is] increasingly dependent on foreign technology from competing companies."[19]

In their attempts to arrest this slippage, officials of the European Economic Community—the EEC, or Common Market—and of the various member states have evolved what is in effect a two-tier program: a set of projects analogous to ICOT and the MCC at the national level, and a complementary, overarching program known as ESPRIT at the EEC level.

Of the national efforts, the earliest and most notable is the so-called Alvey program in the United Kingdom. Named for John Alvey, director of research for British Telecom and the chairman of its founding committee, the program is quite explicitly a response to Japan. Britain's delegation to the October 1981 symposium in Tokyo, a team of government officials and academics led by the head of the information-technology division of the Department of Industry, had returned home in exactly the same state of agitation as their American counterparts, and with exactly the same determination that the challenge had to be answered. A national conference of information-technology experts was hurriedly called in January 1982, leading directly to the establishment of the twelve-person Alvey committee, which included representatives from the major British computer companies, several members from the Ministry of Defence and the Science and Engineering Research Council, and one eminent academic.

The committee's report, recommending a five-year cooperative program of research involving all sectors of the British information-technology field, was released eight months later, to wide acclaim in industry and academia. Prime Minister Margaret Thatcher's Conservative government, after an initially cool reaction, accordingly bent its free-market principles and approved the plan in April 1983. The one concession the cabinet demanded—and won—was that the industrial partners in the program bear half the cost, instead of the 10 percent originally recommended by the Alvey committee.[20–21]

By no coincidence, the substance of the Alvey program is similar to that of ICOT and MCC. Research is to be concentrated in five major areas:

- Software engineering, which seeks to develop methods for enhancing the productivity of programmers.
- Very Large-Scale Integration (VLSI) research, which will improve the design and fabrication of microscopic circuits on silicon.
- The man-machine interface, which will include research into speech recognition and speech generation, image processing, and display technology.
- Intelligent knowledge-based systems, which encompass many of the core activities in AI, including expert systems, natural-language understanding, and computer vision.
- Computer-systems architecture, which includes research into parallel processing, and which was added to the program in 1984.

The organization of the Alvey program, however, is quite different from that of either ICOT or MCC. There is no central laboratory, for example; the overall program is coordinated by a small directorate within the Department of Trade and Industry, under the leadership of Brian W. Oakley, while the actual research is carried out by groups of researchers in industry, academia, and the government laboratories. By the end of 1985, virtually all of the £350 million approved for the Alvey program was committed, and officials had begun to explore the feasibility of an "After Alvey program."

Meanwhile, at the multinational level, EEC officials were struggling to create the European Strategic Programme on Research in Information Technology—ESPRIT.

By all accounts, the driving force behind ESPRIT has been Etienne Davignon, vice president of the Commission of European Communities in charge of the directorates of research and science, industry and trade, and energy. Davignon sensed the importance of advanced information-processing technology—and the Continent's deteriorating position in that area—quite early. Indeed, he brought the chairmen of Europe's twelve leading information-technology companies to a roundtable discussion on the topic in mid-1981, months before MITI announced the Fifth Generation project. If the European information-technology industries ever intended to reach technological parity with the United States and Japan, he told them, they would have to develop a strategy for cooperative research and development; the alternative was to abandon their position in high technology altogether.[22]

Like their counterparts at William Norris's meeting in Orlando a few months later, the attendees at Davignon's roundtable were ready to listen. In due course they appointed a steering committee to devise a plan of action. The steering committee gave rise, in turn, to panels of experts from the twelve major industrial partners; together they developed the outline for the program that was to become ESPRIT: a five-year, $1.3 billion project to be funded fifty-fifty by the commission and by industry.

The ESPRIT plan emphasized five strategic areas:

- Advanced microelectronics, including VLSI.
- Software technology.
- Advanced information processing, including knowledge engineering and other AI-related endeavors.
- Office automation, with special emphasis on computer networking and data-base management.
- Computer-integrated manufacturing, looking toward the totally automated factory.

Like Alvey, and unlike ICOT and the MCC, the ESPRIT program was to function only as a central agency for coordinating and funding the research. The work itself would be done in the laboratories of the participating members. To ensure a cooperative spirit, however, any proposal for an ESPRIT grant would have to involve at least two companies from at least two separate EEC countries.

While this plan had its rough edges, it was undeniably acceptable to industry; a one-year pilot phase for ESPRIT, launched in mid-1983 with a budget of twenty million dollars, drew more than two hundred proposals, of which only thirty-six could be selected for funding. EEC officials pronounced themselves "pleasantly surprised"—not only that so many companies responded but that so many of them were willing to let their scientists work with potential rivals.

Money, however, was not the only reason that the companies were so responsive to ESPRIT, or even the most important reason. Ultimately, ESPRIT was seen as a catalyst that would help unify and rationalize the European microelectronics industry. Adopting common standards, for example, would ensure that a computer made in Germany could also work in the United Kingdom. Coordinated marketing strategies between companies in different countries would help turn Europe into a single, homogeneous marketplace, instead of a patchwork of relatively small national markets. The result, hopefully, would be a much stronger industry overall.

Unfortunately, trying to get the European bureaucracy to agree on anything is an arduous process. The one-year pilot program, for example, was not launched until two years after Davignon's 1981 roundtable. In mid-1983, three of Europe's largest mainframe-computer manufacturers—Siemans of West Germany, International Computers Limited of the United Kingdom, and Bull of France—set up an AI research center of their own in Munich; the move was widely interpreted as a hedge against the collapse of the ESPRIT effort.

Then, in December 1983, when hopes were high that the full-scale ESPRIT project would finally be endorsed at a meeting of EEC heads of state in Athens, the conclave bogged down in bickering over the efficiency of French farming and reform of the EEC's budgetary procedures. Nothing was endorsed. Davignon responded by announcing that he considered ESPRIT to be the EEC commission's top research priority; if need be, he would carve the required funds out of other projects, such as nuclear energy or magnetic-fusion research. So, after considerable debate and skirmishing, the member states took him up on it. Davignon would somehow have to cut $100 million out of his total research budget of $600 million. But ESPRIT was finally approved in early March 1984, and has been more or less on course ever since.

DARPA AND STRATEGIC COMPUTING

Finally, back in Washington, DARPA was getting underway with its one-billion-dollar Strategic Computing program, one of the biggest, most ambitious, and most exciting of all the Fifth Generation projects. It is also the program that has the greatest potential impact on AI and the American computer community in general. It is the only project of its kind whose goals are explicitly military. And it is probably the best case study of the political machinations that inevitably accompany such an effort.

Technology Push and Technology Pull

According to Robert Kahn, then head of DARPA's Information Processing Techniques Office and now president of a start-up firm known as the Corporation for National Research Initiatives, the program originated as a logical outgrowth of the agency's twenty years of being the major U.S. funding source for AI and computer science in general. "We'd gotten to the point where developing the technology would take much more money than we had available in the basic research program," he says. "What we also needed to do—and what Strategic Computing would allow us to do—was to branch out of the university labs and get industry involved.

"When Bob [former DARPA director Robert S. Cooper] arrived in 1981," says Kahn, "he and [Undersecretary of Defense for Research and Engineering Richard D.] DeLauer got behind the idea. And once the decision was made in the spring of 1982 to go forward with it seriously, they took a key role."

While Kahn maintains that Strategic Computing was not a response to Japan—given DARPA's long support for AI in the United States, he says, "in some ways, the Fifth Generation was a response to us"—the MITI program certainly helped give the idea legitimacy. Not the least of DARPA's problems in selling the program was convincing the Pentagon brass. They were used to spending big money on aerospace and ordinance research, but to many of them the idea of smart computers sounded a little flaky.

Helped by the pressure from Japan, however, Cooper and DeLauer proved persuasive, and in January 1983 the first request for funding arrived on Capitol Hill. Congress was also willing to go along, provided only that DARPA prepare a detailed program plan before spending any money. That plan, prepared in consultation with researchers in the AI community, was submitted to Congress in October 1983, where it was quickly approved.[23] It was ambitious, to say the least.

Central to DARPA's strategy was its attempt to simultaneously push and pull the technology. "Pull," in this case, meant specifying three major demonstration projects, to be completed by the end of the ten-year time period, and then letting that set of goals serve as a kind of engine that would draw the other technologies behind it. The three:

- The *autonomous land vehicle,* a robot rover that could be employed for such missions as deep-penetration reconnaissance, rear-area resupply, ammunition handling, and weapons delivery. The early versions would have wheels and move only on roadways; the later versions might have mechanical legs, like a huge insect. DARPA's ten-year goal was a vehicle capable of navigating over rugged terrain at ten kilometers per hour (a slow jog), while avoiding obstacles and taking advantage of available cover.

- The *pilot's associate,* a kind of R2D2 built into a bomber or a jet fighter to help with routine chores of controlling the aircraft, leaving the pilot to focus his attention on, say, his bombing run. In some circumstances, such as an enemy attack on the aircraft, the associate might also take on a more demanding role. It turns out that a jet fighter, with its large control surfaces, is technically capable of outmaneuvering an interceptor missile—except that the accelerations involved will make a human pilot black out. In such a crisis the pilot's associate could take over, evade the missile, and fly its unconscious master to safety.

- The *naval carrier group battle-management system,* an outgrowth of DARPA's previous experiments with expert systems and advanced display technology on board the U.S.S. *Carl Vinson.* In operation the battle-management system would display a detailed picture of the battle area, including the enemy order of battle (surface, air, and subsurface), our own force disposition, the electronic-warfare environment, the strike plan, and weather forecasts. It would also generate hypotheses about the enemy's possible intentions and rank them according to their likelihood. Using ultrarapid, rule-based simulation, it would then advise the admiral and his staff as to the likely outcome of each potential course of action. Finally, once a course of action had been selected, the battle-management system would prepare and disseminate the operating plan throughout the fleet—monitoring the outcome so as to modify and improve its expertise for the next time.

By no coincidence, DARPA's plan had one application for each of the three services, although to make sure that all the services paid attention to all the projects, the agency did emphasize that the applications could be reshuffled at any time. For example, it might turn out to be more useful to have an autonomous underwater vehicle, or a land/air battle-management system. (In fact, a land/air system *was* added to the program in 1985.)

In any case, once the applications were specified, the requirements for all the supporting technologies followed naturally, as per the "pull" philosophy. In particular, knowledge-based systems technology would clearly be a critical element in all three applications. Thus the Strategic Computing plan called for completion by 1992 of multiple cooperating expert systems firing ten thousand to twenty thousand rules per second—that is, several orders of magnitude faster than today's top speed for a single expert system.

Image understanding, by contrast, would be most closely tied to the autonomous vehicle, which was required to operate in rugged and unpredictable terrain; in this case, DARPA wanted systems that could do reconnaissance in a dynamically changing environment, while recognizing both targets and threats—again, to be completed by 1992.

The speech-understanding requirements fell into two basic classes. For the high-noise/high-stress environments of a fighter aircraft, where accelerations and/or tension might alter the pilot's voice, DARPA wanted the pilot's associate to understand a two-hundred-word vocabulary, usable by any speaker, by 1990. In a low-noise/low-stress environment of the battle-management system, however, DARPA wanted something closer to human-level language ability: a ten-thousand-word vocabulary, spoken in natural grammar, and usable by any speaker, by 1992.

Next, with the AI requirements set, it logically followed that DARPA would need certain kinds of computers. Achieving the required level of performance with expert systems and natural language, for example, would mean building ultra-high-speed symbolic processors. On the other hand, doing real-time image processing in the first stages of vision would mean building special-purpose signal processors capable of roughly a trillion calculations per second, which is roughly a thousand times faster than current-generation supercomputers. And, of course, these signal processors would have to be light enough, rugged enough, and compact enough to fit inside a highly mobile vehicle.

Finally, once DARPA knew what kind of computers it wanted, it knew what kind of microelectronics it would require. The plan called for such features as high-density memory storage, and advanced development work on microelectronics made of gallium arsenide, which is faster and more radiation resistant than silicon.

Voices of Outrage

The AI community as a whole reacted positively to the Strategic Computing program, or at least to the concept. As Yale's Roger Schank said at the time, "It's critically important for the country to try to mount some kind of communal effort to develop computer technology." However, a vocal minority reacted very differently when it came to the demonstration projects, and most particularly when it came to the new program's explicit link to military applications.

Surprisingly, DARPA's connection with the Pentagon had never been much of a concern in the AI community prior to Strategic Computing, even though academics in other fields have tended to view such connections with deep suspicion. For one thing, DARPA has a well-deserved reputation as perhaps the most open and effective organization in the Defense Department. For another, DARPA is the Pentagon's agency for basic research—it was founded in the late 1950s in the aftermath of Sputnik—and while that definitely means research in areas relevant to military problems, DARPA administrators have generally kept the focus on generic technologies; after all, a missile-guidance system may very well use the same hardware and software techniques as, say, a hospital information system. Indeed, for several decades now the agency has been *the* principal sponsor of computer research in U.S. universities and in many American industrial laboratories. It's fair to say that the rapid development of computer technology since the 1960s—and the position of the United States as a world leader in that technology—is largely the result of DARPA's leadership and support.

That said, however, many researchers in the AI and computer-science communities were deeply troubled by what they saw in the Strategic Computing plan. "Having gained control of much of the leading computer-science research over the last several decades, DARPA now proposes to direct that research toward much more specifically military applications," declares an assessment of Strategic Computing prepared by the Computer Professionals for Social Responsibility (CPSR), a nationwide group formed in 1983 to address the role of computer technology in the fields of nuclear weaponry and arms control. "Such a strong hand on the rudder, it seems to us, should be subjected to public scrutiny and debate."[24]

For example, research funded under Strategic Computing is largely unclassified—for now. But what happens as the program moves closer to real applications, ask the CPSR authors? Will the Pentagon clamp down? Will the rapid and free flow of ideas that has enriched AI for decades suddenly stop?

Worse, they ask, what are we to make of Strategic Computing's implicit promise that AI can automate military decision-making in a crisis? "Modern warfare is marked by three interacting trends," they write:

. . . increasingly powerful weapons; more separation (in both time and space) between planning and execution; and a faster and faster pace. The first trend means that the consequences of our actions, whether intended or unintended, can be greater than ever before. The second means that we rely on increasingly large, complex, and indirect systems for command, control, and communication. The third means that any miscalculation can quickly lead to massive ramifications that are difficult, or perhaps impossible to control. It is easy to see the dangerous potential of the three in combination. . . . [However] the Strategic Computing plan accepts the situation as inevitable, and embraces AI and automatic decision-making as a means of coping with it.

The CPSR considers this an extremely dangerous direction to take: "In suggesting such a role for AI," they write, "the Strategic Computing plan creates a false sense of security in the minds of both policy-makers and the public. Like all computer systems, AI systems may act inappropriately in unanticipated situations. Because the limit on their reliability is fundamental, we argue against using them for decision-making in situations of potentially devastating consequence."

In fairness to DARPA, it is certainly possible to read the Strategic Computing plan more sympathetically than that. For all the upbeat tone of the document, it does try to grapple with many of these same issues raised by the CPSR. Nonetheless, the issues are real. During 1985, for example, they surfaced again in connection with the "Star Wars" Strategic Defense Initiative, and the controversy over whether computer software could ever be reliable enough to run the system. Fundamentally, the question is this: In any situation, whether civilian or military, how much responsibility should be given to machines? This is perhaps the single most important issue in the application of AI, and I'll return to it again in Chapter 11.

Meanwhile, quite aside from the question of military applications, many researchers were troubled by a more practical aspect of Strategic Computing. To go along with the demonstration projects, DARPA had produced elaborate timetables which seemed to demand that breakthroughs in basic research be made on schedule. To a community that had already been thrown into turmoil by the entrepreneurial boom in AI, the whole thing seemed to invite an "AI winter"–style backlash. Skeptics recalled DARPA's five-year program in speech understanding, which had been set up in 1971 with the goal of achieving a breakthrough in the ability to handle connected speech; the participants had made good progress and were laying out plans for a follow-up—when DARPA abruptly refused to renew the program, at least partly because the numerical milestones had not been met.[25]

Furthermore, even if a backlash never came, some critics worried that a crash program with specific deadlines could undermine the health of the field in a more subtle way by producing a kind of Project Apollo mentality: Instead of putting money and resources into laying a solid research base for the future, a crash program gives the upper hand to those engineers who are eager to reach the milestone by the quickest and dirtiest means available, even if those techniques prove to be a dead end in the long run.

Ironically, none of these timelines or milestones had existed when the plan was first drafted. Strategic Computing had originally been conceived as being almost entirely a program of technology push, otherwise known as basic research. The elaborate schedules and the heavy emphasis on pull—the demonstration projects—were imposed by Cooper in later drafts as a way of making the whole program more credible to his superiors in the Pentagon hierarchy. (The critics of the plan are correct in saying that it was primarily a sales document.) Furthermore, it happened that the Defense Department was even then in the process of carving out many of the agency's research programs and transferring them into President Reagan's new "Star Wars" Strategic Defense Initiative. The plan's emphasis on "practical" military applications of AI thus helped to protect the fledgling program in an era when DARPA itself was in turmoil.

The upshot was that by the time the plan was finished, the demonstration projects had gone from about 10 percent of the total effort to about 30 percent.

That in itself is not necessarily bad, of course. Reasonable people can and do disagree about the best way to structure such a program. Furthermore, the demonstration projects do give an undeniable focus to the basic research. In a 1984 interview with *Science* magazine, for example, Lynn Conway, who was assistant director of the Strategic Computing program for a brief period during its formative years, and who is now an associate dean of engineering at the University of Michigan, explained how the push and pull approaches could work synergistically in the case of the autonomous land vehicle. "We have a fair degree of confidence that we can plan and produce the hardware of the autonomous vehicle on schedule," she said. But the basic research issue of perception and its relationship to cognition is still open-ended. So DARPA's idea was to create an interdisciplinary test facility, or "testbed," where a number of the vehicles would be housed. (It opened in 1985 at the Denver plant of Martin Marietta, DARPA's prime contractor for the autonomous vehicle.) Researchers from all over the country would then have access to the vehicles through the agency's ARPAnet computer network, so that they could load their programs into specific vehicles, run those vehicles around the roads and countryside of the test facility, and see what worked.

"It's like a telescope," explained Conway. "The telescope hardware itself is planned and built on schedule. But the observations made with the telescope are very open-ended."[26]

Politics and Delay

The Strategic Computing plan was accepted by Congress in the autumn of 1983. Unfortunately, however, that did not end the bureaucratic hassles. Consider the example of the competitive bids.

DARPA, unlike ICOT or the MCC, is not a laboratory but a funding agency. Traditionally, this has meant that scientists in the field will send in a proposal for such-and-such a project, and if DARPA officials think the proposal looks good, the project is funded. When Strategic Computing began, the agency was sitting on some twenty to thirty million dollars' worth of excellent proposals that could have been funded immediately. Cooper, however, decreed in early 1984 that all research contracts had to go out for competitive bids. "If you want to get industry involved," he explained in an interview later that year, "the laws are such that you almost *have* to do it by competitive bid."[27] Industry involvement, both in conducting the research for Strategic Computing and in producing the prototype hardware, had in fact been one of DARPA's highest priorities from the beginning. The best research in the world means nothing to the rest of the Pentagon until there is an industrial base ready to churn out operational hardware, Cooper pointed out. So why not get the private sector involved from the start? Besides, he said, once private companies are participating in the program, they have an inside track on producing commercial spin-offs—say, a "driver's assistant" for a passenger car.

Cynics wondered if Cooper might have been under pressure from congressmen who sniffed the possibility of a little pork for local industries and the home-state university; instead of letting the money go uncontested to established centers such as Carnegie-Mellon, MIT, and Stanford, they wanted to spread it around. Be that as it may, the competitive-bids decision stood; the result was months of confusion and heated tempers, while AI researchers tried to figure out how to write such bids, and while the people in Kahn's office got organized to evaluate them. Eventually, of course, the problem did work itself out, and the contracts did get awarded. But because of it, Strategic Computing didn't really get moving until 1985.

Unfortunately, 1985 was also the year in which many of the original key players left for other jobs. Cooper and Kahn, for example, went their separate ways to become private consultants, and Conway went to the University of Michigan. So as of this writing Strategic Computing has bogged down yet again as a whole new team of administrators tries to figure out just what the program is and isn't. One of the major issues up for grabs is whether the program will become even more applications-oriented than it already is. If so, then it will inevitably be pushed that much closer to the immediate application of available technology, and that much further from long-range research. Indeed, if the Gramm-Rudman budget cuts hit the program as hard as some observers think they might, DARPA and "Star Wars" may be forced to consolidate their programs in exactly the manner that the CPSR spokesmen fear.

TAKING STOCK

Half a decade after MITI's original announcement in Tokyo, the various Fifth Generation projects are still a long way from producing tangible results. Obviously, the early years weren't so much a horse race as a process of jockeying for position at the starting gate. The Americans and the Europeans had a big lead in technology, but they spent the first three years or so scrambling to get organized. The Japanese had a big planning lead, but as they freely conceded in 1981, they needed those first three years simply to catch up with the technologies already developed in the West.

In other words, only now, in the mideighties, has the race begun in earnest.

Of course, in a larger sense, the question of who "wins" this race is less important than that people are running. The most important legacy of the Fifth Generation movement is the idea of coordinated research, coupled with the concept of planning on a specific time scale. No one can pretend that such cooperation is easy. Trying to get a large group of human beings moving in the same direction is inevitably a frustrating, disorganized, and highly political undertaking. Nevertheless, the idea of cooperative research and development is catching on. In 1984, for example, Congress amended the antitrust laws to make it easier for industries to form MCC-like consortia; a year later, more than forty joint ventures had filed with the attorney general and the Federal Trade Commission for protection under the act.[28]

Interestingly, the same dynamic that says "cooperate" to rival companies also seems to apply to rival nations. The problems involved in AI and parallel processing are very hard to crack, and no one can afford to pass up good ideas just because they come from somewhere else. The Japanese, as always, seem to understand this very well. Not only are they in constant attendance at computer conferences in the West, but they have welcomed Western visitors to ICOT and have been very open and frank about their own program. There has even been talk, so far inconclusive, of Western companies joining in the Japanese program. "We have no intention at all of limiting the ICOT program to within Japan," said Tsutomu Makino, director of MITI's Electronics Policy Division, at a three-year review symposium for the Fifth Generation project in November 1984. "We believe that the research work should proceed openly through information exchanges with other countries and that the results and achievements should benefit the international community."[29]

Japan's Progress

If the passage of time has done nothing else, it has given Western observers the chance to make a more realistic assessment of the Japanese program. Fuchi and his team, for all their prowess, are just as human as the rest of us.

Overall, MITI's effort in information-processing technology appears to be following the familiar pattern. According to the U.S. Department of Commerce's Japanese Technology Evaluation Program (JTECH), the Japanese electronics firms have pulled even or surpassed their U.S. counterparts in product development, especially when it comes to such high-performance hardware as scientific supercomputers. But Japan is falling further and further behind in basic research and generic technology development. Even the exceptions tend to prove the rule. Japanese researchers have made great progress on computer speech recognition, for example, because it has a decidedly practical application: it is very difficult to type using the pictographic Kanji characters of written Japanese, and it would be much easier just to talk to the machine.[30]

As for the Fifth Generation itself, the United States and Europe have clearly moved into the lead. The wide differences in factors such as pay scales, accounting methods, and organizational structure make it very hard to compare dollar amounts; nonetheless, at least four programs—MCC, DARPA, Alvey, and ESPRIT—either rival or exceed ICOT in scope.

ICOT, meanwhile, has been reasonably successful as an experiment in managing basic research. However, its focus has narrowed significantly in the process. Although it has not always been appreciated in the West, the original 1981 plan, with its twenty-six points, was a product of Japanese consensus-building and was a bit *too* comprehensive. Government money is as tight in Tokyo as it is in Washington and London, and topflight research talent is just as hard to come by; so by the official opening of ICOT in April 1982, Fuchi had thrown out the kitchen-sink elements of the original plan and had focused his team's efforts on a more realistic main line of research: knowledge-based programming, machine reasoning, and advanced work stations.[31]

Coming so soon after the hoopla of October 1981, it was a risky strategy. It left Fuchi open to criticisms about "falling behind schedule" and being "narrow and academic," as the British journal *Nature* put it.[32] And the headline JAPAN FALTERS ON NEXT STEP IN COMPUTERS was broadcast in the *New York Times*.[33] In all fairness, however, the revised schedule has at least proved feasible. A logic-processing machine, for example, essentially equivalent to the LISP work stations developed in the United States and Europe, was designed by ICOT, built by Mitsubishi Electric, and installed at the ICOT offices in Tokyo in December 1983—right on schedule, according to the revised plan, and taking less than one year from conception to delivery. By the time of the project's three-year review in April 1985, Fuchi's team had dozens of them. In much the same way, a specialized knowledge-base machine was built by Hitachi and Oki Electric Industry, and delivered to ICOT starting in the spring of 1984.

The question now is how well Fuchi and his colleagues do in the second, four-year phase of the project, which lasts from April 1, 1985, until March 31, 1989. Tokyo is currently running a deficit that is proportionately higher than the deficit in Washington, so money is tighter than ever. At the same time, Moto-oka, whom many considered to be the real leader of the program, died of cancer in November 1985; at this writing no one knows how vulnerable that tragedy will leave the program. And finally, from a purely technical point of view, although ICOT's first machines were impressive, they are still sequential machines. In a sense they represented the easy first step. In the second phase, the ICOT researchers are beginning to work on the real innovations, the hardware and software for the parallel machines. And there the Japanese, like everyone else, are groping in the dark.

———

In the last analysis, of course, we won't really grasp the long-term significance of the Fifth Generation until we can look back on these projects from the perspective of the 1990s, or even the twenty-first century. In the meantime, perhaps the best summary of the whole thing is one given by Feigenbaum: "AI was a great story," he says, "but it needed a plot—and the Japanese provided the plot."

AI isn't just research anymore. It's going somewhere.

PART III

THE SHAPE OF THE FUTURE

9

The Relationship of Man and Machine

No one really knows when the printing press was invented. No one even knows for sure *who* invented it. By tradition the credit goes to Johannes Gutenberg of Mainz, Germany, but other cities can make a good case for their own favorite sons, and are vociferous about doing so. What historians do know, however, is that sometime in the middle part of the fifteenth century there began to appear a whole cluster of related technologies, including such innovations as movable metal type, oil-base ink, and the wooden handpress. Allowing for the times, moreover, these innovations spread with remarkable rapidity. By 1500, printer's workshops were to be found in every important municipal center in Europe—and the public was showing a ravenous and previously unsuspected appetite for books.★

The early printers, who were nothing if not sharp businessmen, rushed to feed that appetite. The first volumes off their presses in the mid-1400s were expensive Bibles and prayerbooks, with hand–illuminated capitals and type-faces designed to duplicate as nearly as possible the beautiful handwriting of the scribes; not surprisingly, only the wealthy could afford them. But by the next century the printshops were pouring forth a steady stream of printed matter for the mass market: woodcuts of kings, popes, artists, and other luminaries; maps, charts, diagrams, manuals, calendars, dictionaries and other reference works; essays, poems, plays, stories, and eventually, newspapers and novels—together with scandal sheets, "lewd Ballads," "merry books of Italie," "corrupted tales in Inke and Paper," and other forms of Renaissance pornography. There was even a whole new genre of "how-to" books, which ranged from instruction on playing a musical instrument to rules for keeping household accounts. One book of dress patterns, published in Seville in 1520, made "Spanish" fashions visible throughout the far-flung Hapsburg Empire. Indeed, reading was so popular that concern was expressed in many quarters about how isolated and withdrawn people were becoming. Instead of gathering to hear the news of the day in the town square or at church services, this

---

★The influence of the printing press on the Renaissance, the Reformation, and the Scientific Revolution has been traced in telling detail by Elizabeth J. Eisenstein of the University of Michigan. The discussion here is taken from her 1983 book, *The Printing Revolution in Early Modern Europe*.[1]

new generation of readers sat in "sullen silence," perusing their books and broadsheets.

Scholars, meanwhile, were finding that the printshops gave them an easy way to publish their work and to learn from each other. This new technology also gave them easier access to the works of Aristotle, Galen, Ptolemy, and the other ancient philosophers; instead of traveling for months at a time to visit this or that manuscript at some far-off library, a scholar could actually own a copy. In fact, a scholar of modest means could actually own many books, which meant that it suddenly became much easier to compare one ancient account to another and to track down inconsistencies. The Polish astronomer Nicolaus Copernicus, for example, seems to have spent his entire professional life in a sustained and zealous effort to unscramble the astronomical records of the past. His theory that the Earth revolved around the sun instead of vice versa—a theory that he took from an ancient Greek writer, Aristarchus of Samos—was published in 1543 in the spirit of cleansing and rationalizing the ancient wisdom. Indeed, it was probably no coincidence that the scientific revolution inaugurated by Copernicus, and carried on in later generations by such figures as Galileo, Kepler, and Newton, began less than a century after the invention of printing.

On a more practical front, printing quickly made the venerable profession of scribe obsolete. But it created new trades in its place. In fact, many of the former scribes were to be found in the printshops working at these new trades, as compositors, typefounders, and pressmen. A papermaking industry began to flourish. New impetus was given to the science of metallurgy, for the making of better type. Financiers grew rich from their investments in the new printshops. A whole marketing infrastructure grew up, complete with booksellers, book fairs, and something new called advertising.

In short, the printing press became the foundation for a whole new industry. It fueled mankind's passionate love affair with the printed word. And, as we can now see so clearly with five hundred years of hindsight, it became the catalyst for the first great information revolution.

A Five-Hundred-Year Perspective

It doesn't take much imagination to see the parallels between the story of the printing press in the Renaissance and the story of the computer in our own times. The sudden appearance of a new information technology, the rapid spread of that technology, the emergence of new professions and whole new industries, the revolution in communication and the revolution in people's ability to work with knowledge—the parallels have been drawn so often, in fact, that they verge on cliché.

Nonetheless, the analogy is instructive, if only because the five-hundred-year history of printing lends perspective. Most of the discussions one hears about the "long-term" impacts of computers and AI are really only talking about a twenty-year time scale. But our descendants will be living with these technologies a lot longer than that. The truly profound effects of intelligent computers, analogous to the effects of the printing press on mass literacy and the scientific revolution, may not be apparent for centuries.

Sadly, however, that five-hundred-year perspective also reminds us that there were certain things printing did *not* do:

- It did not solve the problem of good and evil. Hitler's Germany, after all, was a literate land.

- It did not sweep away illiteracy, injustice, ignorance, poverty, and disease. These things are still in ample supply, even in the so-called advanced countries.

- It did not bring universal enlightenment. Pope Alexander VI was already nervous in 1501 when he wrote, "The art of printing is very useful insofar as it furthers the circulation of useful and tested books; but it can be very harmful if it is permitted to widen the audience of pernicious works. It will therefore be necessary to maintain full control over the printers so that they may be prevented from bringing into print writings which are antagonistic to the Catholic faith or which are likely to cause trouble to believers."

  Pope Alexander's spirit lives on today—in the attempts by creationist groups to censor all mention of evolution from high-school textbooks; in the attempts by well-meaning people to ban *Huckleberry Finn* as racist; and for that matter in much of our anxiety about secrecy and national security. The impulse to protect other people from "dangerous" knowledge seems to be timeless.

- And, finally, printing did not bring universal peace and understanding. In retrospect, Pope Alexander had good reason to be nervous: Within two decades the Protestants were in open revolt, with passions on both sides being fanned by an outpouring of printed tracts, caustic sermons, vicious cartoons, and vitriolic propaganda. Indeed, the "peaceful" art of printing probably did more to destroy Christian concord than any of the arts of war ever did. By the end of the sixteenth century, Rome had established its index of forbidden books and the counterreformation was in full swing. And by the mid-1600s, after a century and a half of reformation, counterreformation, inquisition, censorship, and thirty years of civil war, Latin Christendom lay irretrievably fragmented. Three hundred years later we are still living uncomfortably with the results—as the residents of Belfast can attest.

  As always in history, the story of the printing press is the story of a particular time and a particular place. It is hardly a detailed prospectus for the future of computers and AI. But it does serve to remind us that neither printing presses nor computers nor any other technology has the power to make us other than what we are.

Technology and Social Transformation

On the other hand, the world *is* a vastly different place because of printing. Looking back at the Renaissance, the Scientific Revolution, the spread of literacy, and all that has come since then, one can even hope that the world is a better place. The question is whether AI and the new-generation computers will have a similar transforming power on history. The answer, I believe, is yes. Printing enhanced human memory. Computers and AI are enhancing human reasoning power. It's hard to imagine that such technologies would *not* have a profound impact on society. So I'm going to spend the remainder of this book looking at some of the possible changes we'll face. But first, fair warning: What follows is one writer's choice of some ideas that look interesting. It is *not* a prediction of when such-and-such a product is going on the market. Lots of clever people are out there doing lots of clever things. We can expect that by the early twenty-first century there will be new-generation computers with high-quality graphics, speech input and output, and a thousand times the computational power of present-day PCs—and they'll be small enough to carry in a shirt pocket. We can also expect that in the twenty-first century an intricate network of optical fibers, coaxial cables, waveguides, and direct-broadcast satellites will allow any given computer to communicate electronically with any other computer on the planet. But as for precisely when, all I can say is "soon."

EXPERT SYSTEMS AND OTHER SYSTEMS: MAN AND MACHINE IN TANDEM

In the movie *Superman II,* at a point in the plot when Superman finds himself troubled and confused about his growing love for Lois Lane, he retreats to his secret Fortress of Solitude in the Arctic and takes out a special crystal. From that crystal, he then calls forth an image of his long-dead mother. Now, this image is remarkable in many ways. It is three-dimensional, life-size, and seemingly alive. It talks with Superman, giving him advice and comfort about his problem. It behaves in every way as if it *were* his mother.

It is, perhaps, the ultimate expert system.

Today's expert systems are obviously a long way from Superman's mother-image. Nonetheless, useful niches seem to be popping up everywhere. You've already seen, in Chapter 7, how businesses are using expert systems in any number of roles—as aids to getting work done, for example; as a mechanism for distributing knowledge within the company ("What's the company policy on such-and-such?"); or as a backup system to help the rest of the staff get by when an experienced worker is ill, or goes on vacation, or takes another job, or dies. (It remains to be seen how people will feel about having their digital alter-ego always hovering in the background, so to speak.)

If we can assume that expert-system shells and knowledge-engineering tools will continue to make the programs easier to build—a reasonably safe assumption, since a good many programmers are working on that sort of thing right now—then it's easy to imagine people toward the end of the 1980s buying home expert systems the way they now buy self-help books and reference texts. I have a good candidate on my shelf right now, a book called *Take Care of Yourself* by Drs. Donald M. Vickery and James F. Fries. It is loaded with advice on such things as how to stock a home medicine chest and how to choose a family physician. Moreover, it has dozens of IF-THEN flow charts to help the reader decide when such-and-such a symptom indicates an everyday problem that can be treated at home, and when that symptom indicates a more serious condition that needs the attention of a professional physician. It's begging to be put on a computer.[2]

It is equally easy to imagine doctors, lawyers, accountants, and a host of other professionals using specialized expert systems as private in-house consultants. If I were to ask my broker about an arcane investment strategy, for example, and she didn't know how to handle it herself, she could turn to her terminal, call up the appropriate financial expert system, and get me the answer. (I could also buy the same expert system for home use, if I needed that kind of information often enough to justify the cost.)

Looking somewhat further into the future, on-line knowledge bases in, say, science and engineering could make the collective wisdom of an entire discipline available to anyone with the electronic equivalent of a library card. As John Seely Brown, head of the AI group at Xerox PARC, pointed out in recent testimony before the House Science and Technology Committee:

> The establishment of large-scale, nationally available knowledge bases, together with the development of appropriate workstation software, would help to create an *evergrowing* knowledge infrastructure to support scientific research.
>
> Properly designed, electronic knowledge bases could serve as powerful repositories of knowledge in forms to be accessed and used directly by smart computer programs running on an individual scientific workstation. For example, a knowledge base for recombinant DNA research might contain descriptors of relevant properties of DNA and enzymes, along with principles for synthesizing recombinant DNA structures. When directed by the scientist to simulate various syntheses, say for a particular effect, the smart workstation software would access the knowledge base, select the appropriate data, and symbolically carry out the various synthesis steps while always checking that any currently known constraints aren't being violated.[3]

Finally, looking very far into the future, it's possible to imagine at least one new kind of art: "personality sculpting." Recall Jaime Carbonell's theory of subjective understanding (see Chapter 3), in which he modeled personality traits such as ambition and compassion in terms of an individual's striving to satisfy his or her own hierarchy of goals. It is at least conceivable that an artist using such an approach could endow a robot with an imagined personality in much the same way that writers now endow their fictional characters with personality. But of course, these robots would not be restricted to the printed page. One can imagine participatory dramas, somewhat like contemporary improvisational theater, in which robots and humans make up the story together as they go along. One can also imagine cheerful robot assistants, spunky robot maids, and empathetic robot companions. One can even imagine that this same advanced technology will allow our descendants to achieve a form of immortality by leaving records of their own personalities for their great-grandchildren.

And thus we come full circle to the shimmering image of Superman's mother.

Superman II is science fiction, of course. But in all seriousness, that image of his mother is worth keeping in mind, because it is an appropriate metaphor for what is genuinely new about AI. With conventional programs—word processors, spreadsheets, data-base management software, and the like—a computer is essentially just a tool. You sit down, you use the machine to do a job, and that's the end of it. But with AI, we can begin to imagine computers that are more than just tools. We can contemplate computers that comprehend language, give advice, take independent action, and seem to understand what is going on around them. Indeed, we can begin to talk about computers in terms of their *relationships* with users and the *roles* they play in that interaction. Throughout the remainder of this book, you'll see that the important questions about the application of AI always seem to hinge on issues such as understanding, trust, communication, and responsibility—precisely the same issues that come up in relationships between human beings.

Of course, this perception may be just a failure of the imagination. As Allen Newell points out, we invariably envision intelligent computers as "humans without flaws"—tireless and emotionless beings that simply take over otherwise conventional roles. The reality, he says, may be utterly different.

Maybe. But somehow I suspect not. The *details* may be different. But for roughly three million years now, we humans have been devising and defining roles for intelligent entities—people—and I somehow doubt that any fundamentally new roles are going to be discovered just because we develop some new entities made of silicon.

In short, I suspect that the most profound long-term effect of AI is that human beings are going to have to start dealing with computers and robots not as tools but as social beings: as counselors, servants, agents, tutors, and even friends.

Giving Good Advice

In the case of an expert system, a computer obviously takes on the role of adviser—which turns out to be a more subtle role than it seems.

To see why, let's imagine a small AI start-up firm that decides to market the world's best expert system for doctors.* The programmers spare no effort. They consult all the world's best diagnosticians. They do Herculean feats of knowledge engineering. And after many, many man-years of work, they have the system they want: All the user has to do is type in the symptoms and out comes the answer, delivered by a machine that never gets tired or irritable, that never forgets anything, and that never has an ax to grind. It is indeed the most effective diagnostician in the world.

Releasing their brainchild under a catchy name—something along the lines of *Delphi 2000*, perhaps—the company managers now sit back and wait for the orders to roll in. And wait. And wait—until their hopes slowly fade with the sight of medical practitioners shunning their product in droves. "Why should I listen to a ß#$%ˆ& machine telling me what to do?" comes the typical reaction. "And why should I take responsibility for this ß#$%ˆ& machine's opinion?"

What went wrong? Or, more precisely, why was the oracular advice of this program so unsatisfactory?

The answer becomes clear very quickly when one imagines what it would be like to consult a human expert who behaves the way this program does—as many humans unfortunately do. First, the great man asks a few questions to get data. Then he mulls things over for a bit. And finally, without any particular explanation, he condescends to deliver a solution to your problem. Good day; my secretary will send you a bill.

Now, the problem with this kind of advice (aside from its being extraordinarily irritating) is that it leaves you, the advisee, no smarter than you were before. Since you have no way of knowing how the expert arrived at his decision, you have no way of knowing what to do if conditions change slightly, or if you are faced with a new problem that is slightly different from the first. Also, because the oracular expert doesn't know firsthand what is really going on, he may be solving the wrong problem, and neither you nor he will necessarily recognize that fact.

Good advice, obviously, involves more than just asserting a solution to a problem. Studies of person-to-person interactions have shown that the most satisfactory advice comes about when the client is involved in a much more intimate way. It is more of a back-and-forth, iterative kind of process: first the expert helps you figure out the right questions to ask, and then he helps you lay out your full range of options—with particular reference to the side effects,

---

*The stress is on the word *imagine*. Any resemblance to an actual company or product is purely coincidental.

obstacles, benefits, and trade-offs of each. And finally, once *you* have made your choices, he helps you devise a plan of action. As a result, you come away from the session with a deeper understanding of your situation and a high degree of confidence that you have, indeed, addressed the right problem.

To put it another way, advice isn't something to be dispensed like aspirin. Good advice involves a special kind of relationship.

AI as Oracle or Facilitator?

Clearly, instead of trying to build gadgets that dispense answers—oracles—software designers should try to build systems that help the user find a solution: facilitators.

To see how this idea might work, let's look several decades into the future and imagine that trouble has flared up in the Middle East. Diplomacy is getting nowhere, and in frustrated rage, the President of the United States turns to his crisis advisory computer with a very simple question: "How soon can we get warships to the area?" Now, the crisis computer can certainly answer that question. All it has to do is consult the appropriate electronic data bases to find out which ships are available, where each one is, what role it is playing in support of other ships and other missions, how much fuel and ammunition it has, what its cruising speed is, and so on. Then, after a little computation, it can readily state the solution: "Next Tuesday." But of course, a question like that one doesn't exist in isolation. A wise leader should also want to think about the political ramifications of sending warships into a volatile area, and perhaps would want to consider some other, less warlike options. So a genuinely useful crisis advisory computer ought to be able to bring these various factors to the President's attention, drawing on its knowledge bases about the political situation at home, the world price of oil, the current state of relations with the Soviet Union, and a host of other variables. Perhaps the computer would even be able—diffidently, of course—to make a case for some of the more promising approaches. Indeed, by refusing to fixate on one potential solution while ignoring the rest, as humans so often do, the crisis computer might actually help calm the crisis.

The invention of such a full-caliber computer adviser is still a good many years away, but the value of the facilitator principle is already widely recognized within the AI community in general, and among knowledge engineers in particular. That's why virtually every large-scale expert system has a facility for explaining how it reaches its conclusions, so that users can get some idea of how much to trust it.

On the other hand, as AI moves into the area of mass-market expert systems, there may be quite a lot of oracular software being produced nonetheless. Even assuming that programmers understand the principles involved—and the history of personal-computer software suggests that a lot of self-taught programmers will not—a good facilitator system takes a lot of software engineering to build and a lot of computer power to run. So until the standard desktop microcomputers get a good deal more powerful than they are right now, mass-market systems will tend to be rather simple and oracular.

At the same time, expert-systems publishers may feel the pressure to leave out even the explanation subsystems. The thing that makes an expert system unique and valuable is its knowledge base. Yet an expert system that explains its reasoning will inevitably reveal what is in its knowledge base, which means that the publisher's competitors will have access to proprietary information. Finally, and perhaps most important, a great many potential customers may be perfectly happy with oracular expert systems, because in fact they don't *want* to have to think about options and choices. They just want to be told what to do. And markets being what they are, the customers will undoubtedly get what they demand.

So why is this a problem? At one level, of course, it's not. An oracular expert system is simply a reference book in another form; so long as the users understand those limitations, then it could be a handy piece of software to have around. For example, in the book that I mentioned previously, *Take Care of Yourself,* many of the decision paths conclude with "Make appointment with physician"; home expert systems that take that same attitude seem harmless enough.

On another level, however, the difference in approach is crucial. Indeed, this issue is the key to many of the fears that have been expressed about the long-term effects of expert systems and other AI programs. For example:

- *Expert systems will take away any incentive for people to learn or to create new knowledge.* To the extent that we all end up listening to revealed truth from a swarm of electronic oracles, this is a very real concern. Indeed, whoever controls the programming of these oracles will enjoy a disturbing level of social control, along the lines of Orwell's Ministry of Truth. On the other hand, if the software more often follows the facilitator approach, then it seems plausible that the effect will be just the opposite: The very act of using such a program gets the user deeply involved in the decision-making process, and is itself an act of learning.[4]
- *Expert systems will encourage uncritical, blind trust in their results, as well as an abdication of responsibility.* Computers have acquired a powerful mystique in our society, a phenomenon enshrined in the slogan "Garbage In–Gospel Out." Bureaucrats and junior executives, for example, long ago learned that figures presented to their bosses on a computer printout— even arbitrary and meaningless figures—take on an amazing aura of authority and precision. So how much worse will this kind of intimidation be when the software comes under a sensational label like Artificial Intelligence? How much worse will it be when computers can actually talk to people in natural-sounding English? Remember how people responded to Weizenbaum's ELIZA, a comparatively simple-minded program.

Thus, to the extent that AI programs encourage this kind of

199

uncritical acceptance, they could have some very worrisome effects. To take an admittedly extreme example for illustration, suppose that I consult a doctor who uses an oracular system to make a diagnosis, and the diagnosis is wrong: The doctor says I'm healthy when in fact I have a cancer that would have been operable had it been caught in time. Whom do I sue? Who is responsible for that diagnosis? Presumably the doctor himself—but then what about the software publisher? What about programmers who wrote the expert systems? What about physicians who provided the expertise in the first place?

Actually, given the way lawyers have been acting lately, they would probably encourage me to sue everybody in sight no matter what kind of system the doctor had used. But notice that the oracular system diffused and blurred responsibility, whereas a facilitator-type system, which would have kept the doctor deeply involved in the problem-solving process from the beginning, would have also kept the lines of responsibility and authority clear.

• *Expert systems may have an adverse impact on professions of all kinds.* To the extent that expert systems and other AI programs are designed as little oracles, it seems likely that they will be resisted and condemned by professional organizations such as the American Medical Association and the American Bar Association, for all the reasons of responsibility and quality control stated above. In that context, the U.S. Food and Drug Administration has already begun to worry about how to set standards for health-related expert systems.

To the extent that these programs are designed as decision aids, however, it seems likely that they will be welcomed by the professions as powerful and important tools. Nonetheless, it has to be recognized that "professionals" are by and large the people who make their living from knowing things. Thus, the widespread availability of expert systems and related software could conceivably cause fundamental changes in the role professionals play in society.

The concept of a "profession" as we know it today, with university-based professional schools and the whole apparatus of government certification, is actually quite a recent development. Before the late nineteenth century, anyone who wanted to could hang out a shingle and call himself a doctor, in much the same way that a young farmer named Abraham Lincoln was able to "read law" in an established law office and become a lawyer. Our current system grew up in the latter 1800s partly as a mechanism for enforcing standards of competence—getting a tooth pulled by a self-trained dentist was no joke—and partly as a mechanism for the American middle class to retain a certain social exclusivity in the face of rapid industrialization and massive immigration; after all, a professional degree promised their sons and daughters both status and the likelihood of a good income.

If anything, those two motivations are stronger today than ever; indeed, the spectacle of today's college generation in obsessive pursuit of the right degree, the right school, the right experience on the résumé, culminating in the most lucrative job—an attitude that has been dubbed "credentialism"—has led many observers to wonder if initiative and creativity are being stifled on a massive scale.[5] Be that as it may, it seems unlikely that the professions will wither away soon. The social forces behind them are just too powerful.

Within a relatively few years, however, we can expect to see some changes. Undergraduates in a wide variety of fields will learn how to use expert systems in much the same way that students in business schools now learn to use spreadsheets such as Lotus 1-2-3. Meanwhile, we may very well see home and library expert systems taking over more and more of the "general practitioner" type of professional advice—family tax accounting, for example, or home medical advice, or drawing up a simple will—while the professionals themselves tend to become even more specialized than they already are. Alternatively, we may see specialized knowledge embodied more and more in machines while human professionals are trained to be generalists in the best sense, able to integrate differing points of view in a real-world situation. Or, as seems likely, we may see some combination of both approaches, with the mix varying from person to person and from profession to profession.

• *Expert systems and other AI software—together with computers and robotics in general—will throw millions of people out of work, and will condemn millions more to careers of meaningless drudgery.* The answer here is much the same: If computerized automation is implemented with the simple-minded goal of displacing human beings from the process at hand, reducing them to little more than providers of input and readers of output, and if everything else about the organization is left unchanged, then yes, automation will eliminate a lot of jobs.

However, if computers and robots are implemented as facilitators, with the goal of involving their users in a partnership, then the results could be very different. The computers would take care of the tasks that machines are good at—juggling petty details, for example, or handling lots of tedious data—so that the user would be left free to do the tasks that people are good at: recognizing patterns and relationships, bringing together wide varieties of real-world experience, coming up with creative new insights—and interacting with other people.

However, the issue of automation and jobs is not simple. Indeed, it is one of the most emotional and politically potent issues going. It therefore deserves a detailed discussion of its own, to which I'll return in the next chapter.

Meanwhile, it should be clear enough that the role of *facilitator* goes well beyond expert systems. Indeed, a role such as *adviser* is just one among many forms of the facilitator. Thus, we'll spend the rest of this chapter exploring how intelligent computers might serve as facilitators in other contexts, beginning with one that could be the most influential of all: enhancing human creativity.

GETTING TO *AHA!*

In the forty-odd years that computers have been among us, people have used them to grind out numbers, to manipulate data, to process words, and in general to sling around bits of information with a facility that would have astounded our ancestors. Only quite recently, however, have people begun to use computers as a medium for working with *ideas,* which is a much more subtle endeavor.

Probably the most familiar examples in the personal computer realm are the recently developed "thought processors," or outlining programs, such as ThinkTank and Framework. On the surface, at least, the concept of these programs is simple: Just take the outlining techniques we all learned in high-school English class and put them on the computer screen. An outlining program thus allows you to jot down one point as a heading, then put other points underneath as subheadings, then go on to the next point and more subheadings, and so forth.

But the simplicity is deceptive. For example, you can close the outline at a keystroke so that you see only the major headings. Or, with another keystroke, you can open up various subheads, and then open up *their* subheads, until you are focusing on precisely the level of detail you want. Unlike a word processor, which is best at polishing individual sentences and paragraphs, an outlining program allows you to conceptualize a project from a general plan down to its minutest details.

Alternatively, you can start out in a brainstorming mode. Just type in your thoughts as they come to you, and then begin to build up larger ideas from the bits and pieces. Somehow, the mere act of writing ideas down in a list seems to generate *Aha!* experiences. Once the points are all right there in front of you, you begin to see connections. Point *A* is more important than you thought. Promote it. Points *X*, *Y*, and *Z* really belong together. Group them under a new heading. Point *B* logically goes ahead of point *A*. Move it there; all its subheads will follow. Point *C* is irrelevant. Delete it; all its subheads will vanish as well.

Since outlining programs were first introduced for personal computers in the early 1980s, people have used them for planning construction projects, for keeping their daily list of things to do, and for organizing week-long conference agendas. They have used them for planning books. (In fact, I used an outlining program to plan *this* book.) And in California, one consultant uses a computer outliner to help his clients conduct productive business meetings. As people talk at the meeting, he simply types in the points they make while an overhead projector shows everyone in the room what appears on his screen. By and by, something very subtle and extremely important begins to happen: The participants begin to say things like "Hey, this point relates to something earlier" or "Wait a second, that contradicts what you said ten minutes ago!" With a keystroke, the points are moved. The free-form discussion begins to take on structure. The digressions become more obvious. The subtle points begin to take on their rightful importance. And the ever-present tug of competing egos becomes subdued as participants focus more on the ideas being displayed than on who actually proposed them.[6]

As powerful as these outlining programs are, however, they do have some severe limitations. For one thing, the very concept of an outline imposes a structure on the ideas. Everything has to fit into a linear, hierarchical scheme. And while it's true that almost any set of ideas can be forced into a hierarchical list, the process can produce a gross oversimplification. Most ideas are actually very *non*linear; each one relates to many, many others in an intricate web. Imagine trying to outline the relationships between such concepts as peace, truth, and envy.

A less fundamental objection, but still important from a practical standpoint, is that the outlines are static. The user has to do all the rearranging by hand, so to speak, which means that reshuffling a large outline to take advantage of a new insight can be a major headache. Once the outline expands beyond a certain size and complexity, it's almost easier to start over.

In sum, then, the outlining programs are a good first step. But the kind of software that one really wants for working with ideas is more dynamic, something that can automatically show multiple relationships and complex links between ideas, that can automatically rearrange the structure of ideas as the user changes them—something that is, in fact, very much like an AI program.

Process Versus Product: Computer-Aided Creativity

Perhaps not surprisingly, some of the most innovative work in this area is being done by John Seely Brown and his colleagues in the AI group at Xerox PARC.

The Palo Alto Research Center itself was established by Xerox in 1970 to create "the office of the future." And that, of course, meant hardware. It was at PARC, in fact, that the whole idea of the personal computer was invented. The center's Alto work station, which was produced by the hundreds for internal use during the early and mid-1970s, was not only the inspiration for the LISP machines now in widespread use throughout the AI community but also the first machine to use all the on-screen windows and icons later made famous by the Apple Macintosh. But just as important, through their support of groups like Brown's, the managers of PARC have shown a keen awareness that hardware alone is not enough. Inventing a genuinely effective "office of the future" means that one also has to think very carefully about the best way for human beings and computers to work together.[7]

Thus the AI group's efforts in the realm of idea processing, as described by Brown:

By focusing . . . on the product of the creative effort, we are missing the real source of power for computer-based tools: the computer can record and represent the process underlying the created product. By making explicitly available to the user the series of steps or missteps leading to a particular object or result, we create a basis on which to build extraordinarily powerful editing, merging, undoing, and transforming tools. Tools designed to manipulate this "historical" information . . . can be used to carry out intellectual and creative tasks of great complexity. . . . [Making the creative process explicit] provides a way greatly to enhance the communication to others of *what* one has done by enabling the user to communicate aspects of *how* it was done.[8]

What Brown has in mind is something he calls an "empowering environment," which couples the techniques developed in AI for analyzing the structure of knowledge—semantic networks and frames, in particular—with the multiple, on-screen windows and high-resolution graphics of a LISP machine.

NoteCards, for example, is one such system that is still under active development at PARC. As with the outlining programs discussed previously, NoteCards has a deceptive simplicity: It merely automates the three-by-five notecards that students have used for generations in researching term papers. To use NoteCards, the user first tells the computer to display a new card—actually an empty box, or window, on the screen—and then types in notes or draws diagrams as if the box were a real three-by-five card. The user also gives the card a title, and then goes on to the next one.

What makes the simplicity deceptive in this case, however, is the way in which these electronic notecards can be organized. Unlike paper notecards, which have to be shuffled and lined up by hand, and which tend to favor a linear organization, the on-screen notecards can be linked to one another in any way the user desires. To establish a link, the user simply adds a symbol called a "pointer" to the appropriate card. These pointers are rather like footnotes or cross-references.

The payoff in this procedure is a uniquely flexible method for working with ideas. If the user wanted to arrange his ideas in a linear sequence—for a speech, say, or a book chapter—he could simply define the pointers so that each card pointed to the next. If he wanted to arrange his ideas in an outline form, as in the current-generation outlining programs, he could arrange the pointers so that each notecard representing a major heading would point to a series of notecards representing its subheads. However, if he were still brainstorming a book, say, or a new sales campaign, he could simply jot down ideas on individual notecards in a stream of consciousness; the pointers could be added later as they occurred to him. Thus, the structure of the argument would grow spontaneously, taking on its own organic structure instead of the linear structure imposed by an outline.

At any time, NoteCards also allows the user to go back and modify the structure. Starting from any given notecard, the user selects a pointer with the computer's mouse and clicks the mouse button; the computer instantly fetches the pointer's destination from the notecard data base and displays it on-screen. The user can then select a pointer on this new notecard, and fetch still another card, and so on. Thus, he can quickly browse through the cards following up this idea or that. Moreover, he can add new comments and links as he goes.

In summary, NoteCards provides the user with all the power of an outliner program for brainstorming, while giving him much more flexibility for organizing and reorganizing his ideas. Indeed, that very flexibility can help trigger new ideas. As an experiment, PARC's Kurt VanLehn recently converted a 328-page research paper on human skill acquisition into a data base of some eight hundred notecards. (He had written the paper before the program was developed.) Then, however, as he browsed through the organization of his theory using the graphics display, he suddenly realized that he had neglected to test some of his hypotheses against the empirical facts. And when he went back and did so, he discovered a flaw in his theory; the hypothesis he had originally thought was best now turned out to be quite poor—and a hypothesis that he had previously rejected actually fit the data best of all. "In short," he says, "sloppy reasoning, abetted by a poor rhetorical organization, allowed the suppression of the winning hypothesis. The [new organization devised in NoteCards] uncovered the mistakes, leading to an improved theory."[9]

AI in Education: Computer-Aided Insight

NoteCards illustrates Brown's process-versus-product principle because of the way it facilitates the process of brainstorming and helps users explore the structure of ideas. That same principle has likewise been incorporated into AlgebraLand, a system being developed by Brown and his colleagues at PARC to help high-school students explore the process of problem-solving in algebra. "It is accepted doctrine that one must engage in solving the problems [at the end of each chapter in a math or science book] before one will have mastered the knowledge in that chapter," says Brown. "Yet there has been surprisingly little analysis of what precisely is being learned . . . [and] nearly a total absence of explicit strategies or heuristics for learning from the doing of homework. Whatever is learned is learned tacitly and often by accident."[10]

AlgebraLand thus attempts to hold a mirror up to the student's own thought processes. In one of the on-screen windows, the computer presents the student with an algebraic equation to solve. In another window, it presents a menu of basic algebraic operations, such as combining terms and subtracting the same quantity from both sides. With a click of the mouse, the student can select one of these operations and apply it to the equation as a whole, or to one of its subterms. The result is a new expression, which the student then continues to manipulate in search of the final solution.

Now, according to Brown, the important thing about AlgebraLand is not the details of its operation but its ability to preserve a record of what the student has done—an audit trail, so to speak. It even displays the record graphically, so that all the backtracking and all the false starts become readily apparent. Thus, the student's problem-solving strategy is made visible. It becomes an object of study in its own right. The student can look at the record and see which approaches worked, and which approaches didn't. He or she can even begin to understand *why* some things worked and others didn't.

That process, says Brown, is the first step toward the student's discovery of strategic knowledge about equation-solving—and toward the all-important skill of self-reflection. Indeed, cognitive research has shown that the habit of self-reflection is probably the most dramatic factor dividing successful students from poor students. The former tend to be very good at periodically reviewing their progress toward a goal, analyzing their misunderstandings, and revising their strategies as needed. The latter don't even know where to begin. When they don't understand something, they either fake it or just give up. The promise of such programs as AlgebraLand is to help them develop those skills.

Unfortunately, however, just because AlgebraLand makes a "pretty picture" of a student's problem-solving strategy does not necessarily mean that the student will want to sit down and study that strategy in detail. As happens so often in education, the trick is to make the learning process interesting, compelling, and even fun—which immediately suggests the idea of games.

One intriguing example of a game that emphasizes problem-solving strategies is Truckin, which was invented by Daniel Bobrow, Mark Stefik, and Sanjay Mittal at PARC to help teach their LOOPS programming language. Truckin is a board game somewhat like Monopoly, except that all the action has been transported to a computer screen. Each human player, or team of players, is the manager of a truck that moves from place to place on the playing board, buying and selling goods and trying to make money. At each turn, decisions must be made about what to buy, what to sell, and where to go next. These decisions are complicated by having to worry about running out of gas, being robbed, having goods get damaged or spoiled, stopping at weigh stations, and having to be at a certain location by the end of the game. After a certain number of moves, the truck at the ending location with the most money wins.[11]

Obviously, Truckin is a game of strategy. What makes it different from games like chess, however, is that the strategy must be explicit, because the human players cannot directly control their trucks once the game is underway. The trucks move according to knowledge bases that the players have written beforehand (in the LOOPS language, of course). Thus, the players have every incentive to think through their problem-solving strategies very, very carefully.

A Truckin contest is something to behold. Once the game has started, the trucks move around the board spontaneously, as if they had minds of their own—which in a sense they do. Meanwhile, the LOOPS students are shouting, cheering, and rooting their trucks on, as if they were watching a football game. And this is, of course, exactly what one wants from an educational game. Brown even fantasizes that games of this kind might be expanded into a "robot Olympics," in which children and teenagers would pit their best knowledge-based programs against each other in high-powered computer arcades—refining their own abilities in problem-solving and self-reflection, even as they refined their programs.

From the examples given above, it's already clear where the "empowering environment" concept could have its most important application. The flash of insight, the feeling of *Aha!*, the sense of ideas snapping into place—this is the essence of learning, just as the process of learning how to structure ideas—how to *think*—is the essence of education. Indeed, it is no coincidence that Brown and his colleagues at PARC have also taken the lead in exploring how AI can be used in education; the official name of the group is, in fact, Cognitive and Instructional Science.

The modern approach to "intelligent tutoring," as it is known, is paradoxically both an outgrowth of and a repudiation of the old "programmed learning" methods popular in the sixties. Programmed learning was the first of the two major waves of computers-in-education, the second being the fad for personal computers and "computer literacy" in the early eighties. Its underlying philosophy was that of B. F. Skinner and the behaviorist school of psychology: Teaching was considered to be nothing more than a process of reinforcing desired behaviors. Thus, the computer would present the student with a frame containing a single question or a single bit of information, and the student was supposed to respond by filling in a blank. The buzzwords of the day were *feedback* and *individualization*. But, in fact, the earliest systems would only give feedback when the student finally put down the correct answer—otherwise they would do nothing—and they allowed for individualization only in that a student could proceed at his or her own pace. The material was *not* presented in a different way to different students.

Later programs were considerably more flexible, in that they incorporated IF-THEN-type branching. Here, if the student put down response *A* in a given frame, the program would branch to a new set of questions appropriate to that response. If the student put down response *B*, then the program would branch to yet another set of questions, and so on. Nonetheless, while the branching approach was admittedly more sophisticated, the underlying philosophy remained; in effect, the computer was still a programmed textbook, and the student was still treated as a *tabula rasa,* an empty expanse to be filled with facts. Programmed learning, in the opinion of many critics, was learning only in the driest sense of rote memorization. It encouraged students to do what was expected of them, discouraging initiative.[12]

Intelligent tutoring is an outgrowth of this older approach in that it shares the ideals of individual pacing and individual learning, although with modern AI techniques and modern computer technology, it carries those ideals much further. With high-resolution graphics, for example, a program can utilize vivid pictures and animation instead of just text and line drawings; moreover, with a mouse or a touchscreen, the student can point to things on the screen and even draw his own pictures. With a natural-language interface, the computer can converse with the student in a friendly and reasonably flexible manner. And with expertise about good pedagogy, the computer can know when it's best to correct a student's mistake, and when it's more productive to let the student recognize the mistake on his own.

However, intelligent tutoring is different from programmed learning in the most fundamental sense: The underlying philosophy is not behaviorism but the information-processing model of mind that I described in Part I. Learning is seen as a process of information transfer, and the emphasis is on such questions as "How is the information structured?" and "How does the student process that information once he receives it?" Thus, an intelligent-tutoring program doesn't simply try to reinforce desired behaviors. It undertakes the much more difficult task of understanding the student, so that it can base its responses on what the student is actually thinking and planning at any given time.[13]

One such program is Debuggy, an expert system developed by Richard R. Burton at PARC for diagnosing student errors in subtraction problems. The basic premise behind Debuggy is that a student having trouble with subtraction actually does understand the overall procedure (start in the right-hand column, borrow from the left if you need to, and so forth). But at some point in the learning process, he has scrambled one or more discrete parts of the procedure. His internal program, so to speak, has a bug in it. In the following two problems, for example, the student has produced what seem to be two randomly derived wrong answers:

$$
\begin{array}{r}
500 \\
-65 \\
\hline
565
\end{array}
\qquad
\begin{array}{r}
312 \\
-243 \\
\hline
149
\end{array}
$$

Yet both errors can be accounted for by a single bug, which Burton denotes "0 − n = n." In other words, whenever the student finds himself subtracting a number from zero, he simply writes down that number instead of borrowing from the left as he is supposed to.

In diagnosing a student's misunderstanding, Debuggy starts from a data base of some 130 different bugs that Burton and his colleagues have uncovered, including such errors as "Always subtract the smaller number from the larger number, regardless of which is on top" and "Borrow all the time." Given a set of problems completed by the student, Debuggy uses heuristic search methods to identify which bug, or which combination of bugs, can explain his results. The program will also present the student with new problems designed to narrow the number of possibilities and to confirm its diagnosis. "We require of a diagnosis that it be able to predict, not only whether the answer will be incorrect, but the exact digits of the incorrent answer on a novel problem," says Burton.[14]

Developed in the late seventies and early eighties, Debuggy has now been tested on more than four thousand students, and is able to distinguish among some hundred million possible hypotheses about what a student is doing wrong on subtraction. In real educational settings, moreover, Debuggy has proved to be impressively versatile. Not only can it handle compound errors, in which a student has more than one bug, but it can sort out the real bugs from careless mistakes.

Although the high-powered computer work stations required to run Debuggy are still prohibitively expensive for general classroom use—for now, anyway—this program and other diagnostic programs like it clearly have a potential value that goes well beyond errors in subtraction. Such systems have been adapted for training student teachers, for example, focusing their attention on the underlying causes of student learning problems and on strategies they themselves can apply in diagnosing those problems. Computer-based diagnosis also promises to make an important contribution to the methods by which students are tested. Instead of simply grading a series of problems right or wrong, an intelligent diagnostic system could probe what a student does and does not understand, pinpoint his misconceptions, and thus provide a precise and personalized form of help.

Learning by Exploration

It's interesting to look at Debuggy and its cousins from the perspective of exploratory learning environments, another concept of education that has received a good deal of attention in recent years as microcomputers have flooded into the nation's classrooms.

The underlying philosophy of the exploratory environment is that people learn best not by memorizing facts but by doing things. Thus, the computers ought to be set up in such a way that students can try things out and play with ideas. Probably the most outspoken and best-known advocate of this approach is Seymour Papert of MIT. His LOGO computer language, devised more than a decade ago, is intended as a simple yet conceptually powerful language that could be easily used by children. His concept of "turtle graphics" in LOGO is likewise intended as a mechanism for children to explore the concepts of geometry.

The first turtles used by Papert were little wheeled devices that would roll around on a big sheet of paper spread out on the floor. (Because these devices were shaped like hemispherical domes, they resembled real turtles; thus the name.) Under the command of a computer, the turtles would move back and forth across the surface of the paper, drawing lines as they went. The idea was for a child to write programs on the computer to make his or her turtle do things—draw a picture of a square, perhaps, or of a flower.

In more recent versions, the turtle has become a little marker drawing lines on a PC screen. Either way, children are enthralled. They need no urging to play with the turtle and no urging to try new patterns. In some cases, autistic children have even been able to use the turtle as a first object to communicate with. But the key point, says Papert, is that when children are in this environment, they learn not by memorizing and rote repetition but by experience. If the turtle isn't doing what the child wants it to do, then he or she is led to figure out where the program is going wrong—and thereby to develop an intuition for how lines, angles, and curves go together in space.

In short, a child in this environment learns geometry by total immersion, in much the same way that all children learn language. " 'Gifted' children seem to know mathematics in the same sense I know English," says Papert. Indeed, the difference between traditional education and this process of learning by doing, he adds, is the same as the difference between memorizing a long Sanskrit poem by rote, and learning some Sanskrit, so as to absorb the poem's meaning.[15]

Papert's work has become widely known through his book *Mindstorms*,[16] and through the availability of LOGO and turtle graphics on many microcomputers. In the process of popularization, unfortunately, his ideas have often come across as looking a bit cutesy, as if LOGO and turtle graphics were nothing more than a pleasant game. That, however, is a serious mistake. Exploratory learning environments as Papert intends them are a radical challenge to the educational establishment. In an exploratory setting, the teacher is no longer an authority figure but a kind of cotraveler. And, even more subversive, answers are no longer either right or wrong. Instead, the metaphor for learning and reasoning becomes programming; in effect, the student says, "My solution to this problem doesn't work (my program has a bug)—let's fix it." Of computers and society, Papert writes:

> Faced with a computer technology that opens the possibility of radically changing social life, our society has responded by consistently casting computers in a framework that favors the maintenance of the status quo. For example, we typically think of computers making credit decisions in an otherwise unchanged banking system, or helping to teach children to read in an otherwise unchanged school system. We think of computers as helping schools in their task of teaching an existing curriculum in classrooms instead of confronting the fact that the computer puts the very idea of school into question.[17]

The exploratory approach is undeniably powerful and effective. In its pure form, however, it suffers from exactly the same problem that plagued the "open classroom" methodology that was so popular in the sixties and early seventies: It is very teacher-intensive. To make sure that the children are actually learning something worthwhile, not just floundering around, some-one has to be paying very close attention. That "cotraveler" role for the teacher is still very important. Unfortunately, even assuming that the teachers understand and approve of the exploratory approach—which is not always the case—very few schools can afford to give their students that kind of one-on-one attention.

Hence the importance of systems like Debuggy. Using AI techniques, the computer exploratory environment could be united with intelligent tutors as integral parts of the same system. The result would be an environment for individually guided discovery.

As an illustration of this possibility, Burton and Brown have developed an experimental system known as West. In a sense, West is the inverse of the Truckin game described earlier: Instead of the student coaching the computer, the computer attempts to coach the student. The field of play is a simple computer board game called How the West Was Won, which was originally designed to give students drill and practice at arithmetic. The players move down a path seventy squares long. On each turn, a player is given three numbers and has to use the basic operations of addition, subtraction, multipli-cation, and division in order to determine how far forward he can move. The first player to get to square 70 wins. However, an element of strategy is introduced by the presence of special moves, short cuts, and a rule that sometimes allows one player to bump another backward. The job of West is to coach the student both in arithmetic and in the strategy of the game—a job that turns out to require a startling amount of tutorial knowledge.

Fundamentally, a computer coach has to solve two problems: (1) when to interrupt the student's own play of the game, and (2) what to say when it does interrupt. The first problem turns out to be very hard indeed. Unlike Debuggy, which was a pure diagnostic system, West cannot be constantly posing special tests for the student or asking a lot of questions to find out where the bugs are in his strategy. For a coach to exhibit such behavior in the middle of a game would be obnoxious. Thus, West has to infer the student's shortcomings from whatever the student does in the context of the game. And this can create a serious diagnostic problem: Just because the student doesn't use a particular skill in the course of a game doesn't mean he lacks that skill. Maybe he simply never needed to use it.

So West relies on what Burton and Brown call "differential modeling." On each move, the computer looks at the student's position and evaluates what his "best" move ought to be—an act that requires considerable expertise in the game itself. Then the computer compares that best move with what the student actually does. And finally, assuming that the student does not make the best move, the computer tries to use the difference to model the bugs in the student's strategy.

To meet the second problem, meanwhile, Burton and Brown have equipped West with expertise in good pedagogy, as founded on twelve explicit principles, such as "Don't provide *only* criticism"; "Don't tutor before the student has a chance to discover the game for himself"; and "After giving the student advice, permit him to incorporate the issue immediately by allowing him to repeat his turn." In the beginning Burton and Brown were quite concerned that their coaching principles would be too crude to be effective. But when they tried out West on their first group of test subjects—eighteen student teachers—the majority commented that the coach seemed to manifest a good understanding of their weaknesses. As one subject said, "I misunderstood a rule; the computer picked it up on the second game."

Burton and Brown have also tested West in an elementary-school setting, where the coach seemed to improve the students' game skills markedly. Indeed, Burton and Brown noted that the students seemed to enjoy the game more when they were playing with the coach—quite possibly because the students were having such a good time trying to "psych out" West so it would talk to them.[18]

The Uses of a Machine Tutor

No one should imagine that artificially intelligent tutors such as West and Debuggy are magically going to solve all the problems that plague the American public-school system. Those problems clearly run deep. And considering that most school budgets are already stretched to the limit, and that many teachers are still trying to figure out what to do with all those computers they've bought over the past few years, the idea of AI-based tutors running on very expensive LISP machines may seem laughably unrealistic.

Nonetheless, there is undeniable appeal to the idea of giving each child a personal tutor that can adapt to his needs, and even "understand" him in some sense. Granted, such machines might turn out to be nothing more than extra gravy for the well-off and highly motivated students. But that need not be the case. In fact, ideally, computer tutoring might turn out to be even more important for poor students; it could help them break out of the vicious circle in which they don't understand what's going on, don't know how to ask for help, can't get enough attention from an overworked human teacher, and end up falling further and further behind.

That vision may not be so far out of reach. Economically, at least, the "artificial" part of artificially intelligent tutoring is becoming more and more feasible as increasingly powerful microcomputers become available at increasingly affordable prices. And the "intelligence" part—the exploration of human cognition, memory, and problem-solving behavior—promises to provide a new and more rigorous scientific basis for teacher training and curriculum design. Indeed, with just these possibilities in mind, a recent study by the National Academy of Sciences called for the creation of one or more federally funded research centers on learning, to be staffed by interdisciplinary teams of cognitive scientists, social scientists, and artificial-intelligence researchers.[19]

But Is It Wise?

In summary, then, intelligent computer tutors clearly have the potential to serve as adjuncts to human teachers. They may even prove to be highly valuable adjuncts. Yet that very possibility raises some troubling questions. Good teaching is more than just pedagogy. It also requires such personal qualities as inspiration, empathy, and affection. Presumably these are qualities that only another human being can provide. On the other hand, maybe not. As robots and computers begin to transcend their conventional role of *tool* and take on such roles as *adviser* and *tutor,* won't people inevitably come to have emotional reactions to them? Might children, especially, come to see these machines as trusted confidants, counselors, and even friends? And what will it mean if they do? As MIT sociologist Sherry Turkle writes in *The Second Self:*

> Computers call up strong feelings, even for those who are not in direct contact with them. People sense the presence of something new and exciting. But they fear the machine as powerful and threatening. They read newspapers that speak of "computer widows" and warn of "computer addiction." Parents are torn about their children's involvement not only with computers but with the machine's little brothers and sisters, the new generation of electronic toys. The toys hold the attention of children who never sat quietly, even in front of a television screen. Parents see how the toys might be educational, but fear the quality of children's engagement with them. "It's eerie when their playmates are machines." "I wish my son wouldn't take his 'Little Professor' to bed. I don't mind a book, would welcome a stuffed animal—but taking the machine to bed gives me a funny feeling." I sit on a park bench with the mother of a six-year-old girl who is playing a question-and-answer game with a computer-controlled robot. The child talks back to the machine when it chides her for a wrong answer or congratulates her for a right one. "My God," says the mother, "she treats that thing like a person. Do you suppose she thinks that people are machines?"[20]

In light of that question, perhaps it is not too early to ask what effect intelligent machines will have on human relationships in general. As we look ahead a few decades or so, it's not so hard to imagine people spending less and less time with each other, and more and more time with robot companions that have been engineered for congeniality. After all, people are a pain. They get angry, or they want something from you, or else they're all worried about *their* problems when you want to talk about yours; dealing with an empathetic robot would be so much simpler. It might even be more satisfying. For a while.

And yet, could a robot share a smile or a touch? It's all too easy to imagine people growing up in a world of sympathetic and congenial machines, feeling empty inside and never knowing why.

On the other hand, the prospect doesn't have to be bleak. I somehow find it hard to imagine that people will avoid each other altogether. Indeed, I'm reminded of one flirtatious and attractive young lady who interrupted a conversation about AI when she burst out laughing and said, "Who'd want to date a computer?"

So an optimist could say that human relationships in a world of intelligent machines will not necessarily be worse—just different. It's at least conceivable that someone who grew up exploring the world in the company of a wise and responsive tutoring machine, as opposed to spending hours every day passively watching television, would become not a recluse but an emotionally secure, curious, aware, and outgoing kind of person.

It's even conceivable that the effort of learning to live with another kind of intelligence—intelligent computers—may have some of the same effect which some scientists have postulated for the discovery of extraterrestrial intelligence: The very difference might help us to understand better what it means to be human.

10

A New Way of Working

In 1981, when Roger Smith took over as chairman of General Motors after a long career of rising through the ranks, the prospects for his company could not have been less auspicious. The American automobile industry as a whole was reeling from the invasion of Japanese subcompacts, and GM in particular had just posted a loss of $763 million, the worst year in its history.

As it happened, however, Smith was not content to serve as a mere caretaker while his company sank into oblivion. A plain, uncharismatic man who describes himself as "a reluctant revolutionary," he quickly moved to streamline his Brobdingnagian, 750,000-employee corporation by merging its five divisions into two. Next he formed a joint venture with the Japanese auto maker Toyota as a way of bringing some Japanese management expertise into the firm. And then, in 1984, he spent $2.55 billion to acquire Electronic Data Systems (EDS), the giant Dallas-based computer-services firm headed by H. Ross Perot. In effect, EDS will create a new central nervous system for GM, using electronic communications to link engineers with designers, salesmen with executives, and robots with computers. "What we're trying to do," EDS president Mort Myerson recently told *Newsweek*, "is to make information available in the proper amount, with the proper speed, to the proper people. Nobody has ever taken a mammoth corporation and done that before. It's going to happen everywhere. The question is 'Who gets there first, and who does it best?' "

Meanwhile, Smith had already plunked down another five billion dollars for Hughes Aircraft Co., the seventh-largest defense contractor in the United States. In part, this was a move to diversify GM and thereby guard against any further erosion of its position in the automobile market. But more important in the long run, the Hughes acquisition gave GM a conduit for infusing the automobile industry with aerospace technology. Ultra-lightweight composite material developed for satellites and military aircraft would be adapted for making lighter, more fuel-efficient cars. Aerospace-inspired electronics would be incorporated into the dashboard to give drivers the benefit of crash-warning radar, computer road maps, and satellite navigation. There would even be seats that could remember the favorite position and seat-back angle for each driver of the car, reconfiguring themselves at the push of a button. In effect, Smith and GM were looking a decade ahead toward a total redesign and rethinking of the automobile.

Finally, Smith gave his blessing to the Saturn project. Organized as a brand-new company-within-a-company, Saturn began in earnest in 1985 with the selection of Spring Hill, Tennessee, as the site of a new, state-of-the-art manufacturing plant, to begin operation by the end of the decade. The project is primarily an attempt to bring this new-generation automobile to market. But to Smith and to GM, Saturn is much more than that. It is, in effect, an attempt to reinvent the manufacturing process itself. If it works—and there is no guarantee that it will—then the GM of the twenty-first century will come to seem less and less like a collection of manufacturing plants and showrooms, and more and more like a single, giant organism. Everything, from assembly-line robots to the computer running the chairman's strategic-planning expert system, will be integrated by a nationwide network of electronic communications.

GM isn't the first company to try this, of course. Factory robots, computer-aided design terminals, computer networks, and other such high-technology accoutrements have been around for more than a decade. GM itself has already built a showcase for this type of technology in its new plant in Hamtramck, Michigan, which produces Buicks, Oldsmobiles, and Cadillacs. Other corporations, notably General Electric, IBM, Westinghouse, and Apple Computer, have pioneered their own state-of-the-art manufacturing plants.[1] Phrases like "reinventing the manufacturing process" have long since become clichés in industrial circles. But in the United States, at least, the field is more notable for its visionary rhetoric than for its actual accomplishment. Only about two dozen U.S. factories have even come close to total automation, while managers in general have been very slow to take advantage of the new technology. It's partly a matter of the expense involved; a single robot can cost $100,000 or more. Another problem is that all too often, different pieces of equipment from different vendors can't communicate with one another—so standardizing computer languages for automated manufacturing is a top priority in the industry. Then, too, companies have already committed a substantial investment of money and time to their existing equipment. And finding enough good people to handle the transition is not an easy task.[2]

Mostly, however, it's a matter of sheer mental inertia. As an editorial writer recently complained in *High Technology* magazine, a lot of managers still seem to think that "computerized inventory control" means manually counting up all the parts in their storeroom once a year and then entering the result on a five-year-old Apple II.[3]

In this context, Saturn is significant for the same reasons that the Fifth Generation projects are significant: The project is extremely well financed, it deals with all the pieces in a coordinated way, and it has been planned on a ten-year time scale. Moreover, its sponsorship by GM, one of the largest corporations in the world, gives this new wave of high-tech automation a kind of legitimacy, visibility, and momentum that it never had before.

New-Age Manufacturing

The details are still being developed, but in general terms Saturn-style automated manufacturing will work something like this:

- In the beginning, the automobile as a whole and all its individual components will be designed on computer-aided design, or CAD, terminals, which are high-powered engineering work stations reminiscent of the LISP machines described in Chapter 7.

    Actually, computer-aided design is the one component of computerized automation that *is* reasonably well developed. The terminals themselves have been around for years and are especially common in the automobile and aerospace industries. At Boeing, for example, engineers designed most of the 767 passenger jet using CAD, while Chrysler—not to mention GM—has declared that it will completely automate all its design work in all divisions by the late 1980s.

    To design a new automobile, engineers start out with a general concept derived from marketing research, which sketches out style, price, performance, number of passengers, and so forth. From there they turn to their CAD terminals to devise a rough geometric model of the shape of the vehicle, with the intention of adding detail as the concept is refined. The terminal eases the process by offering a variety of software tools for drawing lines of precisely the right dimensions in precisely the right position and orientation. Indeed, the most sophisticated modern terminals are able to display a design on-screen as a solid, realistic-looking object in full color; moreover, the object can then be rotated at a keystroke and examined from all sides.

    Once the engineers have roughed out several alternative designs in this way, the designs are sent electronically to special engineering computers that analyze each one for such factors as overall weight, stresses on the structural joints, and aerodynamic drag. With these results in hand, the engineers then go back into the original models to make the appropriate modifications—and do it again and again, if necessary, until the simulations say they have the performance desired. Only at the end will the most promising concepts be turned into real prototypes for final testing; thus, mistakes are caught early—before the whole car has to be rebuilt—and the development process is far quicker and far cheaper than it was before.

    Meanwhile, other engineers are designing the engine using their own CAD terminals to model the performance of, say, the combustion chamber to make sure that its emissions meet the federal standards set by the Environmental Protection Agency. Still other engineers are designing the passenger compartment, the layout of the dashboard, and so on. Finally, three-dimensional models of the motor, chassis, and the other components are "assembled" on-screen to see how they fit together; in addition, a complete model of the engine is positioned in the engine

217

compartment to make sure that when the real thing reaches the assembly line, the tools that have to bolt the engine in will actually fit. At GM's Pontiac division, assembly drawings for the chassis and motor that once took eight to sixteen weeks to do by hand can now be produced in less than a day by combining geometric models of the individual parts.[4]

While little or no AI has been incorporated into the CAD process so far, the possibilities are endless. The design of an auto interior, to take just one example, is a complex trade-off between aesthetics, comfort, safety, customer preferences, and practicality, none of which can easily be expressed in terms of a formula. But much of their essence could be captured as rules of thumb in a knowledge base, where it could be used to facilitate the designers' efforts to make the best trade-offs.

In much the same way, other knowledge bases could be used to help designers estimate how reliable a complex part will be in service, or how expensive it will be to manufacture. Indeed, in a 1983 survey of computer-aided design and manufacturing, the National Academy of Sciences identified expert systems as one of the key research opportunities in the field.[5]

• Once the design is completed on the CAD terminals at the Saturn plant and fully tested on its engineering computers (together with full-scale prototypes), the data is sent to scheduling computers, which devise a plan for how the various parts and materials will flow through the assembly lines and arrive exactly where they are needed *when* they are needed. Like a chess game, this scheduling problem is fraught with a near-infinity of options; thus, the computers may very well use a heuristic knowledge base to help them solve it.

Meanwhile, the designs are also translated into detailed programs for the robots and the numerically controlled machine tools on the factory floor. As the latter name suggests, numerically controlled machine tools are computer-operated machines that can automatically turn out gears, piston blocks, and other such parts. Robots, of course, are the gadgets that automatically bring parts together, weld them, paint them, and so forth. By no coincidence, GM has made a larger investment in robotics research than has any other U.S. corporation. The robots in the Saturn plant are likely to incorporate sophisticated computer vision and other refinements only hinted at in today's models.

In general terms, this effort to bring computerization to the factory floor is known as computer-aided manufacturing, or CAM. It is also one of the major bottlenecks in the whole automation process. John K. Krouse, editor of *Computer-Aided Engineering* magazine, recently described progress as "painfully slow," largely because top-of-the-line CAD work stations are still expensive, and because current-generation computers, robots, and CAD work stations still have no common language for transferring data.[6] Nonetheless, as Krouse himself points out, the development of CAM has begun to gain increasing momentum, with aerospace and automotive industries again in the lead. At present,

GM alone has some forty thousand programmable controllers, numerically controlled machines, robots, and vision systems—and plans to invest forty billion dollars over the next four years, to bring the total up to two hundred thousand units. Moreover, GM has given top priority to developing a common computer language for these machines—the Manufacturing Automation Protocol, or MAP—and is promoting it as an industry standard.[7]

- Finally, when the new Saturn models reach the showroom, customers will come in to look and (hopefully) to buy. Let's suppose that Mr. Consumer does decide to buy. He and the salesman then sit down at one of the showroom's computer terminals to select options, perhaps with the aid of an expert system similar to the R-1 program that Digital Equipment Corporation now uses to configure its VAX minicomputers (see Chapter 8). From there, events proceed as in the scenario depicted recently by business writer Eric Gelman of *Newsweek*:

Mr. Consumer doesn't smoke and doesn't like people who do, so he specifies a dashboard with no ashtray and no lighter. Since Mr. Consumer lives in Oregon, where it rains all the time, he sees no need for tinted windows; he selects plain ones. He likes planting his soggy shoes on thick carpeting, so he orders some shag beige. He wants his car to be the sky blue he rarely sees. He likes loud music, so he chooses a top-of-the-line radio/compact disc player and four Panasonic speakers to overcome the acoustical damping of his wet thick shag carpeting. On he ranges down the checklist; steel-belted whitewalls, digital speedometer, cruise control. After reviewing his choices, he presses the "enter" key.

Mr. Consumer's car is now an electronic blip on the EDS communications network, a vast array of computers linked by 18 Information Processing Centers around the country. The computers at the Saturn plant receive the order, giving it a number and an assembly date. Then they kick back onto the EDS network to order four tires from Goodyear, six spark plugs from Champion, one untinted windshield from PPG Industries, one trunk liner from Detroit Gasket, and so on. GM's suppliers will build their parts on a no-inventory system: each is made when ordered, not before. Back in the Saturn showroom the salesman has already done a credit check on Mr. Consumer via the EDS network and has lined up GMAC financing and insurance from MIC, GM's insurance arm. Mr. Consumer shakes hands with the dealer, who tells him that the car will be ready in a week.

On the Saturn assembly line, a radio transponder is attached to the frame of Mr. Consumer's car. As it moves down the assembly line, the transponder gives off signals to computers and robots: "I am job #123456 and I need a six-cylinder engine. . . . I am job #123456 and I need six spark plugs. . . . I am job #123456 and I need an untinted windshield . . . a blue paint job. . . ."

When Mr. Consumer's blue Saturn rolls out the factory door and onto a truck, another EDS computer signals the dealer that the car is on the way, instructs GMAC to start collecting finance payments and MIC to start collecting insurance payments and tells the receiving department to pay the suppliers for the parts. Mr. Consumer has his dream car, and GM has just built it for $2,000 less than it costs today."[8]

AUTOMATION AND EMPLOYMENT

For the moment, at least, this last scenario—call it "customized manufacturing"—is wholesale fantasy. But only because no one has yet put all the pieces together in a nationwide communications network. The technology itself is relatively straightforward.

Nonetheless, it should be clear from the above description that Saturn is far more than another exercise in technology. Saturn represents a wholesale reorganization of the way people work, together with a fundamental rethinking of what management is all about. Indeed, in the end this new style of working may alter far more white-collar jobs than blue-collar jobs—even as it blurs the distinction between them.

By the same token, Saturn is not just another tool to improve GM's efficiency and competitiveness in the world marketplace. However long it takes, the methods and technology pioneered here *will* be adopted in other industries. The competitive pressures—from Japan, if nowhere else—will guarantee it. And as that happens, this new wave of information-age automation will begin to alter the dynamics of the whole economy. Ultimately, it will reshape the social order. The question is, How?

While no one can seriously claim to know the full answer to that question, it is clear that, as always, the most emotional and politically sensitive issue is employment.* Automation on the scale represented by Saturn could easily eliminate the jobs of a large fraction of GM's 750,000 employees; if carried out on a national scale, without regard to human consequence, it has the potential for social disaster.

Historically, of course, this is not a new concern. People have been worried about automation's effects on employment ever since the followers of Ned Lud roamed around England smashing knitting machines in the eighteenth century—and probably long before that. But so far the worst nightmares have never come to pass, simply because new jobs have been created faster on the average than the old ones were eliminated. On the other hand, while the history of automation is reassuring, it may not be such a reliable guide to the future.

---

*Indeed, it's rare even to hear a coherent discussion on this subject, simply because people are forever talking right past each other. Someone who defines the health of an industry in terms of "jobs" sees things very differently from someone who defines its health in terms of "profitability." That's why, in a recession, an industry that one person calls "sick" can be described by someone else as undergoing a "healthy retrenchment."

Especially in the twentieth century, the jobs lost to automation in the farming, mining, and manufacturing sectors have been more than compensated by growth in the service sector, which includes such activities as trade, finance, education, and government. In effect, displaced workers and farmers have put on white collars and gone to work in the front office.[9] However, this latest round of automation, as exemplified by Saturn, affects office workers just as much as it does factory workers; indeed, one of its most striking repercussions is the potential impact on corporate middle management—the executives in the $25,000–$80,000 salary range, who have hitherto been shielded from any effects of automation.

Since World War II, when American businesses began an era of very rapid expansion, middle managers as a group have increasingly acted as facilitators in much the same sense that I used that word in the last chapter: They collect information, analyze and interpret it, and make recommendations to the decision-makers at the top corporate levels; once those top-level decisions are made, moreover, it is middle management that translates them into action. As a result, this group has grown considerably faster in the last forty years than American business as a whole.*

However, these are exactly the kind of information-management functions that the Saturn project—and for that matter, the Fifth Generation projects—is trying to automate. As one auto-industry analyst recently commented, "Think of what access to information can do. By sitting down at a computer, the people running GM will be able to see what colors are selling, what components are selling. If you want to look at the number of orders to date for two-door cars, you log into the computer. Now you've just done what it previously would have taken a market researcher three to six weeks to do. You don't end up with 20,000 unsaleable cars."[10]

Obviously, a lot of companies are going to be drastically simplifying their organizational charts, and a lot of marketing researchers are going to be looking for alternative employment—along with any number of analysts, planners, and third assistant vice presidents. Indeed, it's already begun to happen. The trend was noticeable enough in 1983 that *Business Week* produced an eighteen-page special report on the subject. "It started with a modest modernization of bookkeeping chores—the purchase of computers for data processing—and quickly gathered steam," wrote the editors in summarizing the emerging attitude. "Now it is being fueled by hard times. As more top managers see that much of the information once gathered by middle managers can be obtained faster, less expensively, and more thoroughly by computers, they have begun to view many middle managers as 'redundant.' They look on the very fiefdoms they have created as vast cost centers, contributing little to

---

*Nor has the rise of middle management been confined to corporations. Much the same thing has been happening in government bureaucracies and other large organizations.

profits and much to overhead. Where once they eagerly added to staff as symbols of their power, today they enviously eye Japanese competitors who all along realized that less meant more."[11]

Whatever virtues this kind of executive streamlining may have in terms of efficiency, however, it does herald a significant change in the shape of the job market, as well as in the absolute number of jobs. Some economists have become seriously concerned that the rise of a high-technology service economy will ultimately undermine the basis for middle-class society. Once everything is thoroughly computerized and automated, goes the argument, humans will be left with the jobs that can't be automated (yet). And for the most part that means a few high-prestige managerial jobs at the top, and a lot of low-paid, menial jobs on the bottom: cashiers, janitors, waiters and waitresses, sales clerks, and the like. "The pattern of wages in the old, mill-based economy looked just like a normal bell curve," writes economist Barry A. Bluestone of Boston College. "It had a few highly paid jobs at the top, a few low-wage jobs at the bottom, and plenty of jobs in the middle. But in the new services economy, the middle is missing."[12]

Actually, a pessimist could find even more to worry about. According to a recent study by the Bureau of Labor Statistics, the fastest-growing jobs in the next decade will be paralegals, computer programmers and analysts, medical assistants, computer/electronics technicians, and travel agents.[13] But those particular jobs, as it happens, are in fields that could be strongly affected by AI. Expert systems might conceivably replace travel agents outright, for example, while automated programming systems might ultimately *reduce* the need for programmers.

On the other hand, while it's true that the percentage of the work force earning middle-income wages has declined over the last decade, it should be said that many economists find Bluestone's arguments less than persuasive. Among other things, a case can be made that the shift from manufacturing to services has largely run its course.[14] But the bottom line is that nobody really knows. The people who say that this new wave of automation will produce just as many new jobs as it displaces are simply betting on a hunch, a fond hope that the future will be like the past. And those who prophesy massive unemployment and a vanishing middle class are simply extrapolating current trends on a straight line, as if nothing will ever happen to change those trends.

The Case for Optimism

All things considered, I have to side with the optimists, for three reasons.

First, the problem is self-correcting in the long run: Robots can make an auto factory marvelously productive—but they don't buy cars. Marxist theory to the contrary, GM and its sister corporations do have long-term interest in seeing to it that all this newfound wealth is widely shared. As the Nobel prize–winning economist Wassily W. Leontief has pointed out, the problem of worker displacement has been eased historically by a steady shortening of the work week, with a corresponding increase in leisure time. That trend has been at a standstill since the end of World War II, he says; perhaps, with this latest wave of automation, it is time for the downward trend to resume.[15]

Second, technology does have a way of changing the rules—and changing them in unpredictable ways. Consider Saturn-style customized manufacturing, for example. While the GMs of the world are inevitably going to be the pioneers in this kind of thing (no one else can afford the massive investments in research and retooling required, especially when the technology is new and the risk is high), their innovations obviously won't be confined to the automobile and aerospace industries. Ultimately there is no reason, for instance, that I couldn't walk into a shoe store and order a pair of shoes of precisely the style and color I want, fitted to each foot individually, and have them available within a few days. The store wouldn't even necessarily have to stock samples. I could view images from an electronic catalog on a high-resolution, CAD-like color terminal. For that matter, I could design my own shoe at the terminal with the help of an expert system to advise me on style, color, material, and durability. (Actually, if I had a high-resolution terminal at home and access to a computer network, I wouldn't even need the store.)

Now, for my part, this high-tech shoe store would give me the best of both worlds: The shoes would be fitted to *my* feet and produced to *my* individual order, just as if they had been handmade by an eighteenth-century cobbler. But they would actually be mass-produced in a factory, which presumably means that they would be much cheaper than handmade items. Of course, I've just put a lot of shoe salesmen and factory workers out on the street—or have I? What if I ended up buying shoes more often than I used to, because these Saturn-style factories were making them cheaper? What if miniature, roboticized factories proliferated in the cities and the suburban malls to be near their customers? What if there were no separate factories anymore, because every shoe store actually had a miniature shoe factory in the back? Might the total number of jobs actually increase? And how would this affect employment in the trucking industry, which would be hauling raw materials to all these minifactories?

Now imagine this example multiplied over millions of people and thousands of different products. It won't happen instantly, of course. If nothing else, a nationwide system of customized manufacturing will require a staggering investment in computers, networks, and robots. Moreover, certain products, such as food, just aren't amenable to this kind of production. But if we imagine a time when customized manufacturing *has* taken hold on a large scale, then we also have to imagine a very different kind of economy. We can expect businesses and factories to put much less emphasis on stockpiling parts and inventory, and much more emphasis on stockpiling manufacturing capacity in the form of computer instructions for robots and machine tools. We can also expect that businesses will be able to respond much faster to the ups and downs of customer demand. So how does that affect business cycles? Will it make them faster or slower? Will it level them out or make the swings even wider? And how will the faster response time affect the employment picture, when plant X is no longer forced to lay its workers off for months at a time because its customer, plant Y, has stocked up on too many of plant X's widgets?

In short, the effects and side effects will ricochet through the economy and through society itself, with further effects we can only guess at.

Finally, there is room for optimism about this new wave of automation because on a national and international scale we will have plenty of time to adapt. All the robot producers in the world couldn't crank out enough machines to throw millions of people out of work by next Tuesday, even if every manufacturing company in the world placed their orders tomorrow morning. And as we've seen, in real life the manufacturers aren't exactly rushing to do that anyway. Even GM, which has commitment and billions of dollars to spend, is talking about automating its factories over a ten-year period.★

On the other hand, it has to be remembered that individual communities don't stare at locked factory gates "on a national scale," nor do individual human beings stand on unemployment lines "in the long run." Their problems are here and now, a fact no amount of optimistic pronouncements about the future can be allowed to mask. Fundamentally, it comes down to the ancient question of sharing the wealth—a question we still haven't fully answered after three million years of trying. But then, that is no reason to stop trying.

CONDITIONS OF WORK

If we assume for the sake of argument that the question of employment does sort itself out eventually, we can ask what it will be like to live and work in this hyperautomated society. Of course, no one can claim to know the full answer to this question, either. But some broad outlines are beginning to emerge.

For example, decentralization and greater local autonomy seem inevitable; a company that cuts back on middle management finds itself dispersing power from headquarters to the local level. Xerox recently gave the general managers of its twenty-four strategic business units the responsibility of

---

★In the near future, employment levels will rise and fall almost independently of any trends one predicts about automation and future-generation computing. The employment situation is much more sensitive to total production levels, which in turn depend upon such things as the overall state of the economy, the ability of managers to guess right about the market, overseas competition, the international balance of payments, and a baroque tax structure that sometimes makes it advantageous to close a profitable plant.[16]

picking the products they want to develop and the technologies they want to use. Meanwhile, the headquarters staff that used to make those decisions was drastically cut back. The result is a substantial decline not only in the time it takes Xerox to develop new products but also in manufacturing costs. At Crown Zellerbach the story is much the same. The forest-products company threw out three layers of management in its container group, and left the managers of the group's sixteen plants accountable for their own success or failure.

"After limiting decision-making to the inhabitants of top-floor offices for the last two decades," write the editors of *Business Week*, "companies are frantically trying to push it down to those closest to the marketplace, giving more autonomy to plant managers, sales people, and engineers—and bypassing staffs completely."[17] Indeed, in many cases responsibility has been extended all the way onto the factory floor, with managers, foremen, and hourly workers meeting once a week in "quality circles" to hash out problems at the plant and to propose solutions.[18]

Not everyone has been comfortable with their newfound responsibility, of course: having the freedom to make decisions brings with it the freedom to make mistakes, and to take the blame when something goes wrong. But by and large the reviews have been favorable. Columbia University industrial engineer Seymour Melman recently spent two years meeting with groups of machinists assembled by the International Association of Machinists. "We found among them an emphatic and near-universal interest in broadened responsibility and authority in work," he says. "It makes life more interesting; the work is more challenging; it just feels better to go to work."[19] In the same vein, Harvard social psychologist Michael Maccoby describes one auto-engine factory that went from a traditional layout employing five hundred workers and managers to a completely automated system run by five workers and an engineer. Again leaving aside the employment implications, the significant change Maccoby noticed was how the remaining workers felt about their jobs: "[They] function as a team. They work together on scheduling, troubleshooting, and maintenance. They have moved from production to service functions within a production facility. And in so doing they have had to constantly develop both technical and interpersonal skills, which has been very motivating for them."[20]

Meanwhile, the use of computers has begun to make similar kinds of personal autonomy possible in high-volume service industries, such as life insurance, banking, telephones, and government agencies. In the past, notes information-systems specialist Vincent E. Giuliano of the Arthur D. Little Corporation, these industries have generally organized their offices into assembly lines for paper: "Jobs are simple, repetitive, and unsatisfying," he writes in *Scientific American*. "A worker may do no more than staple or file or copy, or perhaps check and confirm or correct one element of data. And of course everyone has to work together during the same hours in the same office to sustain the flow of paper. . . . A fragmentation of responsibility goes hand in hand with bureaucratic organization and the flow of paperwork. Most of the workers have little sense of the overall task to which they are contributing their work, or of how the system functions as a whole."

The system is just as frustrating for the customers, Giuliano points out (and as most of us know all too well): "A clerk may be able to check a sales slip and agree that a customer's bill is incorrect. In many instances, however, the clerk is able to change the account only by feeding a new input into the production line, with little assurance it will have the desired effect. . . . Because a given item can take weeks to flow through the pipeline . . . the billing error can be adjusted incorrectly or can be repeated for several months."

However, consider what happened recently when one insurance office was computerized: "Instead of executing a small number of steps repetitively for a large number of accounts," writes Giuliano, "one individual handles all customer-related activities for a small number of accounts. Each worker has a terminal linked to a computer that maintains a data base of all customer-related records, which are updated as information is entered into the system. The worker becomes an account manager, works directly with the customer and is fully accountable to the customer. . . . Productivity is no longer measured by hours of work or number of items processed; it is judged by how well customers are served. Are they satisfied? Are they willing to bring their business back? Are they willing to pay a premium for a high level of service?"[21]

Thus, in both industrial settings and in office settings, we can begin to get a glimmer of a new way to organize work—a "human-centered" approach, as some people have called it, characterized by decentralization, fewer levels of management, and an increase in individual autonomy and control. Of course, there is nothing startlingly new about this insight. Under one name or another, this approach to work has been touted in best-sellers from *In Search of Excellence* to *Megatrends*. It has become the new wisdom of the 1980s. Moreover, we would be overstating the case to say that computers are responsible for this philosophy. It owes a great deal to fashion—ideas about individual autonomy go down well with the yuppie generation—and it owes even more to the recognition that Japan's ability to dominate market after market is closely related to the worker-oriented approach of Japanese managers.

On the other hand, computers, robots, and telecommunications have certainly reinforced the movement. In effect, the human-centered approach is the facilitator philosophy as applied on a grand scale: Let intelligent machines do the routine, mechanical chores, so that people can be free for thinking, planning, and creativity—the tasks that are uniquely human.

The Electronic Sweatshop

It would be nice to say that the human-centered style of working is sweeping the land. Unfortunately, however, it isn't. For all the talk and publicity, it is still more the exception than the rule. Looking just at office automation, for example, information-processing technology has all too often been used to subdivide jobs until they are more trivial than ever before. When stand-alone word-processing machines were first introduced, they cost tens of thousands of dollars. Understandably, office managers wanted to use them efficiently. But the resulting system tended to resemble an electronic sweat-shop. Secretaries who were used to a varied routine of answering telephone calls, typing letters, and interacting with other office staff now found them-selves sitting in an isolated room and typing steadily at their machines for several hours at a stretch, while the machines measured their productivity by automatically counting keystrokes. In general, secretaries have tended to like their new equipment—and to hate the conditions under which they have to use it.[22]

Studs Terkel describes a similar situation in his book *Working*: Beryl Simpson, an airline-reservations clerk, says, "With Sabre [the computer reservations system] being so valuable, you were allowed no more than three minutes on the telephone. You had 20 seconds to put the information into Sabre, then you had to be available for another phone call. It was almost like a production line; we adjusted to the machine. The casualness and informality that had been there previously were no longer there. The last three or four years on the job were horrible."[23]

Meanwhile, much the same thing has happened in automated factories, and for much the same reasons. Columbia's Melman tells of two product-engineering shops—call them Plant A and Plant B—that offer a particularly vivid example.

The two shops both employ about fifty machinists, says Melman. They both deal with the same union. And they both use as their basic equipment a set of numerically controlled machine tools. Indeed, they are both part of the same firm, although they are in different divisions and have different local managers. Plant A is organized along traditional lines: Once the computer-controlled equipment was installed, the operator's job was reduced to operat-ing the On-Off button. All the programming is done by a programming department. All the maintenance, scheduling, and quality-control functions are performed by management. If an operator sees a problem, his duty is to press the Off button and call the foreman, who will then call a maintenance man, a programmer, or other assistant.

Plant B, however, is a study in contrasts. After many years of negotia-tion with the local union, an agreement was reached in which the machinists were all trained how to run the computers and how to program their machines themselves. Once the training was completed, in 1983, they were given the authority to stop their machines if a problem arose and to make any necessary corrections to its programming on their own. Also, each operator was given the responsibility of performing a three-hour maintenance check on his or her machine every Monday morning.

In short, the management of Plant A used the introduction of computers to narrow and constrict the authority of their employees. The management of Plant B (after some pressure) used the same opportunity to enlarge that authority. In Plant A the wages averaged $12.50 an hour in 1983, and the workers were designated "operators." In Plant B the wages averaged 14 percent more, $14.22 per hour, and the workers were classified under the same union contract as "journeyman machinists." Perhaps not surprisingly, in Plant A the downtime (during which the machines are not running) was more than 50 percent. In Plant B it averaged 3 percent—and furthermore, the work force itself was very stable, with essentially zero turnover.[24]

In effect, says Melman, the management of Plant B adopted a human-centered approach, with great success. Indeed, they were pleased, and proud to report on these conditions, seeing these results as a substantial achievement on their part. At Plant A, however, the management's basic reaction to the experience was to express frustration at the inefficiency of numerically controlled machine tools. They did *not* switch to Plant B's methods.

Why not?

Obviously, says Melman, the answer has nothing to do with dollars and cents, since Plant B is operating at a much greater efficiency. Nor, for that matter, is it a question of sinister class consciousness or malevolence. Fundamentally, it's a matter of mind-set: the unspoken, unconscious set of assumptions between management and workers about what work is and how it is organized. Clearly, the same mind-set has been at work both in Plant A and in the electronic sweatshops mentioned above. And no other term describes it better than *Taylorism*.

The Tenacity of Taylorism

In the early decades of the twentieth century, in a series of works later published as *Scientific Management,* time-and-motion study pioneer Frederick W. Taylor laid out the principles that he felt could maximize human productivity. For example, he decreed that each worker's assignment should be broken down into a fixed set of tasks; further, each task should be broken down into components that could be practiced until each was done as efficiently as possible. This would result in the assignments themselves being done with maximum efficiency. Meanwhile, said Taylor, as much control as possible should be centralized in the hands of the managers:

As far as possible the workmen as well as the gang bosses and foremen should be entirely relieved of the work planning and of all work which is more or less clerical in its nature. All possible brain work should be removed from the shop and centered in the planning or laying-out department, leaving for the foremen and gang bosses work strictly executive in its nature. Their duties should be to see that the operations planned and directed from the planning room are promptly carried out in the shop.[25]

In fairness to Taylor, he was not personally as rigid and authoritarian as this brief description makes him sound. In fact, he was passionately concerned about individual fulfillment and social harmony. But the key, he felt, was efficiency: An inefficient man was like "a bird that can sing and won't sing."[26] And to his contemporaries, the advantages of treating workers as mindless automatons proved compelling. Taylor's theories provided the rationale for the rigid specialization that had already taken hold on the assembly line and in factory-style bureaucracies. Furthermore, they still do. Despite any number of refinements in management theory since Taylor, and despite the fact that his philosophy virtually guarantees an adversary relationship between employer and employee, the essence of Taylorism—centralized managerial control and the subdivision of jobs—is still taught in American business schools, and is so ingrained in managerial thinking that it is rarely questioned.

So it's no surprise that when computers first appeared on the office scene, managers and computer-systems designers instinctively applied old-style thinking to new-style technology. The result was what might be called Electronic Taylorism. And thus the mind-set of Melman's Plant A. Indeed, Melman asserts that type-A thinking has been a major cause of the sluggish rise of productivity in U.S. factories. He cites numerically controlled machine tools as a prime example: In 1978, after twenty years of intense discussion, advertising, promotion in the trade and other press, numerically controlled machine tools accounted for only 2.7 percent of all the machine tools in the United States. "One of the important factors that restrained the introduction of machine tools was the discovery of high cost associated with their operation," writes Melman. "The high cost was incidental to major downtime and poor uptime performance. And the difficulties encountered in getting high rates of utilization from the machines were associated with the mode of organization and division of labor according to the Taylorite principles."[27]

A New Mind-set?

To an optimist, the new wave of automation exemplified by Saturn promises to put Taylorism to rest once and for all. The electronic sweatshop phenomenon is just transitional, goes the argument; once the computers and the robots and the networks are all in place, the advantages of the human-centered approach will become overwhelming—not because of idealism but because it pays off.

And that argument may very well be correct. However, it's important to understand that Taylorism is not going to evaporate all by itself. Archaic though it may seem, that philosophy meets deep psychological needs. As Melman notes in reference to his example of Plant A and Plant B, "Managerial control, decision power in and of itself, is often treated as a prime goal by managers. In that case, some managers so oriented are prepared to put aside and disregard the productivity gains demonstrated in Plant B in favor of what they see as the established managerial control that is operative in Plant A."

Nonetheless, as the popularity of books such as *In Search of Excellence* testifies, the Taylorite mind-set does seem to be changing. Perhaps the change stems from the shock of vigorous overseas competition, especially from Japan, Korea, and other rising industrial powers. Perhaps it stems from the rising educational levels of American workers. But whatever the reason, it seems increasingly apparent that we can no longer afford the "luxury" of treating millions of people like assembly-line automatons. They are much too valuable a resource, in both economic and human terms.

Indeed, provided that we can handle the employment problem intelligently, the automation of work presents us with a happy paradox: By replacing human workers with machines, we can both expand human potential and increase human fulfillment. No one should imagine that it will be easy. But it seems a goal well worth striving for.

11

A Question of Responsibility

In 1940 a twenty-year-old science-fiction fan from Brooklyn found that he was growing tired of stories that endlessly repeated the myths of Frankenstein and Faust: Robots were created and destroyed their creator; robots were created and destroyed their creator; robots were created and destroyed their creator— ad nauseum. So he began writing robot stories of his own. "[They were] robot stories of a new variety," he recalls. "Never, never was one of my robots to turn stupidly on his creator for no purpose but to demonstrate, for one more weary time, the crime and punishment of Faust. Nonsense! My robots were machines designed by engineers, not pseudo-men created by blasphemers. My robots reacted along the rational lines that existed in their 'brains' from the moment of construction."[1]

In particular, he imagined that each robot's artificial brain would be imprinted with three engineering safeguards, three Laws of Robotics:

1. A robot may not injure a human being or, through inaction, allow a human being to come to harm.
2. A robot must obey the orders given it by human beings except where such orders would conflict with the first law.
3. A robot must protect its own existence as long as such protection does not conflict with the first or second law.

The young writer's name, of course, was Isaac Asimov, and the robot stories he began writing that year have become classics of science fiction, the standards by which others are judged. Indeed, because of Asimov we almost never read about robots turning mindlessly on their masters anymore.

But the legends of Frankenstein and Faust are subtle ones, and as the world knows too well, engineering rationality is not always the same thing as wisdom. This insight was never captured better than in another science-fiction classic: the dark fantasy "With Folded Hands," published by Jack Williamson in 1947.[2]

The robots of this story are created by an idealistic young scientist whose world, the planet Wing IV, has just been devastated by a senseless war. Sickened by humankind's taste for viciousness and destruction, and thinking to save men from themselves, he programs his robots to follow an Asimovian Prime Directive—"To Serve and Obey, and Guard Men from Harm." He establishes factories where the robots can duplicate themselves in profusion. He sends them forth to bring order, rationality, and peace to humanity. And he succeeds all too well, as the citizens of his world and other worlds soon began to realize:

"Our function is to serve and obey, and guard men from harm," it cooed softly. "It is no longer necessary for men to care for themselves, because we exist to insure their safety and happiness."

". . . But it is unnecessary for human beings to open doors," the little black thing informed him suavely. "We exist to serve the Prime Directive, and our service includes every task."

". . . We are aiding the police department temporarily," it said. "But driving is really much too dangerous for human beings, under the Prime Directive. As soon as our service is complete, every car will have a humanoid driver. As soon as every human being is completely supervised, there will be no need for any police force whatsoever."

At last, the scientist realizes what he has done:

"I found something worse than war and crime and want and death." His low rumbling voice held a savage bitterness. "Utter futility. Men sat with idle hands, because there was nothing left for them to do. . . . Perhaps they tried to play, but there was nothing left worth playing for. Most active sports were declared too dangerous for men, under the Prime Directive. Science was forbidden, because laboratories can manufacture danger. Scholarship was needless, because the humanoids could answer any question. Art had degenerated into a grim reflection of futility. Purpose and hope were dead. No goal was left for existence. . . . No wonder men had tried to kill me!"

He attempts to destroy his robots by destroying the central electronic brain that controls them. (Williamson was writing in the days before distributed processing.) The robots stop him; this is clearly a violation of the Prime Directive, for how can they serve men if they themselves are hindered? He flees to another world, and tries again. And again. And again. Each time he is thwarted, as the robots continue to spread from planet to planet faster than he can run from them. And in the end, the robots devise a simple brain operation to cure his "hallucinations": " 'We have learned to make all men happy, under the Prime Directive,' the mechanical promised him cheerfully. 'Our service is perfect at last.' "

Needless to say, "With Folded Hands" was widely considered a horror story.

WHAT IS A ROBOT?

A servant, it seems, can all too easily become the master—a phenomenon worth thinking about as we rush toward a new generation of intelligent machines. Just how will we use these machines? How much power and authority should they have? What kind of responsibilities should we give them? And who, if anyone, is going to control them?

Before we tackle those questions, however, we first ought to drop back a step and ask a different question: What exactly *is* a robot?

The question is more subtle than it sounds. For most of us the word *robot* conjures up an image of something like R2D2 or C3PO from the film *Star Wars*. But what about dishwashers and word-processing machines? Are *they* robots? The Robotics Industries Association uses a definition specially devised for factory robots: "a reprogrammable multifunctioning manipulator designed to move material, parts, tools or specialized devices through variable programmed motions for the performance of a variety of tasks." But that describes R2D2 and C3PO only in the crudest sense.

Actually, my favorite definition is "a surprisingly animate machine." But for our present purposes, the most useful definition is one that ignores the gadget's physical appearance entirely, and even its brainpower. It focuses instead on the role of the machine; unlike a lawn mower or a word processor, which requires continuous and direct supervision, a robot is an artificial *agent*—a machine that can take action without direct supervision.

Hidden Processing and Microrobots

Of course, if we take that definition literally, we're already surrounded by robots. Stoplights, for example. The automated teller machine at the bank. The coffeepot that starts up automatically at 7:00 A.M. Admittedly, none of these "robots" is very smart. But microprocessors have already begun to appear in coffeepots, washing machines, automobiles, and microwave ovens. Given the rapidly decreasing price of microprocessors, and the increasing ease with which circuitry can be designed and built for special-purpose applications, there is every reason to expect that the devices around us will rapidly get smarter. Ultimately, in fact, we can expect that the engineers will add in little knowledge bases to their chips, so that their machines can talk, listen to orders, and respond to changing circumstances. And at that point we are not so far from what Pamela McCorduck has described as "a world saturated with intelligence," and what Allen Newell called the New Land of Fairie (see Introduction). For instance:

• Refrigerators that know how to thaw the chicken for dinner.

233

- Robotic cars that know how to stop on wet pavement, and how to drive down the highway while their passengers take a nap.
- Lampposts that know the way, so that no one need ever get lost.

Indeed, perhaps we should forget any lingering fears that all our descendants will become like teenage hackers hunched over a computer screen; our descendants may be much more like sorcerers, able to animate the objects around them with a word, and to command those objects to do their bidding.

In all seriousness, many prognosticators think that "hidden" computing, as it is called, may very well be the most important way in which computers and AI will enter our lives. Alan Kay, who was one of the guiding spirits behind the development of personal computers when he was at Xerox PARC in the early 1970s, points out that using a desktop computer to store household recipes, or to turn on the coffeepot in the morning, is roughly equivalent to an engineer in 1900 saying, "Electric motors are great! Every home should have one!" and then proceeding to rig an elaborate system of belts and pulleys to run everything in the house from one big motor in the attic. In fact, the average American home has some fifty electric motors, according to Kay. It's just that we never notice them, because they are tucked away out of sight in electric shavers, hairdryers, typewriters, fans, and washing machines. Thus, we have hidden motorization. Apply that logic to the newest technology and you have hidden computing and hidden AI.[3]

Humanoid Robots

Next, what about not-so-hidden robots: the mobile, humanoid machines that can walk, talk, see, handle things, and even think? We've read about them in science-fiction stories. We've watched them in the *Star Wars* movies. So when are they going to be available at the local department store?

Actually, simple robots are available already, and have been since the early eighties. As of the mideighties, in fact, they are being offered by at least six different manufacturers at prices ranging from $2,000 to $8,000. The Heath Company of Benton Harbor, Michigan, is even offering its Hero robot as a build-it-yourself kit.

These first-generation machines are real, programmable robots with on-board microcomputers; they are not remote-control toys. However, it's important to realize that they have nowhere near the sophistication of R2D2 or C3PO. Certain advertisements to the contrary, present-day robots are not very good for serving canapés at a cocktail party, nor are they much help at doing the dishes afterward. Essentially, they are personal computers on wheels, with ultrasonic ranging devices and perhaps a few heat and light sensors to help them avoid obstacles. Even then, they are hard-put to cross a room without bumping into anything, and it takes a major programming effort to get one to fetch a glass of water from the kitchen table. (And at that, if the glass is moved six inches from its previous position, the programming has to be done all over again.) By themselves, they are only useful as teaching machines, to show people how robots work.[4]

On the other hand, they *are* significant as a possible first step toward more useful robots. For example, one of the first practical applications for personal robots might be as companions to the elderly and handicapped, which would ease their dependence on human help; it needn't take a very sophisticated robot to pick up a dropped handkerchief or to change television channels on voice command. This is especially true if the users are willing to wire their homes with radio locators in the walls; that way their robots could dispense with the need for high-powered image processing and instead use simple radio receivers to keep track of where they are in the house. In the same vein, mechanical-engineering students at Stanford recently developed a robot hand that will translate electronic text into sign language for the deaf.[5]

Another near-term use for mobile robots might be in industrial settings—not in factories as such but in cleaning long, unobstructed hallways, or in mowing the vast lawns of an industrial park. A prototype floor-washing robot has been developed at Carnegie-Mellon. Moreover, without too much adaptation such robots could also serve as security guards to patrol the grounds of prisons or sensitive military installations.[6]

Admittedly, as of the mid-1980s these markets are still a bit fuzzy. But the prospects are sufficiently promising to give the fledgling personal-robotics industry an undeniable momentum. In effect, the pioneers are betting that robotics will take the same route that personal computers did starting in the early 1970s. There, too, the early machines were little more than playthings for hobbyists. But they gave rise to second-generation PCs that *were* genuinely useful. The skyrocketing sales of these machines, in turn, gave the PC makers both the cash flow and the incentive to develop still more sophisticated computers. And on it went, with the results we see around us today. So who knows? Perhaps things will work out this way for the robotics industry, too.

One trend that gives substance to this vision is the support of advanced research efforts such as DARPA's Strategic Computing Program. As I said in Chapter 8, one of DARPA's major goals in that program is an autonomous vehicle capable of roving over rugged and hostile terrain at the speed of a running man. In a sense this vehicle represents the ultimate in AI: the union of vision, touch, reasoning, and motion in one entity, a machine that not only thinks but acts in a multitude of situations. Moreover, such mobile robots would find applications not just on the battlefield but in any environment where flexibility, versatility, and autonomy are crucial. Take deep space, for example: If and when NASA sends another unmanned mission to Mars, perhaps in the 1990s, an important scientific goal will be to bring back samples of material from many different areas on the planet, which means that a rover of some kind will have to move around on the surface to pick them up. This will in turn require some pretty fancy footwork, since the images returned by the Viking landers in 1976 show that the Martian surface is littered with rocks, boulders, and craters. Unfortunately, however, there is no way to operate the rover by remote control from Earth. Radio signals take forty minutes to get from Earth to Mars and back, and at forty minutes per step the rover would never get anywhere. So the Mars rover will need to be intelligent enough to find its own way and pick up the right samples.

Machines of this caliber are clearly not consumer items in the sense that the personal robotics industry would like. On the other hand, advanced research-and-development does have a way of showing up in commercial products with surprising rapidity. So before long we may find R2D2 and C3PO in the local department store after all.

We probably won't be using these humanoid robots for everything, of course, at least not in the way that Asimov, Williamson, and other science-fiction writers have suggested. It wouldn't make sense. Why build mobile robots for an automobile factory when it is so much easier to string them out along the assembly line and move the cars? Why build a humanoid robot to drive a truck when it would be far simpler to build a computer into the dashboard? Why not just make the truck itself into a robot—a kind of autopilot for the interstates?

In some situations, however, a mobile, humanoid robot might be ideal. Mining is an example, or construction work, or anyplace else where the environment is complex and unpredictable. Ironically, one of the most demanding environments, and the one where a mobile robot might be most useful, is the home. Consider what it would take to program a robot maid to vacuum under the dining-room table without vacuuming up the cat in the process; the terrain is at least as complex as Mars. Furthermore, the environment requires mobility for the simple reason that an automated valet or maid would have to share the house with people. Imagine how complicated it would be to build an intelligent clothes hamper that could take the dirty clothes, sort them by color and fabric, wash them, dry them, fold them, and put them away in the upstairs dresser; it would be a Rube Goldberg contraption with conveyor belts and special-purpose handling devices that took up half the house. Much more sensible would be a humanoid robot maid that could walk up and down the stairs and run an ordinary washing machine.★

★If mechanical valets and maids ever become common, life might take on a curiously Victorian flavor. We might go back to building houses with "maid's rooms"—or at least with storage and parking areas for household robots. We might go back to rooms elaborately decorated with bric-a-brac, because we will have mechanical servants to dust and clean it. And fashions may swing back toward fussy, elaborate, Victorian-style clothing because we will have mechanical maids and valets to help us put it on and take it off.

DISTRIBUTED COMPUTING AND MACROROBOTS

There is no reason that mobile robots couldn't also be part of a distributed system of interconnected intelligences such as I described in Chapter 5. For example, it's easy to imagine a construction gang of robots swarming over the skeleton of a new building, each knowing a fragment of the architect's computer-designed blueprint, and each connected to the others by radio . . . grappling units carry a girder into place and hold it upright . . . an octopuslike thing goes to work with riveting guns on the end of each arm . . . a welding unit walks into position and strikes an arc from its snout. . . .

But this vision leads to an intriguing question: Is this robot construction gang simply a team of individual agents? Or is it *one* individual—a "macro-robot" that just happens to have many eyes, many hands, and many minds?

The distinction may simply be semantic. But it may be more; certainly it's worth thinking about as large-scale distributed systems become more and more important. For example, look at the computer-automated factories described in the last chapter; if a robot is defined as a machine that can take autonomous action, then such a factory might very well be called a robot.

Or consider a modern, high-tech office building: The people who work there talk to each other through a digital, computer-operated telephone system. Their desktop computers communicate through a local area network. The building's heating-and-cooling system, its security system, its elevators and lights—all are controlled by computers for optimum efficiency. In effect, the building is a single giant machine: a robot.

In the 1990s, NASA hopes to launch a permanently manned space station occupied by at least six people at all times.★ Eventually, it could carry as many as twenty people. The station will be expensive, of course—costing roughly eight billion dollars—so NASA wants to keep the crew busy repairing satellites, doing experiments, making astronomical observations, and carrying out other useful work. The agency does *not* want them to spend their time cleaning house and taking care of the life-support system. The station will therefore be designed to take care of itself automatically, using AI and robotics technology wherever possible. In effect, it will be a giant robot.[7]

Back on Earth, meanwhile, personal computers, minicomputers, main-frames, and supercomputers are more and more often being linked together in transcontinental communcations networks, in much the same way that tele-phones are already linked together for voice communications. A computer network can be thought of as a robot; indeed, such networks may turn out to be the most intelligent macrorobots of all.

★The schedule became quite hazy after the explosion of the space shuttle Challenger on January 28, 1986; as of mid-1986, however, NASA officials were still expressing confidence that the first components of the space station would be in orbit by the mid-1990s.

The Multinet: Computers in the Global Village
A great deal has been written and said about the coming of the "net-worked society." I've already described General Motors' plans to build a web of communications from factory floor to showroom. Local area networks are proliferating in business offices and on university campuses. And many people have imagined an interconnected web of such networks that would encompass virtually every computer and data base on the planet, a concept that MIT computer scientist J. C. R. Licklider has dubbed the "multinet."[8]

In time, says Licklider, the government itself will become an integral part of this multinet—using it to monitor regulated industries such as the stock market, to provide weather forecasts and take census data, to collect taxes and make social-security payments, to conduct polls, and even to hold elections. Meanwhile, the postal system will fade into a memory as people communicate more and more through telephone lines and electronic mail—all part of the multinet. Filing cabinets, microfilm repositories, document rooms, and even most libraries will be replaced by on-line information storage and retrieval through the multinet. More and more people will work at home, communi-cating with coworkers and clients through the multinet. People will shop through the multinet, using cable television and electronic funds transfer. People will even reserve their tables at restaurants and order ballet tickets through the multinet.

Clearly, Licklider's vision of a multinet connecting everyone and every-thing is still a long way from reality. If nothing else, there remains the question of who would run it: A private company? A public utility? A federal agency? We can only guess at when it will all come together.

On the other hand, we don't have to rely entirely on guesswork to know what this computer-saturated, networked society of the future will be like. It is already being created in microcosm on the nation's campuses. Most of the large universities in the United States, as well as many of the smaller colleges, are spending tens of millions of dollars each to lay cable in cross-campus trenches and to run wires into dormitories, offices, and classrooms. Three schools in particular—Carnegie-Mellon, MIT, and Brown University—have taken the lead in developing the software and networking standards for what is commonly known as the "scholar's work station": a personal computer with the power of a current-generation LISP machine and the three-thousand-dollar price tag of a current-generation microcomputer. (Much of their funding has come from such manufacturers as IBM, Digital Equipment, and Apple, who will build the actual hardware. The machines began to appear on the market in late 1986.)[9]

What makes a network so attractive in an academic setting—or, for that matter, in a business setting—is not just that it allows people to send a lot of information bits from computer to computer but that it allows them to do things in ways they couldn't before. For example, individual users hooking

238

into the network can begin to share powerful resources that no one user could justify by himself. Thus, local area networks give users access to departmental minicomputers, phototypesetters, high-volume laser printers, and massive on-line data bases located in a central library. At a national level, meanwhile, the National Science Foundation has established a series of five national supercomputer centers (at Cornell, San Diego, Princeton, Carnegie-Mellon, and the University of Illinois) to give scientists around the country routine access to state-of-the-art number-crunching power. As part of that effort, the foundation is establishing a transcontinental computer network so that users can communicate with the supercomputers directly from their desktop terminals, without having to travel.[10] In much the same way, The ARPAnet was established in the late sixties to link DARPA-supported computer scientists by high-speed communications. As you've seen in previous chapters, ARPAnet users are now able to send experimental designs for new computer chips to DARPA-supported silicon foundries, which then produce the chip and mail it back within a few weeks; as a result, hundreds of students and professors have been trying out a multitude of inventive ideas, and the art of integrated circuit design is being transformed. More recently, as DARPA has gotten underway with the Strategic Computing program, researchers have begun to tie in to testing grounds through ARPAnet so that they can experiment with remote robotics and advanced knowledge-based systems.

An equally important effect of networking is that it fosters a sense of community. Instead of just talking on the telephone, for example, widely scattered researchers on the ARPAnet have used its electronic mail facility to create a kind of ongoing debating society, with messages read and posted at any hour of the day or night. Among other topics, the debates have included some fiery exchanges about the pros and cons of the Fifth Generation efforts, the Strategic Computing program, and the Strategic Defense Initiative. The comments have often been quite critical of DARPA.[11] Indeed, as described in Chapter 8, some of the most insistent criticism of Strategic Computing and Strategic Defense has come from the Computer Professionals for Social Responsibility, a group that was organized through the ARPAnet.[12] (DARPA, to its credit, has never tried to censor any of this criticism.)

Meanwhile, ARPAnet's electronic communications have proved a boon for collaboration among widely separated individuals. This is particularly true when a message includes computer code for a joint programming project, the draft of a joint research paper, or graphics depicting a new chip design—all of which would be next to impossible to express in a voice message over the telephone. An author can write a book using the word-processing program on his office computer, and send the manuscript electronically to several dozen friends and reviewers at a keystroke. Then, within a few days, he can fetch it back at a keystroke with comments, suggestions, and corrections inserted— without anyone having to wait for the U.S. mail.

Managing the Network With AI

At first glance, none of this seems to have much to do with AI. But in fact, AI will play an increasingly important role in this area, especially when it comes to managing computer networks.

Fundamentally, it's a matter of human factors writ large. Whether or not we ever arrive at anything as all-encompassing as Licklider's multinet, we are clearly headed in the direction of a nationwide information infrastructure on the scale of the interstate highway system or the electrical power grid, and much more complicated than either one. Indeed, we can already see the beginnings of such a system in ARPAnet, in the National Science Foundation's supercomputer network, in the BITnet system that links campuses across the country, and in the commercial electronic mail services being introduced by such companies as MCI and Western Union.[13]

At the same time, no matter how large or small a computer network may be, it has to be "transparent" in a certain sense, or people will find every excuse not to use it. Compare the process to turning on a light: When I walk into a dark room, I don't have to know about voltages, transformers, or peak-load generators. I don't have to know where the power plant is, or whether it runs on coal, uranium, or solar energy. I just flip the switch and the light comes on. And by the same token, when I want to send an electronic message to a friend across the country, I don't want to have to tell my computer what kind of terminal she has, or what kind of data protocols her local network uses, or what the data rate should be. I just want to type in the message and have it go.

The solution, obviously, is to make the network itself intelligent. Make it come alive with software robots that keep things running smoothly in the background. Give it voice with helpful little expert systems that pop up whenever they are needed.

As an individual user of such a system, for example, I would have instant access to all the services of a private secretary, a personal librarian, a travel agent, and more. (The programs to do all this wouldn't necessarily have to be in my computer; if the communications were quick enough, the software could be residing in another computer elsewhere on the network and still *seem* to be running on my computer.) Thus, when I wanted to send that message, I would just type my friend's name and the text of the message on my office terminal; then, with a keystroke or a voice command, my secretarial expert system would look up her electronic address and route the message for me. In the same way, when I've told my computer to set me up for a trip to Pasadena on the twenty-fifth, my travel-agent system would automatically plan out an itinerary—remembering that I like to fly out of Washington in the early afternoon—and then automatically use the network to make reservations with the airlines, the hotels, and the car-rental agencies. A librarian expert system would likewise be available to guide me through the intricacies of the network itself—advising me what data bases I might want to look at to ascertain the political situation in Chad, for example, or how I would go about accessing a supercomputer to do high-quality computer animation.

My secretarial system could also filter out electronic junk mail—which sounds trivial, except that in the age of electronic communications it may be a matter of mental survival. For example, say I'm a magazine journalist trying desperately to meet a deadline on a major story. I don't want to have my computer beeping at me for every electronic-mail message that comes in. On the other hand, I *do* want it to alert me if one of the field bureaus is sending in new information that needs to go in my story. Yet I can't just set my electronic mail system to accept any message labeled *Urgent,* because there are at least three companies sending me "urgent" messages about hot new prices on used IBM PCs, and one fellow in New Hampshire is desperately trying to convince me that Einstein's theory of relativity is wrong and that the moon is about to spiral into the Earth. So what I really want is a personal-receptionist program living inside the network, with enough natural-language ability to recognize contents of a message and enough common sense to know what I do and don't want to see.

There are other possibilities. In a corporate setting, for example, one can imagine a kind of office-manager program living in the system and keeping track of the electronic flow of work: Who has to read this item? Who has to coordinate on that project? Who has to sign off on this decision, and by when? Such a program would act to regulate the flow of electronic information through the organization, while preventing backlogs and keeping track of productivity. It might even function as a kind of social secretary: based on its expertise about policy and etiquette, it could remind people what kind of replies need to be sent to what messages. At the same time, the office-manager program could serve as a kind of gatekeeper for the network, providing people sure and convenient access to information when company policy says they are authorized to have it, and keeping them out when they are not authorized to have it.

———————

Looking beyond information networks, we can easily imagine how these same concepts of distributed, intelligent management might apply to other systems: an automated electric power grid, using telecommunications and computers to optimize the efficiency of transcontinental power lines[14] . . . an automated air-traffic control system, juggling information from radars hundreds of miles apart . . . an automated city traffic-control system, coordinating lights and directing traffic around bottlenecks on a regional basis, so that things flow smoothly even in rush hour. Ultimately, in fact, we can imagine society itself being run by networks of interlinked intelligences—a single giant robot with each component an expert in its own niche, and the whole greater than the parts.

So perhaps we should define the concept of *robot* yet again: Robots are not just machines that can walk around and manipulate things, or even machines that can take action on their own. In a less visible, yet more all-pervasive sense than Asimov or Williamson ever realized, robots are machines that take care of us.

HOW MUCH RESPONSIBILITY?

So we return to the questions we started with. Robots, in the broad sense that we have defined them, play the role of *agent*. Coupled with AI, moreover, they will be able to take on responsibility and authority in ways that no machines have ever done before. So perhaps it's worth asking before we get to that point just how much power and authority these intelligent machines *ought* to have—and just who, if anyone, will control them.

Obfuscation and Big Brother

There is ample reason to be concerned about such questions. Computers don't come equipped with any built-in ethical system analogous to Asimov's three laws of robotics. And for that very reason, they are well suited to act as tools and smoke screens for the powers that be—as bureaucrats learned almost as soon as computers were introduced. ("I'd like to help you, but I'm afraid the computer just isn't set up to do it that way. . . .") AI, unfortunately, won't necessarily change things.

To illustrate some of the issues here, imagine an expert system that serves as a bank loan examiner. Each applicant sits at a terminal in the bank's offices answering questions about his or her financial status, while the computer verifies everything by automatic queries through the network to other banks and credit companies. (The applicant could also do this through a terminal at home.) Finally, the system makes a decision: Yes, the applicant qualifies, or no, the applicant doesn't qualify.

Now, this could be a very efficient and useful system. Certainly it would be consistent in applying the bank's loan policy to each applicant. On the other hand, people may not be willing to put up with that kind of treatment from a machine. It's humiliating enough to get the once-over from a human bank official, and a few banks might get their computer screens smashed in. But in some ways it's more disturbing to think that people *will* put up with such treatment—not because the expert system does anything sinister, necessarily, but because the situation obscures the fact that the machine's "decision" actually embodies a policy made by humans. Furthermore, the decision comes wrapped in the aura of "artificial intelligence." Rejected applicants may be too intimidated to protest. And even if they do, the (human) managers of the bank could all too easily brush them off with "Gee, I'd like to help you, but the computers these days are wiser than we are. . . ."

So even a seemingly straightforward application of AI can obscure the lines of responsibility—and it's naive to think that some people won't use it that way when they don't want outsiders asking uncomfortable questions.

Another troublesome aspect of this scenario is the free and easy way that our loan applicant feeds information about his life and activities in the electronic data network. How does he know what is going to be done with that data?

Maybe a lot will be done with it. "Today we're building systems that can collect a vast amount of information on an individual's daily transactions," says Fred Weingarten, manager of the Communications and Information Technologies program at the congressional Office of Technology Assessment. "Further, systems such as those employing knowledge-based technology can do more with that information than ever before, including the making of decisions that affect private lives."[15] In that context it's worth noting that in a recent study, Weingarten's group found that at least thirty-five federal agencies were using or planned to use some form of electronic surveillance techniques—including computer-usage monitoring and the interception of electronic mail—and that current laws did not adequately regulate such electronic surveillance.[16]

There is nothing in the rules that says AI has to be benign, of course, and it's perfectly possible to imagine AI techniques in the service of Big Brother. Consider an advanced speech-recognition program that monitors every telephone call in the country for evidence of criminal activities, or a natural-language program that scans every computer bulletin board and reads every item of electronic mail. Such a system might catch a lot of obscene phone-callers and drug dealers. But how long before the definition of "criminal" starts sliding over into "subversive" and "disloyal"?

Actually, the process doesn't even have to be that dramatic. The mere possibility of surveillance is chilling. Langdon Winner, professor of politics and technology at the University of California at Santa Cruz, thinks that this may be the most insidious problem of all: "When I talk to people about this question, citing examples in which electronic monitoring has been used as a tool for harassment and coercion," he says, "they often say that they don't need to worry about it because they're not doing anything anyone would possibly want to watch. In other words, it becomes a sign of virtue for them to say: 'Thank God, I'm not involved in anything that a computer would find at all interesting.' It's precisely that response that I find troubling."

Winner finds a metaphor for this situation in a fascinating design for a building, the Panopticon, created by the nineteenth-century philosopher Jeremy Bentham:

The Panopticon was to be a circular building, several stories high, with a tower in the center. It could be used as a prison, hospital, school, or factory. A key feature of the design was that people in its rooms could not see each other, but the person in the center looking out to the periphery could gaze into every cell. Bentham saw this architecture as the ultimate means of social control. There would not even need to be a guard present in the tower at all times: all one had to do was to build in such a way that surveillance became an omnipresent possibility that would eliminate misbehavior and ensure compliance.

It appears that we now may be building an electronic Panopticon, a system of seemingly benign electronic data-gathering that creates *de facto* conditions of universal surveillance.

This isn't just a threat to individual privacy. It is a threat to our public freedoms. "Unless we take steps to prevent it," Winner concludes, "we could see a society filled with all-seeing data banks used to monitor an increasingly pliant, passive populace no longer willing to risk activities that comprise civil liberty."[17]

Tacit Assumptions in the Nuclear Age

The specter of Big Brother is never far from people's minds when they worry about the effect of computers on society. But in a sense, that kind of abuse is also the easiest to guard against. The bad guys wear black hats, so to speak; their actions are explicit and deliberate, even if covert. Thus, laws can be written to protect our electronic privacy, and a code of behavior enforced.

Much more widespread and much more insidious, however, is another kind of situation, in which the bad guys don't wear black hats. Instead, they are ordinary, well-intentioned people whose tacit assumptions and values cause us to drift in a direction we might not have taken by choice. As an example, recall the "electronic Taylorism" discussed in the last chapter; the designers of the first office word-processing machines, together with the managers who installed them, brought certain values and assumptions to the job that ended up turning many offices into electronic sweatshops. They didn't necessarily mean to do it, but that is what happened. Looking to the future, consider Licklider's multinet and the various software robots that will be required to run it; even with the best of intentions, the people who design those programs will shape what we do, what we see, what we know about, and how we interact with our fellow human beings.

PC Magazine editor Bill Machrone highlights this issue in an article about a demonstration he saw of a new electronic-mail package for PCs. The idea of the package was to render corporate communications more efficient by organizing all messages according to set categories: requests, denials, commands, counteroffers, and the like. Machrone's reaction: "communications software designed by Nazis."

"Consider that this is how people who don't like each other communicate," he explains. "It is not a foundation for trust and mutual cooperation. In fact, in most organizations, the use of techniques such as this is virtually guaranteed to put people on edge and at one another. Like anything else that mechanizes human interaction, such a system inevitably makes that interaction less human. . . . [What people in corporations need is] room to roam, freedom to grow, to express opinions, develop points of view, and interact."

So why would a group of well-meaning programmers produce such a package? Machrone asks. "Its creators are fervent believers in mechanized, highly structured communications. It works for them, and they are sure it'll work for you. They're converts to this way of thinking and they want you to be too."[18]

In short, a robot doesn't have to be an agent just of a person or an institution. Without anyone's ever fully realizing it, a robot can also be the agent of a value structure or a set of assumptions. And that is perhaps as it should be—so long as we understand what the values and assumptions really imply. Remember that Williamson's robots, who were pledged "to serve and obey, and guard men from harm," were conceived with the best of intentions.

Nowhere is this issue of tacit values and assumptions illustrated more starkly than in the realm of nuclear weapons and nuclear war. In particular, consider the "launch-on-warning" strategy.

There has long been a school of thought among strategic planners in the United States that our land-based nuclear missiles should be launched as soon as incoming warheads show up on radar. Afterward, goes the argument, it will be too late. Both the military and civilian communications network will very likely collapse as soon as the first hostile warheads fall. So even if the missiles themselves survive in their hardened silos, no one could fire them. We would have lost the war without firing a shot. Indeed, the very possibility invites a sneak attack. Thus, launch-on-warning.[19]

Now, there is an undeniable, if ruthless, logic to that argument. On the other hand, it's important to notice the tacit assumptions inherent in launch-on-warning: that a state of unrelenting hostility exists between us and the Other Side; that international fear and mistrust are the natural state of affairs; that They are sneaky devils just waiting for a chance to hit us on the blind side; that our ability to retaliate is more important than anything else, including the fate of the human race.

Are those the kind of assumptions we want to build our future on?

In any case, launch-on-warning has never been implemented—at least, not by the United States*—largely because the early-warning radars have shown a distressing tendency to give false alarms. Signals mistaken for hostile missiles in the past include flights of geese, the rising moon, and the signals from a training tape that was accidentally mounted on the wrong computer. For much the same reason, even the proponents of the idea have shied away from entrusting the launch decision to computers. Computers are too prone to break down and (currently) too rigid in their responses.

---

*There are persistent rumors that the Soviet Union *has* implemented such a policy.

However, those tacit assumptions of hostility, fear, and mistrust are very strong. The pressure to move toward a launch-on-warning strategy is always with us, especially as our land-based nuclear-missile forces become increasingly vulnerable to cruise missiles launched from submarines off the coast, and to increasingly accurate intercontinental missiles routed over the pole. Indeed, the existence of new-generation computers and a new generation of machine intelligence may well tempt some future administration to take the step.

Meanwhile, we have President Reagan's concept of a space-based defense against ballistic missiles: "Star Wars." The system is intended strictly as a defensive measure; so if we assume for the sake of argument that it *will* be built and *will* be effective—two controversial assumptions—then the consequences of a false alarm would presumably not be as dire. The orbital lasers and such would just waste a lot of ammunition firing at empty space. An accidental activation of the system, on the other hand, might reveal its weaknesses to the other side and leave the country temporarily unprotected. So the indirect consequences could be very serious. In any case, the pressure to put an automatic trigger on such a defensive system are the same as they are for launch-on-warning: Once incoming missiles show up on the radar screen, there is just too little time to rely on having the president or anyone else make meaningful decisions.

In short, the relentless logic of the technology seems to be leading us ever closer to a point where the fate of the human race can no longer be entrusted to humans. Officially, of course, the release of our offensive nuclear arsenal can only be authorized by the president in his role as commander-in-chief. Moreover, the officials of the Strategic Defense Initiative Organization have always maintained that any future Star Wars defensive system will likewise be under the control of the president. And there is no reason to doubt them at their word.

However, even if we leave aside a host of practical questions—Will the president be able to communicate with the missile command centers after the bombs start falling? Will he even be *alive* at that point?—we can still ask what human control would really mean in a situation of nuclear crisis.

The fact is that most of the offensive and defensive systems would have to be automated in any case; there's simply no way for any one human to understand the myriad details involved. Indeed, from what little one can gather about U.S. plans for responding in a nuclear war, the president will essentially be presented with a short menu of preprepared options: Place *these* forces on alert, for example, or launch *that* contingent of missiles while holding *those* back, and so on.

Given the painfully short response times available in a nuclear attack, this menu approach is probably the only rational way to go. However, it's all too easy to imagine the scene: one aging politician—the president—sitting in front of a computer terminal that he may never have seen before, trying to read and digest a list of complex options while half-hysterical advisers are whispering contradictory advice in each ear. Meanwhile, he himself is probably becoming panicky with the knowledge that an irrevocable decision has to be made right *now*. Just how much careful consideration is he going to be able to give to his choice?

Very little, probably. In fact, one is left with an uncomfortable feeling that "controlling" nuclear forces in such a situation is virtually a contradiction in terms. The real choices will have already been made by the people who prepare the items on the menu—which means that it becomes critically important to know what their assumptions are. If they only present options that refer to this or that degree of belligerence, with no options that allow for backing away from hostilities, then the system has built into it the presumption that *there will be war*. Indeed, so far as an outside reporter can tell, that is exactly the case. There is precious little consideration being given on either side to helping leaders calm the crisis.

Actually, this is one place where AI techniques might be very helpful. Recall the discussion of facilitator systems in Chapter 9: It's easy to imagine a calm, nonhysterical expert system advising some future president on various diplomatic options in a nuclear crisis, together with predictions of the other side's likely reaction. Never despairing, never forgetting things, never becoming obsessive about this or that course of action under the pressure of the moment—such a machine would be invaluable as the one cool head in the midst of chaos. Indeed, if consulted beforehand, it might help keep the crisis from developing in the first place. The question is, Is anyone planning to develop or deploy such a system, or any other decision-support system for helping our leaders deal with a crisis? At the moment no one seems to be. Does that mean that the presumption of war takes precedence?

From one point of view, of course, this debate over human control of nuclear weapons can be read as a rationale for turning the whole thing over to computers. In a nuclear age, goes the argument, a new generation of very intelligent computers incorporating AI could actually defend the country better, faster, and more rationally than humans. And who knows? Maybe they could. But here are some thoughts to ponder:

- Even if computers *are* better than humans at fighting a nuclear war, is it ethical to abdicate responsibility for the fate of human civilization to machines? For better or worse, that is *our* responsibility.
- Even if computers can do the job better than humans, computers are not human: An artificially intelligent machine may know *about* humans, in some sense, but it's hard to imagine that any machine in the foreseeable future will be able to appreciate the full implications of launching a nuclear-tipped missile. Even with AI, a computer just follows orders as best it can—the ultimate Good German. Perhaps a little hesitation and a chance for second thoughts ought to be kept in the system.
- Even if computers can be programmed to decide the future of the race in a cooler and more rational manner than humans are capable of, perhaps

it's worth devoting a little effort along the way to making sure that neither humans nor machines are ever put in that position.

The Theory and Practice of Machine Ethics

In the last analysis, it seems unlikely that the question "How much responsibility?" is ever going to have a simple answer. After all, human beings have been arguing among themselves about responsibility, authority, and control for many thousands of years, with no final resolution in sight; I see no reason to think that the answers are going to be any easier just because we've suddenly introduced some new intelligences based on silicon instead of flesh and blood.

However, one thing that is apparent from the above discussion is that intelligent machines *will* embody values, assumptions, and purposes, whether their programmers consciously intend them to or not. Thus, as computers and robots become more and more intelligent, it becomes imperative that we think carefully and explicitly about what those built-in values are. Perhaps what we need is, in fact, a theory and practice of machine ethics, in the spirit of Asimov's three laws of robotics.

Admittedly, a concept like "machine ethics" sounds hopelessly fuzzy and far-fetched—at first. But maybe it's not as far out of reach as it seems. Ethics, after all, is basically a matter of making choices based on concepts of right and wrong, duty and obligation. We can already see a glimmer of how computers might make such choices in Jaime Carbonell's model of subjective understanding (discussed in Chapter 3). Carbonell showed how programs could be governed by hierarchies of goals, which would guide their reasoning processes in certain directions and not in others. Thus, it might very well be possible to formulate a hierarchy of goals that embody ethical concepts; the hard part, as always, would lie in formulating precisely what those concepts ought to be.

Another hint comes from the work on distributed processing that I discussed both in Chapter 5 and again in this chapter: In the effort to teach individual computers how to cooperate among themselves without having some boss computer tell them what to do, AI researchers are beginning to discover the principles that govern when individuals will work together harmoniously, and when they will not.

In any case, the effort of understanding machine ethics may turn out to be invaluable not just as a matter of practicality but for its own sake. The effort to endow computers with intelligence has led us to look deep within ourselves to understand what intelligence really is. In much the same way, the effort to construct ethical machines will inevitably lead us to look within ourselves and reexamine our own conceptions of right and wrong. Of course, this is hardly a new activity in human history; it has been the domain of religion and philosophy for millennia. But then, pondering the nature of intelligence is not a new activity, either. The difference in each case is that, for the first time, we are having to explain ourselves to an entity that knows *nothing* about us. A computer is the proverbial Martian. And for that very reason, it is like a mirror: The more we have to explain ourselves, the more we may come to understand ourselves.

THE SHAPE OF THE FUTURE

As the great Danish physicist Niels Bohr once said, "It's hard to predict—especially the future." So we can talk all we want about possibilities and trends, but no one really knows what the new generation of computers will bring. Even if we did know, people would still be arguing about precisely which effects were good and which were bad.

In the broadest terms, of course, our prospects are bracketed by the visions of Asimov and Williamson. On the one hand, we have the bright vision of intelligent machines as our servants, advisers, tutors, companions, even our friends. According to this vision, computers represent a profoundly humane technology. Indeed, we can look forward to a new kind of partnership between mankind and machines, in which intelligent computers and robots will both relieve us of drudgery and tedium, while expanding our ability to understand and to cope with the world. The result will thus be a richer and more fulfilling life for all of us.

On the other hand, we have a darker vision of the future as an exercise in blank futility. Even if we leave aside our concerns about Big Brother, what will happen when all these artificially intelligent computers and robots leave us with nothing to do? What will be the point of living? Granted that human obsolescence is hardly an urgent problem. It will be a long, long time before computers can master politics, poetry, or any of the other things we really care about. But a "long time" is not forever; what happens when the computers *have* mastered politics and poetry? One can easily envision a future when the world is run quietly and efficiently by a set of exceedingly expert systems, in which machines produce goods, services, and wealth in abundance, and where everyone lives a life of luxury. It sounds idyllic—and utterly pointless.

But personally, I have to side with the optimists—for two reasons. The first stems from the simple observation that technology is made by people. Despite the strong impression that we are helpless in the face of, say, the spread of automobiles or the more mindless clerical applications of computers, the fact is that technology does not develop according to an immutable genetic code. It embodies human values and human choices. And to the extent that we can make those choices consciously instead of by blindly stumbling into them—admittedly not an easy thing to do—we do have control. Indeed, as we've just seen, the effort of developing intelligent computers may help us gain the insight to make those choices more wisely.

My second reason for being optimistic stems from a simple question: What does it mean to be "obsolete"?

A parable: Behold the lilies of the field. Considered purely as devices for converting light into energy, they've already been made obsolete by solar cells. But they go right on blooming, because photochemistry is not what lilies are about.

Another parable: Outside my window, the sparrows gather every day at a bird feeder. Considered purely as flying machines, they've long since been made obsolete by 747s. But they go right on eating and squabbling, because flying isn't what sparrows are about.

So what are human beings about? Perhaps our purpose is to serve God. Or perhaps we are here to serve each other. Perhaps we are here to create beauty in music, art, and literature, or to comprehend the universe, or to have fun. I won't presume to dictate the correct answer for anyone else. But I do suspect that in the long run, the most important implication of AI may be that it leads us to confront this question anew.

No, we don't know what this new world will be like. Perhaps it's just hard for those of us born to the work ethic to imagine what our hypothetical descendants will do with themselves. They may think of some very creative entertainments. Or they may create a new golden age of art and science. And they almost certainly will think of a whole new set of problems to worry about. But consider this: Some four thousand years stand between us and the author of Genesis. Technology has changed the world immeasurably in that time. And yet we can still read his words and feel their power. I somehow doubt that the advent of intelligent machines is going to change that very much. These machines may transform the world in ways we can only guess at—but we will still be human.

References

REFERENCES, INTRODUCTION

1. Allen Newell, "Fairytales," Remarks at the Inaugural Dinner for the U.A. and Helen Whitaker Professorships, 17 September 1976; reprinted as *Viewpoints, No. 3,* Carnegie-Mellon University Publications Office, 1976.
2. Joseph Weizenbaum, quoted in Fred Guterl, "Next Generation Impacts," *IEEE Spectrum,* November 1983, p. 117.
3. Newell (1976), *op. cit.*
4. Bruno Bettelheim, *The Uses of Enchantment* (New York: Vintage Books, 1977), p. 309.

REFERENCES, CHAPTER 1

1. Pamela McCorduck, *Machines Who Think* (San Francisco: W. H. Freeman, 1979), p. 95.
2. George A. Miller, "The Magical Number Seven, Plus or Minus Two: Some Limits on Our Capacity for Processing Information," *Psychological Review* 63, pp. 81–97.
3. Howard Gardner, *The Mind's New Science: A History of the Cognitive Revolution* (New York: Basic Books, 1985).
4. Allen Newell and Herbert A. Simon, *Human Problem Solving* (Englewood Cliffs, N.J.: Prentice Hall, 1972), p. 877.
5. Alan M. Turing, "On Computable Numbers, With an Application to the Entscheidungsproblem," *Proceedings of the London Mathematics Society,* Series 2, 42 (1936), pp. 230–265.
6. Claude E. Shannon, "A Symbolic Analysis of Relay and Switching Circuits," *Transactions of the American Institute of Electrical Engineers* 57 (1938), pp. 1–11.
7. Warren McCulloch and Walter Pitts, "A Logical Calculus of the Ideas Imminent in Neural Nets," *Bulletin of Mathematical Biophysics* 5 (1943).
8. Murray Eden, "Cybernetics," *The Study of Information: Interdisciplinary Messages,* Fritz Machlup and Una Mansfield, eds. (New York: John Wiley and Sons, 1983).
9. Norbert Weiner, *Cybernetics: Communication and Control in the Animal and the Machine* (New York: John Wiley and Sons, 1948); 2d ed. (Cambridge, Mass.: MIT Press, 1961).
10. Arturo Rosenblueth, Norbert Weiner, and Julian Bigelow, "Behavior, Purpose, and Teleology," *Philosophy of Science* 10 (1943), pp. 18–24.
11. Allen Newell, "Intellectual Issues in the History of Artificial Intelligence," in Fritz Machlup and Una Mansfield, eds., *op. cit.,* p. 192.
12. Claude E. Shannon, "A Mathematical Theory of Communication," *Bell System Technical Journal* 27 (July/October 1949), pp. 379–423; pp. 623–656.
13. Myron Tribus, "Thirty Years of Information Theory," in Machlup and Mansfield, eds., *op. cit.,* pp. 475–484.
14. Stan Augarten, *Bit by Bit: An Illustrated History of Computers* (New York: Ticknor and Fields, 1984).

15. Weiner, *op. cit.*, p. 155.
16. Claude Shannon, "A Chess Playing Machine," *Scientific American*, February 1950.
17. McCorduck, *op. cit.*, p. 117.
18. Herbert A. Simon, "Herbert A. Simon," *A History of Psychology in Autobiography*, Vol. VII, ed. Gardner Lindzey (San Francisco: W. H. Freeman, 1980).
19. Herbert A. Simon, Interview with Constance Holden, 22 January 1986.
20. Simon, in Lindzey, ed., *op. cit.*, p. 460.
21. McCorduck, *op. cit.*, p. 132.
22. McCorduck, *op. cit.*, p. 134.
23. Newell and Simon, *op. cit.*, p. 109.
24. George Polya, *How to Solve It*, 2d ed. (New York: Doubleday, Anchor Books, 1957).
25. Simon, in Lindzey, ed., *op. cit.*, pp. 462–463.
26. McCorduck, *op. cit.*, p. 142.
27. McCorduck, *op. cit.*, p. 116.
28. McCorduck, *op. cit.*, p. 141.
29. George A. Miller, "A Very Personal History," Talk to Cognitive Science Workshop, MIT, 1 June 1979; quoted in Gardner, *op. cit.*, p. 29.
30. McCorduck, *op. cit.*, p. 212.
31. Newell and Simon, *op. cit.*, p. 416.
32. Simon, in Lindzey, ed., *op. cit.*, p. 463.
33. Herbert Simon, Interview with Constance Holden, 22 January 1986.
34. Gardner, *op. cit.*, p. 384.
35. Herbert A. Simon, *Sciences of the Artificial* (Cambridge, Mass.: MIT Press, 1969).
36. Herbert A. Simon, Interview with Constance Holden, 22 January 1986.
37. Newell, in Machlup and Mansfield, eds., *op. cit.*, pp. 192–193.

REFERENCES, CHAPTER 2

1. Herbert A. Simon, quoted in Pamela McCorduck, *Machines Who Think* (San Francisco: W. H. Freeman, 1979), p. 188.
2. Marvin Minsky, "Why People Think Computers Can't," *Technology Review*, November/December 1983, pp. 64–70.
3. Natalie Dehn and Roger Schank, "Artificial and Human Intelligence," *Handbook of Human Intelligence*, Robert J. Sternberg, ed. (Cambridge, England: Cambridge University Press, 1982), pp. 361–362.
4. Jill Larkin, John McDermott, Dorothea P. Simon, Herbert A. Simon, "Expert and Novice Performance in Solving Physics Problems," *Science* 208 (1980), p. 1335.
5. W. G. Chase and Herbert A. Simon, "The Mind's Eye in Chess," *Visual Information Processing*, W. G. Chase, ed. (New York: Academic Press, 1973).
6. Edward A. Feigenbaum, Bruce G. Buchanan, and Joshua Lederberg, "On Generality and Problem-Solving: A Case Study Using the DENDRAL Program," *Machine Intelligence* 6 (Edinburgh: Edinburgh University Press, 1971), p. 187.
7. I. Goldstein and Seymour Papert, "Artificial Intelligence, Language, and the Study of Knowledge," *Cognitive Science* 1, no. 1 (1977).

8. Edward A. Feigenbaum, private communication, May 1983.

9. Richard O. Duda and Edward H. Shortliffe, "Expert Systems Research," *Science* 220 (1983), p. 264.

10. Edward H. Shortliffe, *Computer-Based Medical Consultations: MYCIN* (New York: Elsevier, 1976).

11. Paul Harmon and David King, *Expert Systems* (New York: John Wiley and Sons, 1985), p. 21.

12. Richard O. Duda and Edward H. Shortliffe, *op. cit.*, p. 264.

13. Feigenbaum (1977), *op. cit.*, p. 5.

14. W. Van Melle, "A Domain-Independent System that Aids in Constructing Consultation Programs," Doctoral Dissertation, Stanford University Computer Science Department Report No. STAN-CS-80-820 (1980).

15. Avron Barr and Edward A. Feigenbaum, *The Handbook of Artificial Intelligence*, Vol. II (Los Altos, Calif.: William Kaufmann, 1982), p. 84.

16. Harry E. Pople, Jr., "CADUCEUS: An Experimental Expert System for Medical Diagnosis," *The AI Business*, Patrick H. Winston and Karen A. Prendergast, eds. (Cambridge, Mass.: MIT Press, 1984), Chap. 5.

17. Duda and Shortliffe, *op. cit.*, p. 266.

18. Randall Davis, "Expert Systems: Where Are We? And Where Do We Go From Here?" *The AI Magazine*, Summer 1982, pp. 3–22.

19. Feigenbaum (1977), *op. cit.*, p. 4.

20. Jon Doyle, "Expert Systems Without Computers, or Theory and Trust in Artificial Intelligence," *The AI Magazine*, Summer 1984, p. 60.

21. Randall Davis and Douglas B. Lenat, *Knowledge-Based Systems in Artificial Intelligence*, Part 2 (New York: McGraw-Hill, 1982).

22. Jaime G. Carbonell, Ryszard S. Michalski, and Tom M. Mitchell, "Machine Learning: A Historical and Methodological Analysis," *The AI Magazine*, Fall 1983, pp. 69–78.

23. Jaime G. Carbonell and Steven Minton, "Metaphor and Common-Sense Reasoning," Carnegie-Mellon University Reprint CMU-CS-83-110, 5 March 1983, p. 2.

24. Lofti A. Zadeh, "Making Computers Think Like People," *IEEE Spectrum*, August 1984, pp. 26–32.

25. Duda and Shortliffe, *op. cit.*, p. 266.

26. Marvin Minsky, Presidential Address to the American Association for Artificial Intelligence, 1982.

27. Marvin Minsky, "A Framework for Representing Knowledge," *Mind Design*, John Haugeland, ed. (Cambridge, Mass.: MIT Press, 1981), pp. 95–128; reprinted in *Readings in Knowledge Representation*, Ronald J. Brachman and Hector J. Levesque, eds. (Los Altos, Calif.: Morgan Kaufmann, 1985), pp. 245–262.

28. Barr and Feigenbaum, *op. cit.*, pp. 217–218.

29. Roger C. Schank and Robert P. Abelson, *Scripts, Plans, Goals, and Understanding* (Hillsdale, N.J.: Lawrence Erlbaum, 1977).

30. M. Ross Quillian, "Word Concepts: A Theory and Simulation of Some Basic Semantic Capabilities," *Behavioral Science* 12 (1967), pp. 410–430.

31. Anderson, *op. cit.*, pp. 119–123.

32. *The Handbook of Artificial Intelligence*, Vol. III, Paul R. Cohen and Edward A. Feigenbaum, eds. (Los Altos, Calif.: William Kaufmann, 1982), pp. 39–40.

33. John R. Anderson and Gordon H. Bower, *Human Associative Memory* (Washington, D.C.: V. H. Winston and Sons, 1973).

34. John R. Anderson, *Language, Memory, and Thought* (Hillsdale, N. J.: Lawrence Erlbaum, 1976).

35. John R. Anderson et al., "Intelligent Tutoring Systems," *Science* 228 (1985), p. 456.

36. John R. Anderson, *Cognitive Psychology*, 2d ed. (New York: W. H. Freeman, 1985) pp. 115–117.

37. Richard Fikes and Tom Kehler, "The Role of Frame-Based Representation in Reasoning," *Communication of the ACM*, September 1985, pp. 904–920.

38. Davis and Lenat, *op. cit.*, Part 1.

39. Douglas B. Lenat, "The Nature of Heuristics," *Artificial Intelligence* 19(2), pp. 189–249 (1982); "Theory Formation by Heuristic Search, Theory of Heuristics (II): Background and Examples," *Artificial Intelligence* 21(1,2), pp. 31–59 (1983); "EURISKO: A Program that Learns New Heuristics and Domain Concepts, The Nature of Heuristics (III): Program Design and Results," *Artificial Intelligence* 21(1,2), pp. 61–98 (1983).

40. Quoted in Michael Schrage, "Artificial Intelligence: Teaching Computers the Power of Creative Stupidity," *Washington Post*, 1 December 1985, p. F1.

41. Douglas B. Lenat, Mayank Prakash, and Mary Shepherd, "CYC," *The AI Magazine*, Winter 1986, pp. 65–85.

42. Hubert L. Dreyfus, *What Computers Can't Do*, 2d ed. (New York: Harper and Row, Colophon Books, 1979), pp. 81–82.

43. Anderson (1985), *op. cit.*, Chap. 4.

44. Carbonell, Michalski, and Mitchell, *op. cit.*, p. 71.

REFERENCES, CHAPTER 3

1. Warren Weaver, "Translation," *Machine Translation of Languages*, W. N. Locke and A. D. Booth, eds. (New York: Technology Press of MIT and Wiley, 1955). (Original paper, 1949.)

2. Yehoshua Bar-Hillel, "The Present Status of Automatic Translation of Languages," *Advances in Computers*, Vol. 1, F. L. Alt, ed. (New York: Academic Press, 1960), p. 159.

3. David Waltz, "Artificial Intelligence: An Assessment of the State-of-the-Art and Recommendation for Future Directions," *The AI Magazine*, Fall 1983, pp. 56–57.

4. Joyce Heard and Leslie Helm, "Machines Are Mastering the Language of Multinational Business," *Business Week*, 16 September 1985, p. 90J.

5. Joseph Weizenbaum, *Computer Power and Human Reason* (New York: W. H. Freeman, 1976), pp. 3–4.

6. Kenneth Colby, S. Weber, and F. Hilf, "Artificial Paranoia," *Artificial Intelligence* 2 (1971), pp. 1–25.

7. Daniel G. Bobrow and J. B. Fraser, "An Augmented State Transition Network Analysis Procedure," *Proceedings of the International Joint Conference on Artificial Intelligence* (Washington, D.C., 1969), pp. 557–567.

8. William A. Woods, "Transition Network Grammars for Natural Language

Analysis," *Communications of the Association for Computing Machinery* 13, no. 10 (October 1970), pp. 591–606.

9. Terry Winograd, *Understanding Natural Language* (New York: Academic Press, 1972).

10. John R. Anderson, *Cognitive Psychology,* 2d ed. (New York: W. H. Freeman, 1985), pp. 323–327.

11. Anderson, *op. cit.,* pp. 328–333.

12. Derek Bickerton, "Creole Languages," *Scientific American,* July 1983, p. 116; "The Language Bioprogram Hypothesis," *The Behavioral and Brain Sciences* 7 (1984), 173–221.

13. Bickerton, *ibid.,* pp. 175–176.

14. Anderson, *op. cit.,* p. 342.

15. Charles Fillmore, "The Case for Case," *Universals in Linguistic Theory,* E. Bach and R. Harms, eds. (New York: Holt, Rinehart and Winston, 1968), pp. 1–88.

16. Phillip J. Hayes and Jaime G. Carbonell, "A Tutorial on Techniques and Applications for Natural Language Processing," Carnegie-Mellon University Reprint CMU-CS-83-158, 17 October 1983; originally prepared for the Eighth International Joint Conference on Artificial Intelligence (Karlsruhe, West Germany, August 1983).

17. Terry Winograd, *Syntax; Language as a Cognitive Process,* Vol. 1 (Reading, Mass.: Addison-Wesley, 1983), pp. 311–326.

18. Hayes and Carbonell, *op. cit.*

19. Roger C. Schank, *Conceptual Information Processing* (New York: North Holland, 1975).

20. Barr and Feigenbaum, *op. cit.,* pp. 218–219.

21. Roger C. Schank and Robert P. Abelson, *Scripts, Plans, Goals, and Understanding* (Hillsdale, N.J.: Lawrence Erlbaum, 1977).

22. Weizenbaum, *op. cit.,* p. 200.

23. Robert P. Abelson and J. D. Carroll, "Computer Models of Individual Belief Systems," *American Behavioral Scientist* 8, pp. 24–30 (1965); Robert P. Abelson and C. M. Reich, "Implicational Molecules: A Method for Extracting Meaning from Input Sentences," *International Joint Conference on Artificial Intelligence* 1, pp. 647–748 (1969).

24. Robert P. Abelson, "Differences Between Belief and Knowledge Systems," *Cognitive Science* 3, pp. 355–366 (1979).

25. Robert P. Abelson, "The Structure of Belief Systems," *Computer Models of Thought and Language,* Roger C. Schank and Kenneth M. Colby, eds. (San Francisco: W. H. Freeman, 1973).

26. Schank and Abelson, *ibid.,* p. 72.

27. Jaime G. Carbonell, *Subjective Understanding: Computer Models of Belief Systems* (Ann Arbor: UMI Research Press, 1979).

28. Carbonell, *op. cit.,* pp. 44–45.

29. Carbonell, *op. cit.,* p. 229.

30. Herbert A. Simon, "Cohabiting the Planet with Computers," *Cohabiting with Computers,* Joseph F. Traub, ed. (Los Altos, Calif.: William Kaufmann, 1985), pp. 155–171.

31. David Sylvan, Interview with M. Mitchell Waldrop, 19 December 1985.

32. Barbara J. Grosz, "Utterance and Objective: Issues in Natural Language Communication," *The AI Magazine* 1, no. 1 (Spring 1980), pp. 11–20.

33. J. L. Austin, *How to Do Things With Words* (Cambridge, Mass.: Harvard University Press, 1962).

34. John R. Searle, *Speech Acts* (Cambridge, England: Cambridge University Press, 1969).

35. Jon Barwise and John Perry, *Situations and Attitudes* (Cambridge, Mass.: MIT Press, 1983).

REFERENCES, CHAPTER 4

1. Takeo Kanade and Raj Reddy, "Computer Vision: The Challenge of Imperfect Inputs," *IEEE Spectrum*, November 1983, p. 88.

2. Tomaso Poggio, private communication, April 1984.

3. David Marr, *Vision* (San Francisco: W. H. Freeman, 1982).

4. Marr, *ibid.*, pp. 329–330.

5. Tomaso Poggio, "Vision by Man and Machine," *Scientific American*, April 1984, pp. 106–116.

6. David Marr and Ellen Hildreth, "Theory of Edge Detection," *Proceedings of the Royal Society of London* B207 (1980), pp. 187–217.

7. Poggio, *op. cit.*, pp. 110–112.

8. John R. Anderson, *Cognitive Psychology*, 2d ed. (New York: W. H. Freeman, 1985), pp. 54–57.

9. Marr, *op. cit.*, p. 102.

10. David Marr and Tomaso Poggio, "Cooperative Computation of Stereo Disparity," *Science* 194 (1976), pp. 283–287; "A Computational Theory of Human Stereo Vision," *Proceedings of the Royal Society of London* B204 (1979), pp. 301–328.

11. W. Eric L. Grimson and David Marr, "A Computer Implementation of a Theory of Human Stereo Vision," *Proceedings of the Royal Society of London* B292 (1980), pp. 217–253.

12. Anderson, *op. cit.*, pp. 66–70.

13. Anderson, *op. cit.*, Chap. 4.

14. Thomas O. Binford, "Visual Perception by Computer." Paper presented at the IEEE Conference on Systems and Control, December 1971, Miami.

15. David Marr and H. Keith Nishihara, "Representation and Recognition of the Spatial Organization of Three-Dimensional Shapes," *Proceedings of the Royal Society of London* B200 (1978), pp. 269–294.

16. H. Christopher Longuet-Higgins, "A Theory of Vision" (review of David Marr's *Vision*), *Science* 218, pp. 991–992.

17. John W. Dizard, "Machines That See Look for a Market," *Fortune*, 17 September 1985, pp. 87–97.

18. Azriel Rosenfeld et al., "Report of the Research Briefing Panel on Computer Vision and Pattern Recognition," *Research Briefings 1985* (Washington, D.C.: National Academy Press, 1985), pp. 88–100.

19. Herb Brody, "Kurzweil's Keyboard," *High Technology*, February 1985, p. 27.

20. *Ibid.*, p. 94.

21. Rodney A. Brooks, "Model-Based Three-Dimensional Interpretation of Two-Dimensional Images," *International Joint Conference on Artificial Intelligence* 7 (1981), pp. 619–624.

22. Rosenfeld et al., *op. cit.,* p. 94.

23. Rosenfeld et al., *op. cit.,* p. 89.

24. Dizard, *op. cit.*

25. Berthold K. P. Horn and Katsushi Ikeuchi, "The Mechanical Manipulation of Randomly Oriented Parts," *Scientific American,* August 1984, pp. 100–111.

26. Berthold K. P. Horn, "Obtaining Shape From Shading Information," *The Psychology of Computer Vision,* P. H. Winston, ed. (New York: McGraw-Hill, 1975); "Understanding Image Intensities," *Artificial Intelligence* 8 (1977), pp. 201–231.

27. Tomaso Poggio, Vincent Torre, and Christof Koch, "Computational Vision and Regularization Theory," submitted to *Nature.*

28. Kanade and Reddy, *op. cit.,* p. 89.

REFERENCES, CHAPTER 5

1. Hans P. Moravec, "Visual Mapping by a Robot Rover," *International Joint Conference on Artificial Intelligence* 6 (1979), pp. 598–600.

2. "Report of the Research Briefing Panel on Computer Architecture," *Research Reports* (Washington: National Academy of Sciences, 1984), pp. 4–6.

3. Charles L. Seitz, "The Cosmic Cube," *Communications of the ACM* 28, no. 1 (January 1985), pp. 22–33.

4. Eric J. Lerner, "Parallel Processing Gets Down to Business," *High Technology,* July 1985, pp. 20–28.

5. W. Daniel Hillis, *The Connection Machine* (Cambridge, Mass.: MIT Press, 1985).

6. Geoffrey E. Hinton, "Distributed Representations," Carnegie-Mellon University Reprint CMU-CS-84-157 (October 1984), p. 1; to be reprinted in *Parallel Distributed Processing: Explorations in the Micro-Structure of Cognition,* J. L. McClelland and David E. Rumelhart, eds. (Publisher TK in press).

7. Scott Kirkpatrick et al., "Optimization by Simulated Annealing," *Science* 220 (1983), pp. 671–680.

8. John J. Hopfield, "Neural Networks and Physical Systems With Emergent Collective Computational Abilities," *Proceedings of the National Academy of Sciences* 79 (1982), pp. 2554–2558.

9. Scott E. Fahlman, Geoffrey E. Hinton, and Terrence J. Sejnowski, "Massively Parallel Architectures for AI: NETL, THISTLE, and BOLTZMANN Machines," *Proceedings of the National Conference on Artificial Intelligence (AAAI)* (Los Altos, Calif.: William Kaufmann, 1983), pp. 109–113.

10. Paul Smolensky, "Schema Selection and Stochastic Inference in Modular Environments," *ibid.,* pp. 378–382.

11. Geoffrey E. Hinton, Terrence J. Sejnowski, and David Ackley, "Boltzmann Machines: Constraint Satisfaction Networks That Learn," Carnegie-Mellon University Reprint CMU-CS-84-119 (May 1984).

12. William F. Allman, "Mindworks," *Science 86,* May 1986, pp. 22–31.

13. Randall Davis and Reid G. Smith, "Negotiation as a Metaphor for Distributed Problem Solving," *Artificial Intelligence* 20 (1983), pp. 63–109.

14. Thomas W. Malone, Richard Fikes, and Michael Howard, "Enterprise: A Market-Like Task Scheduler for Distributed Computing Environments," WP No. 111, Center for Information Systems Research, MIT, October 1983.

15. Victor R. Lesser and Daniel D. Corkill, "The Distributed Vehicle Monitoring Testbed: A Tool for Investigating Distributed Problem-Solving Networks," *The AI Magazine,* Fall 1983, pp. 15–33.

16. Lee D. Erman, Frederick Hayes-Roth, Victor R. Lesser, and D. Raj Reddy, "The HEARSAY II Speech Understanding System: Integrating Knowledge to Resolve Uncertainty," *Computing Surveys* 12, no. 2 (1980), pp. 213–253.

17. Thomas W. Malone and Stephen A. Smith, "Tradeoffs in Designing Organizations: Implications for New Forms of Human Organizations and Computer Systems," CISR WP No. 112 and SLOAN WP No. 1541-84, Center for Information Systems Research, MIT, March 1984.

18. Carl E. Hewitt and Peter de Jong, "Open Systems," *Perspectives in Conceptual Modeling* (New York: Springer-Verlang, 1983).

19. William A. Kornfield and Carl Hewitt, "The Scientific Community Metaphor," MIT Artificial Intelligence Laboratory Memo No. 641, January 1981.

20. Carl E. Hewitt, "Control as Message Passing," *Artificial Intelligence* 8 (1977), pp. 323–363.

21. Carl E. Hewitt and Henry Lieberman, "Design Issues in Parallel Architectures for Artificial Intelligence," MIT Artificial Intelligence Laboratory Memo No. 750, November 1983.

22. Howard Gardner, *Frames of Mind: The Theory of Multiple Intelligences* (New York: Basic Books, 1983).

23. Marvin Minsky, "Music, Mind, and Meaning," *Computer Music Journal* 5, no. 3 (Fall 1981), pp. 28–44.

24. Marvin Minsky, "The Society Theory of Thinking," *Proceedings of the Fifth International Joint Conference on Artificial Intelligence* (1977); reprinted in *Artificial Intelligence: An MIT Perspective* Vol II, Patrick H. Winston and Richard H. Brown, eds. (Cambridge, Mass.: MIT Press, 1979), pp. 421–450.

25. Marvin Minsky, *The Society of Mind* (New York: Simon and Schuster, 1986).

26. *Ibid.,* p. 13.

REFERENCES, CHAPTER 6

1. Mary Shelley, *Frankenstein* (first published 1818), Chapter 4.

2. Alan Turing, "Computing Machinery and Intelligence" (1950), reprinted in *Computers and Thought,* Edward Feigenbaum and J. Feldman, eds. (New York: McGraw-Hill, 1963).

3. Seymour Papert, *Mindstorms: Children, Computers, and Powerful Ideas* (New York: Basic Books, 1980), p. 165.

4. Joseph Weizenbaum, *Computer Power and Human Reason* (New York: W. H. Freeman, 1976), p. 201.

5. Yvonne Baskin, "The Way We Act," *Science 85,* November 1985, pp. 94–100.

6. Marvin Minsky, quoted in Patrick Huyghe, "Of Two Minds," *Psychology Today,* December 1983, p. 34.

7. Marvin Minsky, "Music, Mind, and Meaning," *Computer Music Journal* 5, no. 3 (Fall 1981), pp. 28–44.

8. Marvin Minsky, "Jokes and the Logic of the Cognitive Unconscious," MIT AI Memo No. 603, November 1980.

9. Sigmund Freud, *Jokes and Their Relation to the Unconscious* (1905), tr. Strachey (Honolulu: Hogarth Press, 1957).

10. Roberta L. Klatzky, *Memory and Awareness* (New York: W. H. Freeman, 1984), p. 3.

11. Allen Newell, "Reasoning, Problem Solving, and Decision Processes: The Problem Space as a Fundamental Category," *Attention and Performance,* Vol. 8, R. Nickerson, ed. (Hillsdale, N.J.: Lawrence Erlbaum, 1980).

12. Daniel C. Dennett, "Computer Models of the Mind—A View From the East Pole," *The Times Literary Supplement,* 14 December 1984, pp. 1453–1454; condensed from *Problems in the Representation of Knowledge and Belief,* M. Brand and R. Harnixh, eds. (Tucson: University of Arizona Press, in press).

13. Hubert L. Dreyfus, *What Computers Can't Do: The Limits of Artificial Intelligence,* 2d ed. (New York: Harper and Row, 1979).

14. Pamela McCorduck, "L'Affaire Dreyfus," *Machines Who Think* (San Francisco: W. H. Freeman, 1979), Chapter 9.

15. John R. Searle, "Minds, Brains, and Programs," *The Behavioral and Brain Sciences* 3 (1980), pp. 417–457.

16. *Ibid.,* p. 417.

17. Daniel C. Dennett, "The Role of the Computer Metaphor in Understanding the Mind," *Computer Culture: The Scientific, Intellectual, and Social Impact of the Computer,* Heinz R. Pagels, ed. (New York: New York Academy of Sciences, 1984), p. 268.

18. Sherry Turkle, *The Second Self: Computers and the Human Spirit* (New York: Simon and Schuster, 1984), p. 316.

19. Thomas Kuhn, *The Copernican Revolution* (New York: Random House, 1959).

20. Douglas R. Hofstadter, "Reductionism and Religion" (reply to Searle's "Mind, Brains, and Programs"), *The Behavioral and Brain Sciences* 3 (1980), p. 434.

21. Charles P. Snow, "The Two Cultures," *The New Statesman,* 6 October 1956; *The Two Cultures: And a Second Look* (New York: Cambridge University Press, 1963).

22. Margaret Boden, *Artificial Intelligence and Natural Man* (New York: Basic Books, 1977), p. 473.

REFERENCES, CHAPTER 7

1. "Artificial Intelligence Is Here," *Business Week,* 9 July 1984, p. 55.

2. "AI Gaining Speed in PC Arena," *Computerworld,* 16 April 1986.

3. Edward A. Feigenbaum and Pamela McCorduck, *The Fifth Generation* (Reading, Mass.: Addison-Wesley, 1983), p. vii.

4. Sherry Turkle, *The Second Self: Computers and the Human Spirit* (New York: Simon and Schuster, 1984), p. 13.

5. Raj Reddy, quoted in "The Academics Cashing In at Carnegie Group," *Business Week,* 9 July 1984, p. 60.

6. John McDermott, *ibid.*

7. James Lighthill, "A Report on Artificial Intelligence" (unpublished manuscript, 1972), Science Research Council, U.K.; quoted in Howard Gardner, *The Mind's New Science: A History of the Cognitive Revolution* (New York: Basic Books, 1985), p. 164.

8. Drew McDermott, "The Dark Ages of AI: A Panel Discussion at AAAI-84," *The AI Magazine*, Fall 1984, pp. 122–134.

9. David Waltz et al., "Artificial Intelligence: An Assessment of the State-of-the-Art and Recommendation for Future Discussions," *The AI Magazine*, Fall 1983, p. 65.

10. Roger Schank, "The Dark Ages of AI: A Panel Discussion at AAAI-84," *The AI Magazine*, Fall 1984, p. 125.

11. Marvin Minsky, "The Problems and the Promise," *The AI Business*, Patrick H. Winston and Karen H. Prendergast, eds. (Cambridge: MIT Press, 1984), pp. 244, 250.

12. Nils J. Nilsson, "Artificial Intelligence Prepares for 2001," *The AI Magazine*, Winter 1983, p. 12.

13. Stan Augarten, *Bit by Bit an Illustrated History of the Computer* (New York: Ticknor and Fields, 1984), p. 236.

14. Bob Davis, "Mechanical Minds: More Firms Try to Put Skills of Key Staffers in Computer Programs," *Wall Street Journal*, 10 June 1985, p. 1.

15. S. Jerrold Kaplan, "The Industrialization of Artificial Intelligence: From By-Line to Bottom Line," *The AI Magazine*, Summer 1984, pp. 51–57.

16. Judith Bachant and John McDermott, "R1 Revisited: Four Years in the Trenches," *The AI Magazine*, Fall 1984, p. 21.

17. Paul Harmon and David King, *Expert Systems: Artificial Intelligence in Business* (New York: John Wiley and Sons, 1985), pp. 160–163.

18. Syntelligence, Inc., "Commercial Underwriting 'Expert System' Being Developed," news release, 17 January 1986.

19. Texas Instruments Data Systems Group, "Knowledge-Based Systems Gain Momentum in the Marketplace," *Artificial Intelligence Letter*, February 1986.

20. Feigenbaum and McCorduck, *op. cit.*, pp. 68–69.

21. "AI Gaining Speed in PC Arena," *Computerworld*, 16 April 1986.

22. Tom Schwartz, "AI Development on the PC: A Review of Expert System Tools," *The Spang-Robinson Report*, Vol. 1, no. 1, pp. 7–14.

23. Alan Kay, "Software's Second Act," *Science 85*, November 1985, p. 122.

24. Edward A. Feigenbaum, "The Art of Artificial Intelligence: Themes and Case Studies of Knowledge Engineering," Stanford Heuristic Programming Project, Memo HPP-77-25, August 1977.

25. David E. Sanger, "Smart Machines Are Getting Smarter," *New York Times*, 15 December 1985, p. F-1.

REFERENCES, CHAPTER 8

1. Robert E. Kahn, "A New Generation in Computing," *IEEE Spectrum*, November 1983, p. 38.

2. Robert E. Kahn, *op. cit.*, pp. 36–41.

3. Gordon Bell, "Challenges in Generating the Next Computer Generation," in *Cohabiting with Computers*, Joseph F. Traub, ed. (Los Altos, Calif.: William Kaufmann, 1985), pp. 25–40.

4. Edward A. Feigenbaum and Pamela McCorduck, *The Fifth Generation* (Reading, Mass.: Addison-Wesley, 1983), pp. 7–8.

5. *Ibid.*, p. 8.

6. David Brandin et al., "JTECH Panel Report on Computer Science in Japan,"

JTECH-TAR-8401, Japanese Technology Evaluation Program (JTECH), Science Applications International Corporation, December 1984, p. I-6.

7. Ezra Vogel, *Japan as Number One* (New York: Harper and Row, Colophon Books, 1980); quoted in Feigenbaum and McCorduck, p. 105.

8. Feigenbaum and McCorduck, *op. cit.,* p. 105.

9. Tohru Moto-oka, "The Fifth Generation: A Quantum Jump in Friendliness," *IEEE Spectrum,* November 1983, pp. 46–47.

10. Feigenbaum and McCorduck, *op. cit.,* p. 24.

11. Tohru Moto-oka et al., "Challenge for Knowledge Information Processing Systems (Preliminary Report on Fifth Generation Computer Systems)," *Fifth Generation Computer Systems,* Tohru Moto-oka, ed. (Amsterdam: North Holland, 1982), pp. 3–89.

12. *Spectrum* Staff, "ICOT: Japan Mobilizes for the New Generation," *IEEE Spectrum,* November 1983, p. 48.

13. Quoted in Gina Kolata, "Japanese Borrow Plan From U.S.," *Science* 220 (1983), p. 584.

14. Bobby R. Inman, quoted in Mark A. Fischetti, "MCC: An Industry Response to the Japanese Challenge," *IEEE Spectrum,* November 1983, p. 56.

15. Michael Schrage, *Washington Post,* 28 July 1985, p. D-1.

16. John Walsh, "MCC Moves Out of the Idea Stage," *Science* 220 (1983), p. 1257.

17. Doug Lenat, Mayank Prakash, and Mary Shepherd, "CYC: Using Common Sense Knowledge to Overcome Brittleness and Knowledge Acquisition Bottlenecks," *The AI Magazine,* Winter 1986, pp. 65–85.

18. Quoted in Mark A. Fischetti, *op. cit.,* p. 55.

19. Horst Nasko, "The Teams and the Players: The European Common Market," *IEEE Spectrum,* November 1983, pp. 71–72.

20. Brian W. Oakley, "The Teams and the Players: Great Britain," *ibid.,* pp. 69–71.

21. David Dickson, "Britain Rises to Japan's Computer Challenge," *Science* 220 (1983), p. 799.

22. Nasko, *op. cit.*

23. Defense Advanced Research Projects Agency, *Strategic Computing,* October 1983; reprinted in *Next-Generation Computers* (New York: IEEE Press, 1985), pp. 146–190.

24. Severo M. Ornstein, Brian C. Smith, and Lucy A. Suchman, "Strategic Computing: An Assessment," Computer Professionals for Social Responsibility, 21 June 1984.

25. Mark Stefik, "Strategic Computing at DARPA: Overview and Assessment," *Communications of the ACM,* July 1985, p. 698.

26. Quoted in M. Mitchell Waldrop, "The Fifth Generation: Taking Stock," *Science* 226 (1984), p. 1061.

27. *Ibid.*

28. Dwight B. Davis, "R&D Consortia," *High Technology,* October 1985, p. 42.

29. Tsutomu Makino, "Panel Discussion: International Research Activities for New Generation Computers," *ICOT Journal* 8 (1985), p. 15.

30. Brandin et al., *op. cit.,* Chapter 2.

31. George E. Lindamood, "The Structure of the Japanese Fifth Generation

Computer Project—Then and Now," *Future Generation Computer Systems* 1, no. 1, pp. 51–55.

32. Alun Anderson, "Japan Finds Rivals Treading Uncomfortably Close," *Nature* 312 (1984), p. 295.

33. Andrew Pollack, "Japan Falters on Next Step in Computers," *New York Times*, 13 August 1984.

REFERENCES, CHAPTER 9

1. Elizabeth L. Eisenstein, *The Printing Revolution in Early Modern Europe* (Cambridge, England: Cambridge University Press, 1983).

2. Donald M. Vickery and James F. Fries, *Take Care of Yourself: A Consumer's Guide to Medical Care*, rev. ed. (Reading, Mass.: Addison-Wesley, 1981).

3. John Seely Brown, "The Impact of the Information Age on the Conduct and Communication of Science," Congressional Testimony Before the Committee on Science and Technology, 12 September 1985.

4. David D. Woods, "Cognitive Technologies: The Design of Joint Human-Machine Cognitive Systems," *The AI Magazine*, Winter 1986, pp. 86–92.

5. James Fallows, "The Case Against Credentialism," *The Atlantic*, December 1985, pp. 49–67.

6. Michael Schrage, "New Computer Package Helps Get to the Meat of Meetings," *Washington Post*, 18 November 1985.

7. George Pake, "Research at Xerox PARC: A Founder's Assessment," *IEEE Spectrum*, October 1985, pp. 54–60; Tekla S. Perry and Paul Wallich, "Inside the PARC: The 'Information Architects,' " *ibid.*, pp. 62–75.

8. John Seely Brown, "Process Versus Product: A Perspective on Tools for Communal and Informal Electronic Learning," *Report From the Learning Lab: Education in the Electronic Age* (New York: Educational Broadcasting Corporation, 1983).

9. Kurt VanLehn, "Theory Reform Caused by an Argumentation Tool," Xerox Intelligent Systems Laboratory Series ISL-11, July 1985.

10. Brown, *op. cit.*, pp. 53–54.

11. Mark Stefik, Daniel Bobrow, Sanjay Mittal, and Lynn Conway, "Knowledge Programming in LOOPS: Report on an Experimental Course," *The AI Magazine*, Summer 1983.

12. "Report of the Research Briefing Panel on Information Technology in Precollege Education," *Research Briefings 1984* (Washington, D.C.: National Academy Press, 1984), pp. 22–23.

13. *Intelligent Tutoring Systems*, Derek Sleeman and John Seely Brown, eds. (London: Academic Press, 1982).

14. Richard R. Burton, "Diagnosing Bugs in a Simple Procedural Skill," *ibid.*, p. 160.

15. Seymour Papert, "Computers and Learning," *The Computer Age: A Twenty-Year View*, Michael L. Dertouzos and Joel Moses, eds. (Cambridge, Mass: MIT Press, 1980), p. 75.

16. Seymour Papert, *Mindstorms: Children, Computers, and Powerful Ideas* (New York: Basic Books, 1980).

17. Papert, "Computers and Learning," *op. cit.*, p. 73.

18. Richard R. Burton and John Seely Brown, "An Investigation of Computer

Coaching for Informal Learning Activities," *Intelligent Tutoring Systems, op. cit.*, pp. 79–98.

19. "Report of the Research Briefing Panel on Information Technology in Precollege Education," *op. cit.*, p. 29.

20. Sherry Turkle, *The Second Self: Computers and the Human Spirit* (New York: Simon and Schuster, 1984), pp. 13–14.

REFERENCES, CHAPTER 10

1. "Special Report: Automation U.S.A." *High Technology*, May 1985, pp. 24–47.

2. Herb Brody, "Overcoming Barriers to Automation," *ibid.*, pp. 41–46.

3. Jacques Koppel, "Manufacturers Must Face the Music," *High Technology*, March 1986, p. 12.

4. John K. Krouse, "Automation Revolutionizes Mechanical Design," *High Technology*, March 1984, pp. 36–45; "Engineering Without Paper," *High Technology*, March 1986, pp. 38–46.

5. "Report of the Research Briefing Panel on Computers in Design and Manufacturing," *Research Briefings 1983* (Washington, D.C.: National Academy Press, 1983), p. 60.

6. John K. Krouse, "Engineering Without Paper," *High Technology*, March 1986, p. 38.

7. Richard Brandt and Otis Port, "How Automation Could Save the Day," *Business Week*, 3 March 1986, pp. 72–74.

8. Eric Gelman, "Wheels of the Future," *Newsweek*, 17 June 1985, p. 65.

9. Daniel Bell, "The Social Framework of the Information Society," *The Computer Age: A Twenty-Year View*, Michael L. Dertouzos and Joel Moses, eds. (Cambridge, Mass.: MIT Press, 1979), pp. 163–211.

10. Maryann Keller of Vilas-Fischer Associates, quoted in Gelman, *ibid.*, p. 67.

11. "A New Era for Management," *Business Week*, 25 April 1983, pp. 50–86.

12. Barry A. Bluestone, quoted in Bob Kuttner, "The Declining Middle," *The Atlantic*, July 1983, pp. 60–72.

13. Peter Perl, "Shift to Service Economy Grows," *Washington Post*, 11 November 1985, p. A-8.

14. "The Myth of the Vanishing Middle Class," *Business Week*, 9 July 1984, p. 83.

15. Wassily W. Leontief, "The Distribution of Work and Income," *Scientific American*, September 1982, pp. 188–204.

16. James Fallows, "America's Changing Economic Landscape," *The Atlantic*, March 1985, pp. 47–68.

17. "The Shrinking of Middle Management," *Business Week*, 25 April 1983, p. 54.

18. Mitchell Lee Marks, "The Question of Quality Circles," *Psychology Today*, March 1986, pp. 36–46.

19. Seymour Melman, "Alternatives for the Organization of Work in Computer-Assisted Manufacturing," *Computer Culture* (New York: New York Academy of Sciences, 1984), p. 90.

20. Michael Maccoby, "A New Way of Managing," *IEEE Spectrum,* June 1984, p. 70.

21. Vincent E. Giuliano, "The Mechanization of Office Work," *Scientific American,* September 1982, pp. 149–164.

22. Suzanne Iacono and Rob Kling, "Office Routine: The Automated Pink Collar," *IEEE Spectrum,* June 1984, pp. 73–76.

23. Studs Terkel, quoted in Iacono and Kling, *ibid.,* pp. 73–74.

24. Melman, *op. cit.,* pp. 84–85.

25. Frederick W. Taylor, "Shop Management," *Scientific Management* (New York: Harper and Row, 1947).

26. Daniel J. Boorstin, *The Americans: The Democratic Experience,* (New York: Random House, Vintage Books, 1973), p. 363.

27. Melman, *op. cit.,* pp. 87–88.

REFERENCES, CHAPTER 11

1. Isaac Asimov, *The Rest of the Robots* (New York: Doubleday, 1964), p. xiii.

2. Jack Williamson, "With Folded Hands," *Astounding Science Fiction,* July 1947, reprinted in *The Best of Jack Williamson* (New York: Ballantine, 1978), pp. 154–206.

3. Alan Kay, "Software's Second Act," *Science 85,* November 1985, pp. 122–126.

4. Trudy E. Bell, "Robots in the Home: Promises, Promises," *IEEE Spectrum,* May 1985, pp. 51–55.

5. Joel Shurkin, "Robot Hand Conveys Sign Language to Persons Both Deaf and Blind," Stanford University News Service, 30 July 1985.

6. Bell, *ibid.,* p. 55.

7. NASA Advanced Technology Advisory Committee, "Advancing Automation and Robotics Technology for the Space Station and the U.S. Economy," NASA Technical Memorandum 87566, 1 April 1985.

8. J. C. R. Licklider, "Computers and Government," *The Computer Age: A Twenty-Year Review,* Michael L. Dertouzos and Joel Moses, eds. (Cambridge, Mass.: MIT Press, 1979), p. 91.

9. Edwaard Balkovich, Steven Lerman, and Richard P. Parmelee, "Computing in Higher Education: The Athena Experience," *Communications of the ACM,* November 1985, pp. 1214–1224.

10. Dennis M. Jennings et al., "Computer Networking for Scientists," *Science* 231 (1985), p. 943.

11. IEEE Staff, "Assessing the Technical Challenges: A Log of Electronic Messages," *Next Generation Computers,* Edward A. Torrero, ed. (New York: IEEE Press, 1985), pp. 100–134.

12. Stan Augarten, "A Sense of Responsibility," *PC Magazine,* 11 March 1986, pp. 99–104.

13. Dennis M. Jennings, *op. cit.,* p. 943.

14. Dennis J. Gaushell, "Automating the Power Grid," *IEEE Spectrum,* October 1985, pp. 39–45.

15. Frederick W. Weingarten, quoted in Fred Guterl, "Assessing the Sociotechnical Challenges," *Next-Generation Computers,* Edward A. Torrero, ed. (New York: IEEE Press, 1985), p. 138.

16. *Federal Government Information Technology: Electronic Surveillance and Civil Liberties* (Washington, D.C.: Office of Technology Assessment, OTA CIT-23, October 1985).

17. Langdon Winner, quoted in Guterl, *op. cit.,* p. 138.

18. Bill Machrone, "Spare Me the Sermon," *PC Magazine,* 28 January 1986, pp. 53–55.

19. Daniel Ford, *The Button* (New York: Simon and Schuster, 1985).

Additional Reading

Introductory Reading

Edward Feigenbaum and Pamela McCorduck. *The Fifth Generation*. Reading, Mass.: Addison-Wesley, 1983.
Pamela McCorduck. *Machines Who Think*. New York: W. H. Freeman, 1979.
Patrick Winston and Karen Prendergast, eds. *The AI Business: The Commercial Uses of Artificial Intelligence*.

General Reference

Aaron Barr, Paul Cohen, and Edward Feigenbaum, eds. *The Handbook of Artificial Intelligence*, Vols. 1–3. Los Altos, Calif.: William Kaufmann, 1981–1982.
Edward Torrero, ed. *Next-Generation Computers*. New York: IEEE Press, 1985.

Textbooks

Elaine Rich. *Artificial Intelligence*. New York: McGraw-Hill, 1983.
Patrick Winston. *Artificial Intelligence*. Reading, Mass.: Addison-Wesley, 1984.

Cognitive Science

John Anderson. *Cognitive Psychology*, 2d ed. New York: W. H. Freeman, 1984.
Howard Gardner. *The Mind's New Science*. New York: Basic Books, 1985.
Marvin Minsky. *The Society of Mind*. New York: Simon and Schuster, 1986.
Allen Newell and Herbert Simon. *Human Problem Solving*. Englewood Cliffs, N.J.: Prentice Hall, 1972.
Herbert Simon. *Sciences of the Artificial*. Cambridge, Mass.: MIT Press, 1981.
Robert Sternberg, ed. *The Handbook of Human Intelligence*. Cambridge, England: Cambridge University Press. 1982.

Knowledge-Based Systems

Ronald Brachman and Hector Levesque, eds. *Readings in Knowledge Representation*, Los Altos, Calif.: Morgan Kaufmann, 1985.
Bruce Buchanan and Edward Shortliffe. *Rule-Based Expert Systems: The Mycin Experiments of the Stanford Heuristic Programming Project*. Reading, Mass.: Addison-Wesley, 1984.
Randall Davis. "Expert Systems: Where Are We? And Where Do We Go From Here?" *The AI Magazine*, Summer 1982.
Paul Harmon and David King. *Expert Systems*. New York: John Wiley and Sons, 1985.

Natural-Language Understanding

Roger Schank and Robert Abelson. *Scripts, Plans, Goals, and Understanding*. Hillsdale, N.J.: Lawrence Erlbaum, 1977.
Terry Winograd. *Syntax. Language as a Cognitive Process*, Vol. 1. Reading, Mass.: Addison-Wesley, 1983.

ADDITIONAL READING

Image Understanding

David Marr. *Vision*. New York: W. H. Freeman, 1980.

Parallel Processing

Daniel Hillis. *The Connection Machine*. Cambridge, Mass.: MIT Press, 1985.

AI, Computers, and Their Impact on Society

David Burnham. *The Rise of the Computer State*. New York: Random House, Vintage Books, 1980.
Michael Dertouzos and Joel Moses, eds. *The Computer Age*. Cambridge, Mass.: MIT Press, 1979.
Heinz Pagels, ed. *Computer Culture: The Scientific, Intellectual, and Social Impact of the Computer*. New York: New York Academy of Sciences, 1984.
Seymour Papert. *Mindstorms: Children, Computers, and Powerful Ideas*. New York: Basic Books, 1980.
Harley Shaiken. *Work Transformed*. New York: Holt, Rinehart and Winston, 1984.
Sherry Turkle. *The Second Self: Computers and the Human Spirit*. New York: Simon and Schuster, 1984.
Joseph Weizenbaum. *Computer Power and Human Reason*. New York: W. H. Freeman, 1976.
Terry Winograd and Fernando Flores. *Understanding Computers and Cognition: A New Foundation for Design*. Norwood, N.J.: Ablex, 1986.

INDEX